舞踏

作品不明 60年代
土方巽（左）、大野一雄（右）
Title unknoun, 1960s
Tatsumi Hijikata (left), Kazuo Ohno(right)

Something Called Butoh

舞踏という何か

『禁色』(1959)のリハーサル
写真:大辻清司

in Forbidden Color's rehearsal
Photo : Kiyoji Ohtsuji

目次
Contents

6 はじめに
Foreword

13–32
舞踏ディアスポラ
Butoh Diaspora

14 田中トシ
Toshi Tanaka

18 Oguri

22 ゆみうみうまれ
Yumi Umiumare

27 吉岡由美子
Yumiko Yoshioka

33–64
舞踏リサーチ
2017-2019 報告書
A Report of Butoh Research
2017-2019

34 調査目的
Research Objectives

調査の変遷
Survey History

35 調査概要
Survey Summary

36 調査結果
Survey Results

63 まとめ：成果／
アンケートを経ての展開
Summary: Results/
Post-Survey Plans

64 アンケート質問項目(2018)
Survey Questions (2018)

Butoh Researchers' Comments

46 ケイトリン・コーカー
Caitlin Coker

60 マーゴ・オリボー
Margot Olliveaux

65-139
舞踏スクリーンショット2019
A Snapshot of Butoh 2019

精神のリレー2019
A Spiritual Relay 2019

76 石井則仁
Norihito Ishii

86 伊藤キム
Kim Itoh

96 鈴木ユキオ
Yukio Suzuki

106 笠井瑞丈
Mitsutake Kasai

114 大橋可也
Kakuya Ohashi

124 高松真樹子
Makiko Takamatsu

137 向雲太郎
Kumotaro Mukai

140 索引
Index

はじめに
Foreword

本書をNPO法人ダンスアーカイヴ構想が行った舞踏現況調査の報告書として刊行する。報告に入る前に、まず「舞踏」について簡単におさらいしておこう。

We have published this book as a report on Butoh surveys conducted by the Dance Archive Network. But before we go into the report, let us briefly review the term "Butoh".

舞踏は、1959年に現代舞踊協会新人公演で発表された、土方巽の『禁色』から始まったと言われている。土方巽の演出による、土方と大野慶人が踊る、短いデュオ作品だった。ホモセクシュアルがテーマで、舞台上で鶏を絞め殺すように見えるシーンがあったこともあり、一大スキャンダルを巻き起こしたらしい。しかし、その時はまだ「舞踏」という名前ではなかった。「舞踏」という呼び名が定着するのは、60年代半ば以降のことのようだ。

Tatsumi Hijikata's *Kinjiki*, performed as part of the All-Japan Art Dance Association's Annual Program of New Dancers in 1959, is often cited as the beginning of Butoh. Directed by Tatsumi Hijikata, it was a short debut performed by Hijikata and Yoshito Ohno. With the theme of homosexuality and a scene in which a chicken appears to get strangled, it caused a huge scandal. However, at the time it was not yet called "Butoh". The term "Butoh" does not seem to have been established until the mid 1960s.

この『禁色』を皮切りに、土方作品に大野一雄を初めとする舞踊家や他分野の芸術家が加わり、次々と実験的な舞台が生まれていく。舞踏の創世記だ。では、土方の踊りはどんなものだったのか、当時の一連の作品をつぶさに見ていた澁澤龍彥の言葉を引用してみよう。

As a result of *Kinjiki*, first Kazuo Ohno, and then other dancers and artists from other fields, joined Hijikata in his creations, giving rise to several experimental works. This was Butoh's genesis. Let's look at the words of Tatsuhiko Shibusawa, who saw this series of performances, to see what kind of dance Hijikata's Butoh was.

> **舞台の上に、裸の男がごろりとひっくり返って、背中をまるめ、手脚をちぢめている。それは生の方向と死の方向とを同時に暗示した、未生の胎児の眠る姿のようでもあり、またカフカの短編のなかの甲虫のようでもある。やがて裸の男はむくむくと起きあがり、一本一本かぞえられそうな肋骨を浮き出させて、からだを屈伸させはじめる。ふいごのように胸と腹がおおきくはずむ。そうかと思うと、小児麻痺のように痙攣的な、衝動的な不均整な動きを示しつつ、ぎくしゃくとした足どりで**

> ***A naked man curls up on the stage, rolling his back and shrinking his limbs. With implications of both birth and death, he appears as a sleeping foetus, or the beetle from Kafka's novella. Eventually the naked man slowly bulges up, extending ribs perceptibly, and begins pulsing his body. He heaves his chest and stomach like a pair of bellows, then starts convulsing with impulsive irregularity like a child having a fit, shuffling around the stage with jerky movements, at times stopping suddenly with legs stiff as rods, and letting out short and***

土方巽『疱瘡譚』(1972)
写真:鳥居良禅
Tatsumi Hijikata, *Smallpox Story*
Photo:Ryozen Torii

舞台の上を歩き出したり、脚を棒のようにして急にたちどまったり、意味のない短い叫び声をあげたりする。
それは、私たちが親しく目にしている私たち自身の日常的な動作、あるいは私たちが知りつくしている古典バレエのリズミカルな、様式的な動作への期待を完全に裏切る、今まで私たちが一度として想像したこともないような、奇怪な肉体行動の可能性を暗示した驚くべきダンスであった。

土方巽『病める舞姫』初版所収
「土方巽について」より(白水社、1983年)

土方のグループは、所謂「舞踊団」ではなく、「暗黒舞踏派」というような、耳慣れぬ「派」という命名が暗示するとおり、独自の運動体を形成していく。澁澤が指摘するような動きだけでなく、舞踏は、ビジュアルも言葉も、生き方も、何から何までユニークづくめで、それまでダンスなどには関係のなかった多くの人々を引きつけた。それはとにかく、誰の目にも、新しかったのである。

前衛から頂点へ向かう舞踏

70年代に入り、舞踏は舞台芸術作品として最高潮を迎える。土方の『四季のための二十七晩』(1972)、大野一雄の『ラ・アルヘンチーナ頌』(1977)、山海塾の『金柑少年』(1978)などは、20世紀の舞踊史に輝く金字塔と言って過言ではない。同時に、この頃から、舞踏家は海外に雄飛する。室伏鴻の最初のパリ公演『最後の楽園』は1978年に行われた。

80年代から、現在に繋がるような国際化が始まる。きっかけは、1980年のフランスのナンシーで行われた国際演劇祭だ。このとき、大野一雄、笠井叡、田中泯、山海塾が日本特集という枠組みでそれぞれ大きく取り上げられた。このあたりから、「舞踏」

meaningless cries.
It was a shocking dance that foretold the bizarre potential of physical movements previously never even imagined, completely betraying our expectations for movements borne of our own familiar daily motions, or the rhythmical and stylised movements of classical ballets.

From Tatsumi Hijikata's *Yameru Maihime*, first edition
"On Tatsumi Hijikata" (Hakusuisha, 1983)

Hijikata's group was not so much a "dance-*dan* [troupe]" but more like a "dark dance-*ha* [faction]" which, as "*ha*" (an unusual word in the arts) implies, did not work in the same ways as a normal dance group. Butoh is not only the movements as pointed out by Shibusawa, but also visuals, words, lifestyle, unique in all aspects, and drew in all kinds of people who until that point had nothing to do with dance. In this way, it was new in everyone's eyes.

Butoh from the Avant-garde to its Zenith

The 1970s were the golden years of Butoh as a performing art. It is not an exaggeration to say that Hijikata's *Shikino tame no nijunanaban* [Twentyseven Nights for Four Seasons] (1972), Kazuo Ohno's *Admiring La Argentina* (1977) and Sankai Juku's *Kinkan Shonen* (1978) were some of the highlights of 20th century dance history. Around the same time, Butoh dancers started going overseas. Ko Muroboshi's *Le Dernier Eden* debuted in Paris in 1978.

In the 1980s, internationalisation began to bring Butoh closer to what it seems to be today. The catalyst was the international *Festival Mondial du Théatre de Nancy*, held in France in 1980 with Kazuo Ohno, Akira Kasai, Min Tanaka and Sankai Juku each headlining as a Japanese special feature. From around this time "Butoh" began channelling its way into the Western dance world, as though a circuit cycling round the world had

『形而情學』(1967)
笠井叡(左)
高井富子(右)
写真:中谷忠雄

Keiji Jogaku
Akira Kasai (left)
Tomiko Takai (right)
Photo:Tadao Nakatani

作品不明 60年代
Title unknoun, 1960s

が欧米のダンス界の動脈に流れ込み、世界中をぐるぐると循環していくサーキットが生まれたように思う。

一方日本ではどうだったか。舞踏は芸術的に高い評価を得ながらも、知る人ぞ知るマイナーなハイアートにとどまっていた。また、舞踏家たちは生業としてはキャバレーやストリップ小屋で踊ってもいたから、ローアートシーンにも、生活を懸けて関わっていた。しかしいずれにしても、大多数を占める一般観客の視野に入っていたとは言いがたい状況だった。

世界へ浸透するBUTOH

90年代以降、時代の変化と共に国際化がさらに加速し、グローバルにはより広範な層に舞踏が知られるようになった。世界各地で舞踏家の活動は活発で、公演もワークショップも数々行われている。今日舞踏は、どんどんその領域を広げているようにも見えるが、時代を分節するような事象にはやや乏しい。あまりにも自由に広がりすぎて、舞踏とは何なのかと問われると、どう答えていいかわからない状況だ。本調査の動機付けはこの点にある。日本に生まれ、世界に受容された舞踏とは何なのか、そう問う前に、世界で何が起きているのか、舞踏家は何を考えているのか、調べてみようということだ。

そこで調査にあたっては、国内外の舞踏の実践者たちに幅広く声がけし、できるだけ多くの人からの回答を得られるよう努めた。また、舞踏が世界に広がった要因として、海外に根を下ろして活動する舞踏家の存在が大きいことを認識し、調査への協力を求めるとともに、彼らの活動について寄稿を求めた。さらに、国内で活動する第三世代の舞踏家たちには、アンケート調査に加えて、「精神のリレー」というテーマで、師から受け継いだことについて原稿を依頼した。「精神のリレー」は、土方夫人の元藤燁子さんがしばしば口にしていた言葉だ。

sprung into existence.
But what about Japan? Even though Butoh had become artistically acclaimed, it remained a niche fine art only known by a few. That said, as many Butoh artists made their livings dancing in cabarets and strip clubs, it can also be said that they were more involved in the popular culture scenes. Either way, it was not widely seen by the general public.

Butoh's Progression into the World

Since the 1990s, globalisation has accelerated the pace of change, and Butoh has become more widely known around the world. Numerous Butoh performances and workshops are being held in all kinds of places. However, although it may appear as if Butoh is continuing to expand, it is no longer the groundbreaking phenomenon it once was. Having spread so far without limits, it is difficult to know how to answer when someone asks what Butoh is. This was the main motivation behind this research. But before we ask *what* Butoh is, besides an art born in Japan before spreading around the world, we decided to see what is happening in the world and what Butoh dancers are thinking.

As such, in this research we have endeavoured to get as many responses to our surveys as possible by contacting numerous practitioners all over the world. In recognition of Butoh spreading throughout the world thanks to the activities of those who have settled and work abroad, we also decided to seek the cooperation of some of these overseas Butoh dancers, and asked them to write about their activities. Additionally, we have requested some third generation Butoh dancers in Japan to write about what they have inherited from their mentors under the theme of "A Spiritual Relay". This "spiritual relay" is something that was often mentioned by Hijikata's wife, Akiko Motofuji.

There have recently been some remarkable changes in Japan's Butoh scene.

大野一雄『ラ・アルヘンチーナ頌』ポスター撮影
写真：細江英公

Kazuo Ohho, A photo session for the Poster of *Admining La Argentina*
Photo:Eikoh Hosoe

さて近年、日本国内で舞踏をめぐる状況には顕著な変化がある。
ひとつは、2017年度に新国立劇場が舞踏公演を初めて主催したことだ。世界の代表的な劇場が毎年のように舞踏作品を制作し、上演しているなかで、新国立劇場は1997年10月に開館以来、じつに20年間舞踏公演を自ら打ったことがなかった。初の舞踏公演主催はたいへん画期的なことに思える。

また、2020年度文化庁が文化芸術振興費補助金によって行う舞台芸術創造活動活性化事業の助成対象活動募集要項において、「助成の対象となる活動」の舞踊分野ジャンルに「舞踏」が加えられた。ちなみに、同時に募集される、独立行政法人芸術文化振興会による現代舞台芸術創造普及活動助成のジャンルには、「舞踏」はない。国の文化行政が関わる公的なプログラムや助成申請書類のなかで、「舞踏」に対する見方に、これまでと異なる点が具体的に見られることは、たいへん興味深い。本書に報告される調査は、時期的には、このような変化と同時並行に行われたことも銘記しておくべきだろう。

本書では、調査の経過を含め、結果の詳細をできるだけ直感的にわかるようまとめた。言うまでもなく、舞踏は変化を続け、社会も変化を続けている。そういう中で、舞踏の歴史を大きく切り取る一断面として見てもらえるといいと思う。本調査は手作りの、手探りの試行であり、偏りも不備もあるに違いない。その脆弱性へのご批判は甘受しつつ、これまで行われたことのない情報の集積に目を向けてもらえればと願う次第だ。

末尾となったが、アンケートにご協力頂いた皆さまに、心からの感謝と敬意を、そして今後の活動に力一杯のエールを送りたい。

溝端俊夫
NPO法人ダンスアーカイヴ構想

One is that in 2017, the New National Theatre Tokyo organised a couple of Butoh performances for the first time. Despite theatres world over putting on Butoh performances on a yearly basis, the New National Theatre Tokyo hadn't put on a single Butoh performance from the time it opened 20 years ago in October 1997. Their organisation of these Butoh performances was a real breakthrough.

Additionally, in 2020 the Agency for Cultural Affairs included “Butoh” as one of the “genres eligible for subsidy” in the dance category of their guidelines for activities eligible for an Arts & Cultural Promotion subsidy. Incidentally, “Butoh” is not listed in the Japan Arts Council's categories eligible for grants for the Creation & Promotion of Contemporary Performing Arts. It is interesting to see how views on “Butoh” have changed in the eyes of the national cultural administrations through their public programs and grant application guidelines. It should also be noted that the surveys in this report have coincided with these changes.

In this book, we have compiled the progress of the survey and details of the results in as clear a way as possible. It goes without saying that Butoh will continue to change, as will society. It is under such circumstances that we have attempted to consolidate a large portion of Butoh's history. This survey was put together by trial and error, and no doubt contains some biases and errors. While we are open to critical feedback regarding this weakness, we hope you will still appreciate this compilation of never before conducted research.

Last but not least, I would like to express my sincerest appreciation and regards to all those who took part in the surveys, and send forth encouragement for all future activities.

Toshio Mizohata
Dance Archive Network

Butoh Diaspora

舞踏ディアスポラ

舞踏ディアスポラ
Butoh Diaspora

田中トシ
Toshi Tanaka

Camin de Lua, Casa do Vento, 2007

私は1994年にサンパウロに移り住んで以来、日本へ帰ることは幾度もありましたが、現在までほとんどすべての生活と活動の場をこちらにおいています。ブラジルの大地に初めて足を着けた頃、「これでやっと舞踏から離れられる」と思ったものです。もしかしたら誰にもそんな時期があるのかもしれませんが、私にとっては大きな距離が必要だったのかも知れません。

日系ブラジル人である妻は、結婚前には大野一雄氏の公演に触発され、大学（ダンス専攻）卒業後日本に渡り、一年ほど大野一雄舞踏研究所に通っていました。そしてその時期に別のところで出会うことになり、やがて家庭を持ち現在に繋がっているわけです。そのことを辿り直してみると「離れられる」と思ったのは大きな錯覚で実はやっと私たちにとっての「舞踏の現場」に足を踏み込んでいたのだと気づくようになりました。

90年代、その頃こちらでは楠野隆夫、フェリーシア・オガワ御夫妻が精力的に活動されており、ご自身達の作品をブラジル人ダンサーたちに振り付け公演し、一方で幾人もの舞踏に関わりのあるアーティストを招聘し紹介するという偉業を為されていました。もしお二人の存

Although I have returned to Japan many times since moving to São Paulo in 1994, almost all of my life and work in now based here. When I first set foot in Brazil my thought was “I can finally get away from Butoh”. This may be something that happens to everyone, or it may be that for me I needed to create some large distance.

Before we were married, my Japanese-Brazilian wife was inspired by Kazuo Ohno’s performance and went to Japan to study at the Kazuo Ohno Dance Studio for one year after graduating from university (dance major). We met around the same time under different circumstances, and eventually moved together. Looking back, I have come to realise that “getting away” was a big illusion; we were in fact setting foot in our own “field of Butoh”.

In the nineties, partners Takao Kusuno and Felícia Ogawa were very active here. By choreographing performances for Brazilian dancers, and inviting many Butoh artists, they achieved the feat of introducing Butoh to Brazil. If it had not been for

Caminho da Lua, Casa do Vento, Photo: Carla Angulo

在がなかったとしたら、ブラジルにおける舞踏の受容のされ方も大きく違っていたのではないかと思います。そして世紀の変わり目にお二人は前後して他界されました。

また近年大野慶人氏がこちらで公演された折にお聞きしたところ、もう十数回もブラジルに足を運んでいるとのことで驚いたのですが、一方改めてその歴史性を思いました。公演に触れワークショップに参加した人の数は計り知れず、また歳月の中で人々の体の中にその経験が浸透し、力となり形となるのを私たちは見て来ました。その事実は、あたかも情報が氾濫し、あらゆる物事がお金に関わるような現代の状況の中で、六百年ほど前に世阿弥が残した「心より心に傳ふる」という言葉を思い起こさせるものです。にわかに表に現れては来なくとも、私たちダンスに携わる者たちのどこかで支えとなり勇気となりして、世代を越え、ゆったりと流れるものを感じています。それはブラジルに訪れていただく多くの舞踏ダンサーにも共通していることは言うまでもありません。
大学教授であるクリスチーネ・グレイネル女史は、長年学術的な観点から舞踏および広く日本文化を研究されており、両国を股にかけて授業や講演、出版、企画等を続けています。一般的に理論と実技が繋がりを持ち難いまま進行しがちなアカデミックの現場で、女史は柔軟な感性で多くの生徒たちを引きつけ育成しています。そう言う私自身も、同大学に招聘され授業を持って19年目になります。

こちらブラジルにおいて語るべき多くの人物がおり、同時代の仲間たちとともに私たちの活動もあるのですが、それは雨の後の筍のような現れ方ではなく、興味を持った者たちが伝を辿って舞踏に至るようなところがあるような気がします。また先に触れたサンパウロカトリック大学に限って言わせていただけば、私どもは四年制の身体芸術コース（Comunicação e Artes do Corpo）の中で、ダンスのみならず、演劇とパフォーマンスの分野も含んだ授業を担当しています。従ってそこでは舞踏から学んだ体との関わり方を、他の分野の基礎として適応させて行くことになります。例えば、裸足で床の上をその感覚の変化を察知しながら一足一足歩いて行く、と言うようなことがあるとすると、舞踏のフォルムとは関係なく、それは俳優の存在感を強めてくれます。踊りの発生に向かう眼差しは必ずしもダンサーのみならず、

these two, I think Butoh would have been interpreted very differently in Brazil. They passed away shortly before and after the turn of the century.

A few years ago Yoshito Ohno came to perform here, and I was surprised to hear that he had already set foot in Brazil over 10 times. It got me thinking about the history again. Countless people have attended workshops after being touched by a performance, and over the years we have seen how this experience permeates into people's bodies and strengthens and shapes them. In the modern world where everything is flooded with information and concerned with money, it brings to mind the words of Zeami from 600 years ago to "convey from heart to heart". Even if it is not immediately clear, I feel the support and courage of those involved in dance flowing across the generations. In this I of course include the Butoh dancers who come to visit Brazil.

University professor Christine Greiner has been studying Butoh and Japanese culture extensively from an academic point of view for many years, and continues to conduct classes and lectures and write publications in both countries. In an academic environment which typically progresses with little connection between theory and practice, she attracts and nurtures students with a flexible sensitivity. I was invited to work at the same university and have been teaching there for 19 years.

There are many people in Brazil worth mentioning, as well activities that both we and our contemporaries are are involved in, but this is not to say that they all sprang out of nowhere; I feel that most people that take an interest have followed a path that somehow led them to Butoh. At the Pontifical Catholic University of São Paulo we have a four year Comunicação e Artes do Corpo (Body Arts Course) which includes theatre and performance as well as dance. There, I adapt my Butoh training as a basis for other fields of study. For example, if you walk on the floor barefoot one step at a time aware of changing sensations, regardless of Butoh form this heightens the presence of any performer. I think observations

Casa do Vento Photo: Calra Angro

親と子の関係や幼児の教育の場に携わるものにとっても、多くの気づきを与えてくれると思います。

最後になりますが、調査報告に見る各国から寄せられた短いコメントは、あたかも舞踏という種子が世界のそれぞれ違う状況の中に散らばって行き、その中で懸命に生きようとしているようで感動しました。どうもありがとうございました。

made from dance can not only teach dancers but would also be hugely beneficial to those involved in working with parent-child relationships and young children's education.

Last but not least, I was impressed to see from the short comments of people from other countries, that the seeds of Butoh have scattered to various different parts of the world, and are working hard to stay alive. Thank you very much.

田中トシ

造形芸術、禅、書、能楽を学ぶ。ジャパン・フルクサス、オルタナティヴ・ロックバンドTACO等に関わる中で、舞踏を知る。81-84年、原田伸雄率いる舞踏青龍會に参加。94年、ブラジル・サンパウロに拠点を移す。96年、Fu Bu Myo In group結成。03年より、シーサ・オノと共にパフォーマンス風楽を始める

Toshi Tanaka

Studied plastic arts, zen, sho and Noh. Came across Butoh while a part of Japan-FLUXUS and alternative rock band Taco. Joined Butoh Seiryu-kai with Nobuo Harada 1981-84. Moved to São Paulo, Brazil in 1994. Formed Fu Bu Myo In group in '96. Been doing fugaku performance with Ciça Ohno since 2003.

舞踏ディアスポラ
Butoh Diaspora

Oguri

1983年、東京中野Plan-Bで土方巽の作品に出会ったのが舞踊を始めたきっかけです。85年に田中泯主宰の舞塾参加、同時に山梨県白州町での身体気象農場創設に加わり、90年まで有機農業を実践しながら国内外の公演活動及び地元白州でのアートフェスティバル現場制作、ライブスペースPlan-Bでの企画運営を担っていました。これらの経験が後年日本を離れてからの活動の原動力となっています。
91年、平成になって米国LAに移り住み。まもなく、ダウンタウンにある女性ホームレス避難施設からの、「敷地内の使われていないチャペルをダンススタジオに改装して、入所者に踊りを教えてくれないか」という要請を引き受

I started Butoh after seeing Tatsumi Hijikata's performance at Plan-B in Nakano, Tokyo in 1983. I joined Min Tanaka's dance school in 1985 and his Body Weather Farm in Hakushu, Yamanashi, and performed both in Japan and abroad, as well as creating works in Hakushu, managing Plan-B and doing organic farming until 1990. These experiences helped propel my lifestyle when I left Japan later on. In 1991, I moved to LA, USA and was presently approached by a downtown women's homeless shelter asking me to "renovate an unused chapel into a dance studio and teach the residents dance". I accepted their request and so my life in LA began.

Façade of Time 2019 at Venice, California Photo: Marco Moo

けLAでの活動を始めました。
入退所者が頻繁な中、滞在が長期になる婦人は、一緒にトレーニングを続け、赤ん坊の子守を引き受けてもくれました。LA暴動の時には、辺りは焼け落ちる中、なんとか略奪、焼失を免れました。
週3回のワークショップで増えた仲間と自主公演を重ねて、2年目頃から地元のあちこちから招かれるようになり、はじめてのソロ公演のカーテンコール、観客のやや大げさな反応は僕にとっては驚きでした。LAには外部からの新参者をとても親切に受け入れているくれる土壌があり、楽屋でも多くの人々が訪れて下さり、歓迎の言葉をもらい、当時はダンスコミュニティーがこじんまりしていて、

Among the frequent participants were long-term residents, who trained with me and sometimes even took care of my baby. Somehow we escaped the flames and looting during the LA riots, while everything around us burned.
As a result of the friends I made in those thrice weekly workshops and my independent performances, from my second year I began getting invitations to various places. I was shocked by the reactions at my first solo curtain call; LA is very warm towards newcomers, and I had many visitors in the dressing room with words of encouragement. The dance community at the time was small, so it was a

皆お互いに支えあっている状況でした。
93年の秋に大野一雄さんの全米公演時は、このスタジオでワークショップデモンストレーションをしていただき、まだヨチヨチ歩きの僕の長男を大野先生が抱き上げてくれたことを覚えています。95年に泯さんがいらしたときは、客席を倍に増やしてソロを踊っていただきました。

近年はベニスビーチに位置する小劇場のレジデンスアーティストとして迎えられて週2回のワークショップと定期公演を続けています。先日、ベニスの市街地での野外公演を、公的機関の協賛を得て企画実行しました。ワークショップを一か月間行い、30人程集まりました。公演に際して更に一般から募った30人は、老若男女LGBTQ人種、国籍、体型の異なるユニークな集まりで、まさにご当地の縮図です。リハーサルから本番にかけてカリフォルニアでは珍しい悪天候でしたが、参加者達の途切れない集中力、そして目的を達成させるという意思の逞しさを垣間見ることができました。

簡易レポートを拝見させていただいて、各人、違った切り口でBUTOHを語っているのは伝わりました。ただし、その個人の仕事のユニークな部分、例えば"違った風土に咲いている花"のようなものが見たかったと思います。「アフリカ大陸にだって"東北"はある」わけですから。
最近ワークショップで人と接し感じることは、皆、特に若い人の豊富な知識と学習速度の早さを実感します。映像、Podcastとかを倍速でプレイして吸収しているからでしょうか、その反面、他人の身体に接するのは苦手になっているような気がします。YogaとかPilates等を習得

supportive environment.
In the fall of 1993 when Kazuo Ohno performed in the US, he gave us a workshop and demonstration in this studio, and I remember how he held my still toddling eldest son. When Min came in 1995, he danced a solo for us and we had to double the number of seats for the audience.

Over the last few years I have been a resident artist at a small theater in Venice Beach, where I hold workshops twice a week and organise regular performances. We recently had some public funding to do an outdoor performance. A unique gathering of 30 people of all races, nationalities, body types, genders, ages and LGBTQ - a veritable microcosm of this area - joined for a month of workshops. Despite the rare spell of bad weather for California throughout the rehearsals and performance, I got to glimpse the uninterrupted focus of the participants and their motivation to achieve their goals.

Having read the initial report, it is clear that everyone talks about Butoh from a different perspective. However, I would have liked to have seen some of the uniqueness of the works of each individual, as "flowers that bloom in different climates". After all, "even Africa has a *Tohoku*".
In recent workshops I've been finding that everyone, especially young people, has a vast knowledge and learning speed. Perhaps this due to videos and podcasts etc. that can be absorbed at double speed.

していて自分の体のことには注視できているのにかかわらず、他人の身体に接したときの戸惑いがあると感じます。多分、もっとじっくりと他人の身体に接することが必要だと思います。
数年前、泯さんの白州での最終の集中ワークショップに数日だけ参加させてもらう機会があり。「土方巽は自分のカラダの内側に梯子をかけて内側に降りて行けと言うが、そのハシゴを昇って自分のカラダを外側に運び出して他者と対峙してみたらどうだろうか」と泯さんが言っていたのがとても印象的でした。

僕のダンス活動は日本での舞塾当時から“舞踏”とは名乗らずに続いています。ワークショップでは常に“身体気象”を掲げて行っています。
土方巽が考えていた舞踏は踊ること、パフォーマンスの事だけを指しているのではないと思っています。
僕は“舞踏”は土方巽、大野一雄、両先生の魂とともに昇華したと思っています。否、未だ内側の梯子から外へ向かって、昇華は続いているのでしょう。

However people also seem to be becoming less accustomed to interacting with others. It is possible to get to know your own body through yoga or pilates and such, but there is confusion when it comes to knowing others. I think it is necessary to get more in touch with others' bodies.
A few years ago, I had the opportunity to participate in Min's final intensive workshop in Hakushu for a few days. His words there left a great impression on me. "Tatsumi Hijikata said to lean a ladder and climb down inside yourself, but what if we were to climb up that ladder, and bring that self outside to confront others?"

I continue, as I have since my dance class days in Japan, to not call my dance "Butoh". My workshops are always carried out as "Body Weather".
I don't think that the Butoh Tatsumi Hijikata envisioned was only about dancing and making performances.
For me, "Butoh" evaporated with the souls of Tatsumi Hijikata and Kazuo Ohno. Or rather, they continue to evaporate from their inner ladders out even now.

Oguri

1985年、田中泯が主宰する「舞塾五期／身体気象農場」に参加。91年に渡米、ロサンジェルスを拠点にBody Weather Laboratory -Los Angelesを立ち上げ、以来市や郡の助成を受けながら活動を継続。2009年、ARCANE Collective を結成。カリフォルニア大学ロサンジェルス校（UCLA）、ベニントン・カレッジでも教鞭を執る。

Oguri

Participated in the 5th *Body Weather Farm* with Maijuku founded by Min Tanaka in 1985. Moved to the USA in 1991 and set up Body Weather Laboratory-Los Angeles, which he continues with the help of public funding. Founded ARCANE Collective in 2009. Also teaches at the University of California, Los Angeles (UCLA) and Bennington College.

Façade of Time 2019 at Venice, California Photo: Moses Hacmon

舞踏ディアスポラ
Butoh Diaspora

ゆみうみうまれ
Yumi Umiumare

DasSHOKU SHAKE!　Photo:Vikk Shayen

私は、1991年に大駱駝艦のオーストラリア公演に参加した後、93年よりメルボルンに移住し、オーストラリアの国内、アジア圏、日本、ヨーロッパ、南米で公演やワークショップを中心に活動して来ました。ダンス、演劇、映像など様々な分野にわたって作品創りをしてますが、舞踏に関しては、3年前から、国や芸術ジャンルを超えた、Butohのスピリットや本質を探るために、ButohOUT!というミニフェスティバルを立ち上げ、毎年、舞台製作、ワークショップ、フォーラムなどを行ってます。1年を通して行っているワークショップには、短期集中型から、寝食を共にする合宿まであります。キャンプスタイルで毎年行われる舞踏合宿は、オーストラリアならではの大自然の中で4-5日間過ごすプログラムになっています。スタジオ内だけでなく、砂漠や岩山、こちら独特の乾燥しきった大地など、日本とは極端に違うオーストラリアの自然との関わりを通して踊りを体験し、また、この土地から生まれてくる「舞踏性」のようなものは何なのを探っています。アボリジニーのダンスを見て、日本の観光客が「舞踏の真似だ!」とコメントしたという、冗談のような本当の話を聞いたことがありますが、5万年の

After performing in Australia with Dairakudakan in 1991, I moved to Melbourne and have been working on workshops and performances in Australia, Asia, Japan, Europe and South America ever since. Although I work in various fields including dance, theatre and film, three years ago I started a mini festival called *ButohOUT!* in which we hold performances, workshops and forums to explore the spirit and essence of Butoh which transcend national and artistic boundaries.
Throughout the year, we hold everything from short intensive workshops to overnight *gashukus*. A camp-style Butoh *gashuku* programme is held every year for 4-5 days in the Australian wilderness. We experience dancing in connection with Australian nature to explore what kind of Butoh is born out of this place, which is completely different to Japan, not only in the studio but also in the desert, on rocky mountains and on dry lands unique to this area. I once heard an unbelievable yet true story of a Japanese tourist who saw an Aboriginal dance and commented "it's

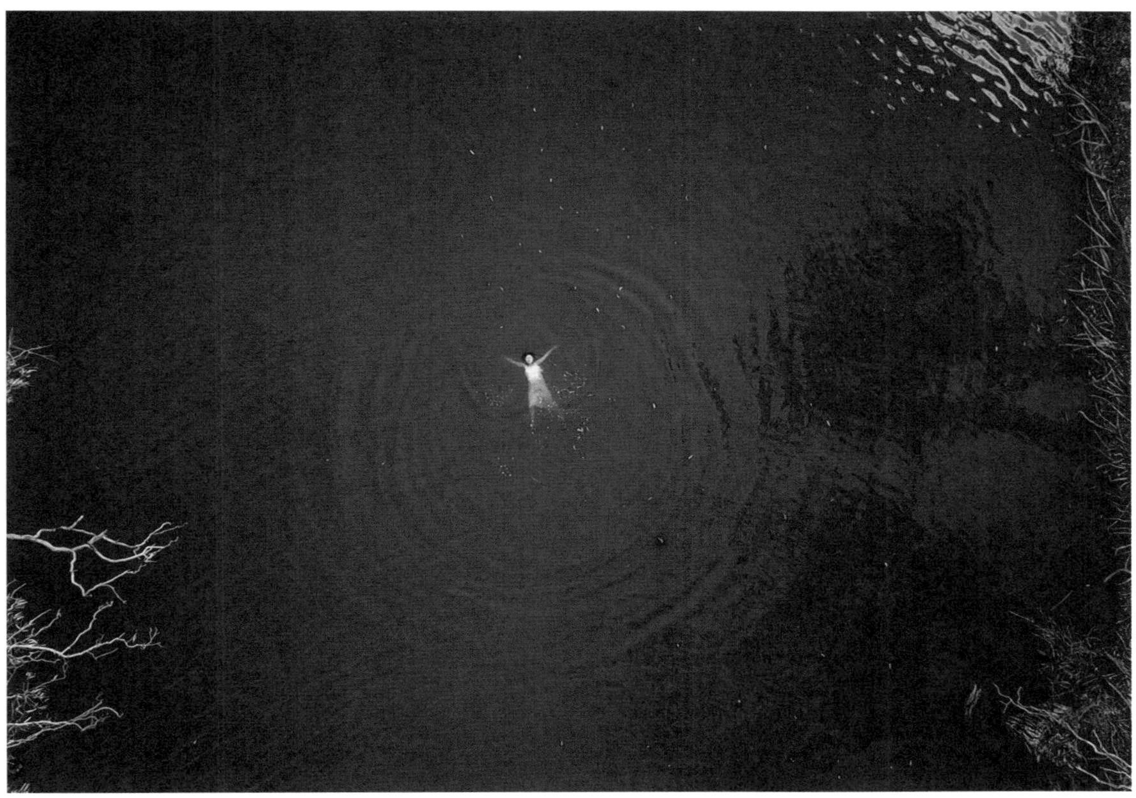

歴史を持つアボリジニー文化や、彼らの身体性（立っているだけで重力を数十メートル落としているような存在感や、自然に溶け込む一体感など）から学ぶことは多大です。
振付家としては、舞台経験がない人々や、難民生活をしている多国籍の人々、身体障害を持つ人々、ギャンブル中毒の人たちや、性的に強制労働をさせられて来た人など、社会的に苦しい状況にある人たちと共に演劇制作するプロジェクトに多数関わってきました。参加者の壮絶な体験談や逸話を、演出家が物語にしてゆく設定の中、振付家はそこに生まれる風景やイメージ、また、体のあり方などを抽象的に織り込み、動きや踊りにしてゆくのですが、彼らの経験して来た暗黒（Darkness）とその肉体が舞台ににじみ出た時、ものすごい「舞踏性」が感じられたことを記憶してます。現代の暗黒舞踏（Dance of Darkenss）は、私たちが今、生きている世界や社会に潜む「暗黒」や「闇」の中に潜んでいるかのように感じられた瞬間でした。そして自分が関わる舞踏は、そのような闇と共存しながら、そこに光を注いでいく明るいものでありたい、と感じ現在に至っています。

copying Butoh!", but there is a lot we can learn from the 50,000 year old Aboriginal culture and their physicality (such as their weighted presence, dropping tens of metres into the ground, and their sense of unity with nature).
As a choreographer, I've worked on a number of projects with people who have no stage experience, or who are from difficult social backgrounds, such as refugees, people with disabilities, gambling addicts, and victims of sex trafficking. I remember how, when directors turn the participants' stunning experiences and anecdotes into stories, and choreographers interpret the atmosphere, images and bodies into abstract movements and dance, the darkness (*ankoku*) of their experiences and the effects on their bodies flow out into a great "Butoh feeling" onstage. It was a moment that felt like modern *Ankoku Butoh* (Dance of Darkness), with the "ankoku" or "darkness" of the world and society we live in today. The dance I do aims to coexist with such darkness, pouring light into it.

私がメルボルンに移住した93年ごろは、舞踏を知らない人が多数でしたが、現在はアートに関わる人は、ほぼ皆知っているようになりました。私なりに客観的に考えますと、近年の舞踏には大きく分けて二通りの流れがあるように感じられます。ひとつは舞踏譜やそのメソッドを忠実に学び踏襲して行きたいとい古典回帰の流れと、もうひとつは、私が上に述べたような、古典的舞踏ではないがその舞踏性のコアになるものを探ってゆこうとする流れです。
前者は、極端にいうと舞踏を歌舞伎、能、文楽と並べ、とてもTraditional（古典的）なものと捉え、歴史の深いメソッドとしてマスターしたいという流れで、一部の欧米圏やオーストラリアでもよく見かけます。後者は、いわゆる古典的な舞踏や、表面的に受け継がれかねないステレオタイプな形態に興味をやや失いながらも、舞踏を舞踏たらしめているという、その揺るぎない「舞踏性」を探っている（答えが出るかでないかは別ですが）踊り手、アーティスト達。または舞踏のことは全く知らなくても、こちらから言わせてもらうとバリバリの「舞踏性」を持って存在している作品、身体、アーティスト達です。個人的には、これからの舞踏は、既成概念を超え、国境、時空を超えて存在し、そのコアになるスピリットを探り、継承し、深めていけたら素晴らしいのでは、と感じます。
調査報告の中で、舞踏は「言葉や形にできないもの」「Formのないもの」のようなコメントが日本語英語共にあり、印象に残っています。ネットやアプリで何でも手に入り、舞踏もYouTubeで見れる今の時代にこそ、見えないものに感覚を開き、沸き起こったものをカタチにし、そうしたと思ったら一瞬にしてそのカタチが消えてしまう舞踏の面白さが、世界あちこちで表出してゆけば楽しいだろうなと思います。

When I moved to Melbourne in 93, most people had not heard of Butoh. Yet recently, almost everyone involved in the arts has come to know of it. From my objective point of view, it seems that two types of Butoh have developed in recent years. One attempts to continue a 'classic' Butoh by faithfully following methods such as *Butoh-fu* (notations), and the other, as I have described above, is not 'classic' Butoh but aims to discover something that can be considered Butoh's 'core'.
At its most extreme, the former considers Butoh as something very traditional, like Kabuki, Noh or Bunraku, and a desire to master it by way of a method with a long history is often seen in some Western countries and Australia. The latter tends to be dancers and artists who search an unwavering "Butoh nature" in their dance (regardless of whether there is an answer), but have no interest in creating traditional or superficial stereotypes. On the other hand there are also works by people who know nothing about Butoh, and yet from my perspective have an incredibly "Butoh" feeling about them. Personally, I think it would be magnificent if Butoh could transcend established concepts, borders and space-time, and go on to explore, transmit and deepen.
From the initial reports, I was impressed to see multiple comments such as Butoh "is something that cannot be expressed in words or shape", or "has no form" in both Japanese and English. Especially in a time where anything, even Butoh, can be found on the Internet, I think it would be great if the fun of Butoh that goes out of reach *just* after having opened your senses to the invisible and turning them into a form, can go on being expressed here and there around the world.

ゆみうみうまれ
クラシックバレエやモダンダンスを学び、1989年大駱駝艦に参加。大駱駝艦の91年豪州ツアーに参加したことをきっかけに、93年メルボルンに移住。舞踏キャバレエ「DasSHOKU」プロジェクト、ButohOUT!を主宰。近年は「踊り」「お茶」「スピリット」の三本柱で活動を深める。

Yumi Umiumare
Studied classical ballet and modern dance, joined Dairakudakan in 1989. Moved to Melbourne in 1993 after touring Australia with Dairakudakan in 1991. Founded Butoh cabaret project DasSHOKU and ButohOUT!. Has recently been focussing on "Dance", "Tea" and "Spirit".

舞踏ディアスポラ
Butoh Diaspora

吉岡由美子
Yumiko Yoshioka

100 Light Years of Solitude photo: Edgar Gutiérrez Calvillo

1977年の11月、アリアドーネの會のダンサーとして、生まれて初めての海外、パリを訪れた。

Jardinという高級キャバレーで、カルロッタ池田振付、室伏鴻演出で構成された2部ショーを、私たち3人で3ヶ月間上演する予定だったが、なんと初日でクビになった。青筋立てて楽屋に飛んできたマネージャーの話では、私たちの踊りが上品なキャバレーには強烈過ぎたらしい。ダンサーたち20人も腕組みをして私たちのことを睨みつけていた。
麿赤兒さん、天児牛大さん、大須賀勇さん、田村哲郎さん等、当時の大駱駝艦の舞踏家達に羽田空港で餞別までもらってパリを訪れた手前、日本に帰るに帰れず、幸い、アパートの家賃はキャバレーのオーナーが払ってくれることになり、3ヶ月のサバイバル案をあれこれ3人で模索した。運よく、知り合いの紹介で，サーカス学校所属の Nouveau Carré Silvia Monfort 劇場（客席数99）にて、78年1月27日から舞踏作品を1ヶ月の契約で上演できることになり、必死に創作、稽古し、1ヶ月後 “LE DERNIER EDEN— PORTE DE L'AU DELA”（最後の楽園—彼方の扉）という作品の幕開きとなった。初めの週の客数は7人～15人程度、しかも殆ど友人、知人という寂しい状況だったが、2週目後半から客数はうなぎ上りになり、3週目には毎日売り切れ、4週目にはチケットの争奪戦まであったそうだ。揉み手して楽屋を訪れた劇場のマネージャーにせがまれ、2週間延長とまでなった。パリの人々は、初めて体験する舞踏公演に衝撃を受けたらしい。終演後、楽屋に飛び込んできた

In November 1977, I travelled abroad for the first time to Paris as a dancer with the Ariadone Company.

I was with Carlotta Ikeda (choreographer) and Ko Murobushi (director), and the 3 of us had plans to create a two-part show over three months in a high-class cabaret called Jardin, but were fired on the first day. According to the furious manager who marched into our dressing room, our dance was too intense for an elegant cabaret. Twenty dancers glared at us with arms folded.
Having been seen off from Haneda airport by Akaji Maro, Ushio Amagatsu, Isamu Osuga, Tetsurō Tamura and other Butoh artists, and even receiving *senbetsu*, we couldn't return to Japan. Fortunately, the cabaret owner agreed to pay the rent for our apartment, and the three of us sought a three month survival plan. Luckily, we got a one month contract through an acquaintance to perform at Nouveau Carré Silvia Monfort, a 99-seat circus theatre due to open one month later on 27th January 1978, and began frantically creating and rehearsing *LE DERNIER EDEN–Porte de l'au-dela* (The Last Eden - Door to the Beyond).
In the first week we had 7~15 audience members, mostly friends and people we knew, but in the second week that number rose, the third week was sold out and in the fourth there was even a fight over tickets. The theatre manager came to the dressing room begging for us to extend an extra two weeks.

Le Dernier Eden Poster 1978 supplied by Yumiko Yoshioka

Butoh Festival in Germany 2015 Phto:Beatriz Guzman

見知らぬ男性にギューっと抱きしめられたり、涙を流して喜ばれたり、スタンディングオベーションなど、日本では考えられない熱い反応に、私たち3人も戸惑いながらも嬉しい達成感を味わった。瓢箪から駒、あの公演が、奇しくも劇場における初の海外舞踏公演となったわけだが、そのような目的や野心は私たちには全くなく、ただ、3ヶ月を生き延びるのに必死だった。
"Butoh? 苦悶の踊りは一回見れば沢山…" と言われることもある昨今、あの時代、あの空気、今でも懐かしく思い出す。
今、同じ公演をしても、あのセンセーショナルな反応は決してないだろう。
その当時に書かれた、リベラシオン紙か、ル・モンド紙の舞台評にも「原爆から生まれた舞踏という苦悶の表現」という記述があり、初めはそのような決めつけに違和感を覚えた。愉快なシーン、エロティックなシーンもあるのに、何故そういう短絡的な見方をするのか、と初めは不思議だったが、西洋の人たちは歴史的観点から現象の起源を探っていく、という観念的な洞察があり、私たち日本人の感情的、感覚的な物の捉え方とは違うパースペクティブがあるのではないか、と思うようにもなった。それはそれで面白い。私は西洋に憧れたわけでは決してなく、ただ自分にないモノの捉え方、感じ方をする"異国"に住むことにチャレンジしたくなった。81-82年にわたる"Zarathustra"(カルロッタ池田振付、室伏鴻演出)ヨーロッパ巡演の後に、私は一人パリに残ることに決めた。(注:アリアドーネの會は、82年で一回解散し、その後83年ごろに池田さんが新メンバーで再開した)

あのパリ時代から幾星霜の月日が流れ、様々な紆余曲折があり、いま、私はベルリンを拠点に、主にヨーロッパ、

It seemed the Parisian's first experience with Butoh had left a great impact. Complete strangers ran into the dressing room post-show and squeezed us tight, shed tears of joy, gave us standing ovations; such passionate reactions were unthinkable in Japan, and though we were embarrassed, the three of us enjoyed a sense of accomplishment. Unexpectedly, this turned out to be the first Butoh performance staged in a theatre outside Japan, even though we had had no such purpose or ambition, we had just been surviving.
Although these days I sometimes hear "Butoh? Seeing that dance of agony once is enough…", I still remember that time and atmosphere with fondness. We wouldn't get the same sensational response if we did that performance again now.
In reviews at the time, even newspapers such as Le Monde and Liberation described Butoh as "an expression of agony born of the atomic bomb", which made me uncomfortable at first. I found it strange that they had such a closed perspective when there had been such funny and erotic scenes, but it turned out that Westerners have insightful ideas about exploring historical origins, and I began to wonder if there may be a different way to perceive emotional and sensual things than the way we Japanese do. This was interesting. I had never had any desire to live in the West, but this made me want to take on the challenge of living somewhere "foreign", where they felt and perceived something I didn't. After *Zarathustra* in 1981-82 with Carlotta Ikeda (choreography) and Ko Murobushi (director), I decided to stay alone in Paris. (Note: Ariadone

Hibrido dance project with the local dancers in Peru 2013　Photo: Yayo Lopez

eX..it Fancy Party small　Photo:Yumiko Yoshioka

アジア、南米を旅しながら生活している。 カンパニー、デュエット、ソロ公演、作品の振り付けや演出、ダンスフェスティバルのアートダイレクションも手がけているが、ワークショップ（Body Resonance—based on Organic Movement and Butoh）が生業の中心となっている。 様々な出自の人たちと出会い、切磋琢磨し、命の交感をするなかで、私の踊りも少しづつ変容していった。例えば、アリアドーネ時代は振り付けされた踊りしか体験しなかったが、パリ、ベルリンに住むようになって、即興やコラボの難しさに揉まれ、それを楽しめるようにもなってきた。

よく聞かれる質問が、"国や地方による人々の肉体や動きの相違"だ。
わたしの答えは、same same but different。
個人差、地方差もあれば、共通する特性も勿論ある。
共有できる何かがあるから人々は繋がることができるし、また相違があって多様だから世界は面白い！

去年訪ねたインドネシアの村の少女たちの身体能力の高さには舌を巻いた。股割りの強靭さには私もついていけなかった。中国本土、マカオ、香港、マレーシアでは、中国人の稽古の熱心さには、いつも頭がさがる思いを味わう。今年2月の広州のワークショップでは、1日7時間の講習を頼まれたが、生徒たちはしっかりついて来ていた。アジア人は一般に即興に慣れていないのか、振り付けされた動きの方が得意という傾向もあるようだ。ちなみに、ヨーロッパや北米の人たちは、最近、体力が落ちて来ているのと、なんでも短く早くするデジタル時代の影響を受けてか、一日4時間でも訓練や稽古に集中するのが難しくなって来ているのを感じる。
メキシコや南米の人々が自然にできるリズム感溢れる動

disbanded once in 1982, and was later restarted by Carlotta with new members in 1983.)

Since those Parisian days much time has passed, and through various twists and turns I am now based in Berlin, and make my living while travelling around Europe, Asia and South America.
Although I still make group, duo and solo performances, choreograph, direct and work as artistic director at dance festivals, my "Body Resonance - based on Organic Movement and Butoh" workshops are now my main livelihood.
Through various encounters, hard work and life experience, my dance has changed, little by little.
For example, with the Ariadone Company I had only experienced choreographed dancing, but living in Paris and Berlin I encountered the difficulties of improvisation and collaboration and began to enjoy them.

I often get asked about the bodies and movements of people from different places.
My answer is "same, same but different".
While there are individual and regional differences, there are of course also common characteristics.
People connect because of that *something* we share, and the world is interesting because of all the diversity!

I was impressed by the physical abilities of the young girls from an Indonesian village I visited last year.
Even I couldn't do their perfect splits.
I find myself humbled by the Chinese enthusiasm

Stranger in the Garden Choreographed by Yumiko Yoshioka Photo:Ron Lau

Stranger in the Garden Choreographed by Yumiko Yoshioka Photo:Ron Lau

きは、北欧や北米の人々には難易度高く、逆に彼らは、キラキラ光る知性の刃でイメージに切り込み、マインドフルな動きや踊りを作り上げていく。ちなみにわたしのワークショップでは、structured improvisationとして、イメージや構成を与え、各自そこからインスピレーションを受けて体から湧き出てくるものを即興する稽古もしている。振り付けよりも、こう言う即興が好きなヨーロッパ人は多い。ただ、ドイツやオーストリア、北欧には頭でっかちで体ガチガチの人も多いので、まず頭を空っぽにし、阿呆になったり、水袋になったり、という稽古から入り、彼らの頭と体の硬さをほぐすことから初めている。肉体派のわたしには、地平線を見晴るかすような視野の広さと洞察力の深いドイツ人に創作の視点を学ぶことも多い。日本でドイツ人と共に作品を上演した際に、「舞踏は日本人にしかできないよ」と、冷たく突き放すように言われ、辛いこともあった。そんな中で、個人感情を超えて連帯する西洋のアーティストたちの寛容性に、胸の奥がジワーッと膨らんで行く思いだった。

万国共通、"パッションが人を動かす"。南米リマの大学でワークショップした際に、チリのサンチアゴから36時間、バスに乗って参加してくれたチリ人舞踏家たちがいた。金欠の彼らは宿泊所からリマの大学まで、毎日歩いて1時間、往復2時間かけて通ってくれた。チリの舞踏家の人々の両親は、独裁者ピノーチェ時代に迫害されたり殺害されているケースが多く、彼らの肉体にもその負の記憶が刻印されている。Butohは、彼らを闇の迷路から解き放つ手段になっているかのように、作品のテーマは人権や歴史に絡んだ社会的なものが多いのも特徴だ。懐は寒くても心の熱い南米の人々には毎回励まされている。

公演に関していえば、"Butoh Performance"と銘打つこともあるが、時に"ダンスシアター",時に"インスタレーションとのコラボレーション"と称することもあり、公演内容や場所によって様々だ。苦しみや痛みに光をあて、メタモルフォーゼすることも大切だが、未知のものを紐解いていきたい好奇心、体を動かし変身を楽しむ、いのちの喜びも観客と共有したいというのが私の願いだ。

訪れる人々やその場に共振する魂との出会いを求めて来たので、あまりラベルには拘っていない。別の言葉で言えば、舞踏は、人種、言語、性別、信条、社会的文化的条件などを超えて、魂の根源を震わせる踊り

for practice in Mainland China, Macau, Hong Kong and Malaysia. At a workshop in Guangzhou in February this year I was asked to teach seven hours a day, and the students kept up. Asians generally seem unaccustomed to improvisation, and tend to be best at choreographed movements. On the other hand, Westerners more recently seem to be lacking stamina, perhaps an influence of the digital age where everything is short and fast, but I feel they struggle to concentrate for even four hours a day.

The rhythms that come naturally to Mexicans and South Americans are difficult for Nordic and North American people, yet they create thoughtful movements and dance out of images with razor sharp intelligence. In my workshops I do structured improvisation by providing images and compositions, from which each person takes inspiration and improvise on the movements that flows out of them. Many Europeans prefer this kind of improvisation to choreography. However, in Germany, Austria and Northern Europe, there are many people with full heads and stiff bodies, so first we practise emptying the head, being fools or bags of water, to begin loosening the mind and body. As a physical person, I often learn from the broad views and creative perspectives of German insight. I was once told to say bluntly that "Butoh can only be done by Japanese" after a performance with a German in Japan, and felt pleased. In that moment, the tolerance of Western artists who put aside personal feelings in solidarity made my heart soar.

Universally, "passion moves people". When I did a workshop in Lima, South America, there were Butoh artists from Santiago, Chile who had taken a 36 hour bus ride to participate. Out of pocket, they walked one hour each way from their accommodation to the university every day. In many cases the parents of these Chilean participants had been persecuted or killed during Pinochet's dictatorship, and their bodies bear these negative memories. A feature of their work is often related to society, on themes of human rights and history; it is as though Butoh unleashes them from their dark pasts. I am always encouraged by the passion of South Americans.

だから、人間が人間でいる限り、時代や国境を超えて存在し続けると思う。

土方巽が言ったように"東北はどこにでもある"し、舞踏は普遍性を持っているから、これだけ世界中に種子が飛び、それぞれの花を咲かせ、百花繚乱になっているのではないか。初めは"かたち"のコピーで、"いのち"が伴っていない空疎なものも多かったが、最近はユニークな"自分の踊り"を探る源泉としてのButohになってきていると思う。

舞踏の将来についてもよく聞かれるが、私にはこれからどうなっていくのかは正直言ってわからない。体に潜む螺旋の記憶が、踊りとなってポンと飛び出す、その至福の驚き。私たちはどこから来てどこへ行くのだろう。その永遠の謎への問いかけは、人類共通だ。血湧き肉躍り心震わす魂の踊りとして、舞踏は形や内容を変えても、そのスピリットは受け継がれてゆくと思う。仮に、Butohという名前が消え去っても、その精神は残るのだ。
そして、変身！は楽しい！

Depending on the content and locations, performances are sometimes called "Butoh Performance", "Dance Theatre", or "Collaborative Installation". Although it is important to shine light on and metamorphosize pain and suffering, my wish is to share the joy of life with the audience, explore the unknown and enjoy transformations with the body. As I go looking to get to know people, and the souls connected to places, I tend not to label. In other words, Butoh is a dance that shakes the roots of the soul beyond race, language, gender, creed, social or cultural backgrounds, and so I believe it will continue to exist beyond time and borders for as long as humans live.

As Tatsumi Hijikata said, "Everywhere has a *Tohoku*". Butoh is universal, and as such its seeds spread across the world, planting themselves variously and blossoming into hundreds of flowers. Although at first many simply copied the "shapes" and lacked "life", I think recently Butoh has become a source for people to find their own unique dance.

I'm often asked about the future of Butoh, but to be honest I'm not sure what will happen.
The surprise of a wound up spring inside the body bounding out in dance.
Where do we come from, where will we go? This is the eternal mystery of all humankind.
As a dance that makes the blood flow, flesh flutter and soul shake, I think the spirit of Butoh will continue, even if its shape or content changes.
Even if the name "Butoh" disappears, this spirit will continue.
And, transforming! Is fun!

吉岡由美子
1974-81年、アリアドーネの會の創立メンバーとして活動（芸名：ミゼール花岡）、海外の公共劇場では初の舞踏公演となる『最後の楽園』パリ公演に参加。88年ドイツに移住。tatoeba THÉÂTRE DANSE GROTESQUEののち、94年TEN PEN CHii art labor結成。95年よりデルタ・ライと共に「eX...it！ダンス交流フェスティバル」を4年毎に開催する。

Yumiko Yoshioka
Founding member of Ariadone Company 1974-81 (stage name: Mizelle Hanaoka), performed in the first Butoh performance overseas *Le Dernier Eden*. Moved to Germany in 1988. Formed tatoeba THÉÂTRE DANSE GROTESQUE, followed by TEN PEN CHii ART LABOR in 1994. Been holding *eX…it!, a Butoh-Related eXchange Festival* every four years with delta RA'i since 1995.

A Report of Butoh Research 2017–2019

舞踏リサーチ2017-2019報告書

調査目的
Research Objectives

舞踏は80年代以降、世界中の舞踊、演劇、アートフェスティバルから招かれるようになり、舞台芸術の枠組みを超えて広く影響力を発揮してきた。日本で行われる舞踏のワークショップにも世界各国から参加者が集まり、様々な国で舞踏を実践する者たちの存在を窺い知ることができるが、その活動の全体像は未だ明らかになっていない。また舞踏は、その発端が明確である一方で、「舞踏とは何か」という問いに対する統一された答えはなく、第三者に対する説明は容易とは言えない。今後さらに、舞踏の始まりに立ち会った歴史の証人がいなくなる状況を迎えることを考えると、舞踏の「アーカイヴ」への意識を高め、議論を深めていくことが急務と言えるのではないだろうか。

舞踏に関係する資料は、これまでも各所で収集・蓄積され、確かなアーカイヴの取り組みが行われてきている。しかし、舞踏固有の魅力を、国境を超えて次世代にも伝え続けていくためには、舞踏をアーカイヴすることの可能性／不可能性と向き合いながら、過去の保存だけには留まらない、未来志向の積極的かつ創造的な取り組みを継続していくことが求められる。個人の枠に留まらない横断的かつ体系的なアーカイヴ構築のためには、世界各地で多種多様に展開する舞踏の現況を把握することが不可欠である。その足がかりとして、本法人はまず、国内外の舞踏の実践者を対象にした複数年にわたるアンケート調査に取り組んだ。今まさに起きている現象を捉え、可視化することで、舞踏という無形の財産の継承に向けた議論を開くことを調査の最終目標とする。

本調査は、アーツカウンシル東京（公益財団法人東京都歴史文化財団）の平成29年度東京芸術文化創造発信助成【長期助成プログラム】の助成を受けて実施した。

Butoh has been invited to dance, drama and art festivals around the world since the 1980s, and has exerted a wide influence beyond the performing arts framework. People gather from all over the world at Butoh workshops in Japan, and can meet practitioners from many countries, but we still do not have an overall picture of what they all do. Additionally, although Butoh has a clear starting point, there is no unified answer to the question "What is Butoh?", and it is not easy to describe. As we head towards a time where we no longer have those who were there at the beginning of Butoh's history with us, it is becoming necessary to raise awareness of Butoh archives, and engage in deeper discussions.

Efforts to source, collect and archive Butoh-related materials are already being made in various locations. However, in order for Butoh to be passed on not only abroad but to future generations, we need to think about what is possible in trying to archive Butoh, and consider not only preserving the past, but how to continue our active and creative initiatives in the future. To create an archive that is inclusive of many viewpoints and systems, it is essential to grasp the current situation of Butoh all over the world. In order to achieve this, our organisation has started by conducting a survey of Butoh practitioners internationally over the course of several years.

The main aim of this study is to capture and visualise what is happening in Butoh at the moment, and to open discussions about the succession of this intangible *something* called Butoh.

This survey has been supported by the Arts Council Tokyo Grant Program [Long Term Grants] from the Arts Council Tokyo (Tokyo Metropolitan Foundation for History and Culture).

調査の変遷
Survey History

調査は、2017年度・2018年度・2019年度の3ヶ年にわたって行った。うち2017・2018年度は不特定多数に向けてアンケートを頒布し、2019年度は過年度の回答者のみを対象とした。以下に続く本報告書では、2017・2018年度のデータを主に取り上げる。調査の性質が異なる2019年度分については、本稿末尾「まとめ」の欄で言及する。

2017年度は日本国内で活動する舞踏家を対象とし、2018年度は国内調査の継続と並行して、国外へも調査対象を拡大した。2018年度の国内版では、前年度の回答者と新規回答者のフォームを分け、前者については「前年度と同じ」という選択肢を設け、重複する設問への回答を省略できる形にした。また2018年度のアンケートは、前年の回答結果を踏まえて、質問項目の再構成を行なった。2018年度版において前年度と大きく異なる点は、以下の3つである。

These surveys were been conducted over 3 years in 2017, 2018 and 2019. The 2017 and 2018 surveys were sent to a large, unspecified number of people, but in 2019 only previous survey respondents were contacted. This report focuses on the surveys conducted in 2017 and 2018. The nature of the survey 2019 was different, and is referred to in the "Summary" at the end.

The 2017 survey was conducted only among Butoh dancers based in Japan, and was then expanded overseas in 2018. In 2018, respondents from the previous year were contacted separately, and had the option to answer questions with "same as last year" to prevent duplicate answers.

Additionally, the 2018 survey had some restructuring based on answers from the previous year. There were 3 main differences between in the 2018 survey and the year before:

1. 定期的に活動を行うプロフェッショナルの実践者のみならず、様々な形で舞踏を実践するアマチュア層にも回答してもらえる設問と対象者抽出方法にする
2. 舞踏の捉え方や魅力など、「舞踏とは何か」について回答者個々人の多様な考え方や価値観を汲みあげることができる設問にする
3. 現状についての聞き取りだけでなく、舞踏の継承やアーカイヴのあり方についての考えを問う質問を設ける

1. Inclusion of amateurs practising Butoh in a variety of ways as well as regularly performing professionals, with questions they could answer.
2. Inclusion of the diverse thoughts and values regarding "what Butoh is" in the form of questions on Butoh interpretation and its appeal.
3. Inclusion of questions regarding thoughts on the succession of Butoh and archiving it.

調査概要
Survey Summary

アンケート対象者
舞踏家あるいは舞踏に影響を受けて様々な形で舞踏を実践する人たち

対象者抽出方法
①NPO法人ダンスアーカイヴ構想および大野一雄舞踏研究所のメーリングリストでの配信　②ワークショップ等を行う舞踏家への情報拡散依頼　③「舞踏」「Butoh」等のキーワードを用いてインターネットやSNSで検索、直接連絡　④NPO法人ダンスアーカイヴ構想公式ウェブサイト、SNSアカウントでの情報拡散

調査方法
ウェブフォーム　および書面によるアンケート

言語
アンケートでの使用言語：日本語、英語、中国語
回答受付言語：日本語、英語、フランス語、ドイツ語、イタリア語、スペイン語、ポルトガル語、中国語、インドネシア語

Survey Target Audience
Butoh dancers and those who practise or are influenced by Butoh in a variety of ways

Distribution Method
(A) Through the Dance Archive Network and Kazuo Ohno Dance Studio mailing lists (B) Distribution by request to Butoh dancers holding workshops (C) Contacting people via searches on the Internet and social media using the keyword "Butoh" (D) Sharing information through the official Dance Archive Network website and social media

Survey Method
Online surveys and paper surveys

Languages
Survey languages: Japanese, English, Chinese
Response languages: Japanese, English, French, German, Italian, Spanish, Portuguese, Chinese, Indonesian

調査結果
Survey Results

調査結果の中から、注目すべき項目を紹介する。
Some notable points regarding the survey results.

活動拠点地
Base of Activities

活動拠点地を教えてください。
Where are you based?

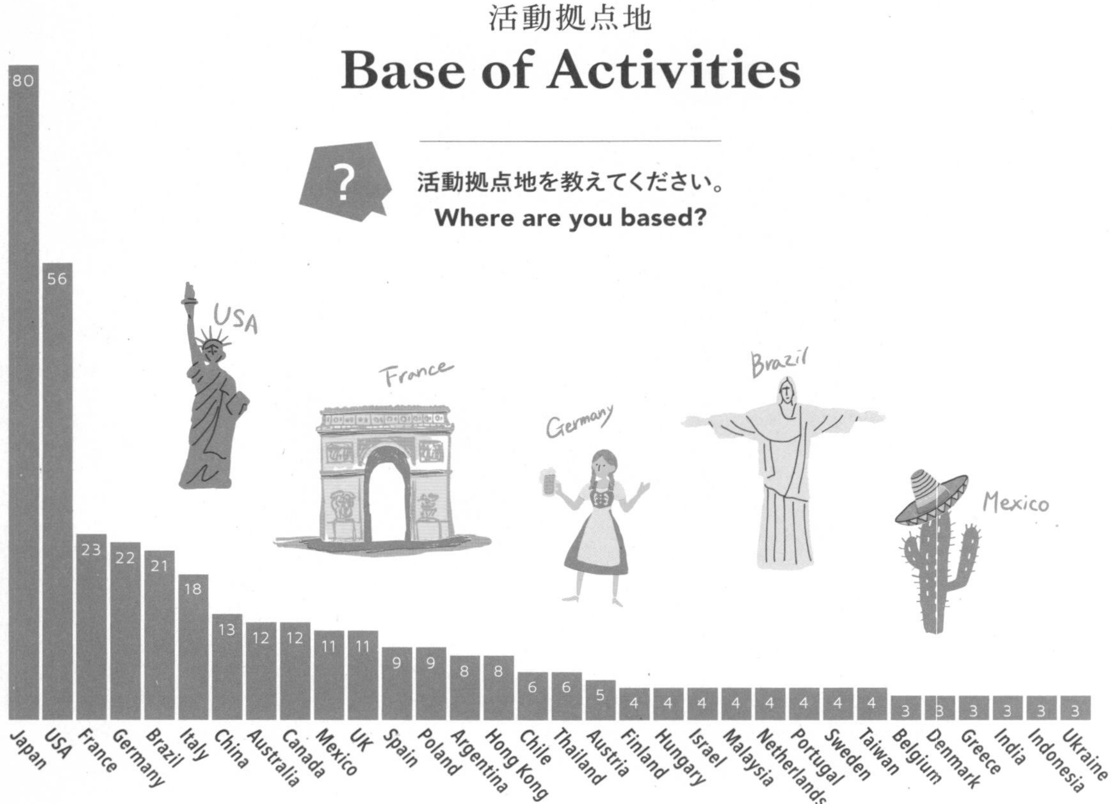

(Butoh Research 2018 国内&国外 | Japan & International)

2018年度に日本国外を対象に実施したアンケートでは、50ヵ国から332件の回答が寄せられた。アメリカの回答数が最も多く、次いでフランス、ドイツ、そして南米のブラジルからとなった。南米は他にも、メキシコやアルゼンチン、チリからの回答もあり、舞踏実践者あるいはそのコミュニティーの確かな地盤を感じさせた。アフリカは少ないが、マダガスカルとナイジェリアからそれぞれ反応があった。欧米圏よりは少ないが、中国からも一定数の回答が得られた。アンケートの拡散の程度が地域によって異なることから、当データが各国における舞踏の浸透度合いを反映しているとは必ずしも言えないが、インターネットとSNSの普及により本調査が可能となり、それぞれの地域で、舞踏の実践者が紛れもなく存在することが確認できた。これまで実感としてはありながらも、あくまで印象として語られてきた「舞踏(の実践者)が世界に広がっている」という現状の一端を可視化することができた。

The 2018 international survey received 332 responses from 50 different countries. The highest number of responses came from the USA, followed by France, Germany and Brazil. From South America there were also responses from Mexico, Argentina and Chile, giving a sense of a solid network of Butoh practitioners or communities there. Although there were not many responses from Africa, there were a few from Madagascar and Nigeria. Although fewer than Europe or the USA, there was also a number of responses from China. This survey is not enough to say to what extent Butoh has spread in each country, but the expansion of the Internet has made it possible to conduct this survey and confirm the existence of Butoh practitioners in these various areas. There had until now been a general feeling of "Butoh (practitioners) spreading throughout the world" but now we are able to visualise some of them.

活動形態

Activity Engagement

2018年の活動の主な形態について、教えてください。(3つ選択可能)
What were your main activities in 2018? (Choose up to 3)

活動形態 / Activity	国内 Japan	国外 International
公演への出演 Performance Appearances	50	226
ワークショップ・レッスン講師 Workshop/Lesson Instruction	26	151
公演での演出 Performance Direction	23	134
ワークショップ・レッスン受講 Workshop/Lesson Participation	18	94
自主的な稽古 Personal Practice	24	74
振付または演出(外部オファー) Choreography/Direction (by Invitation)	10	60
映像出演(外部オファー) Film Appearance (by Invitation)	6	56
(大学など)教育機関での教鞭 Teaching In Educational Institutions (e.g. University)	6	45
プライベートで踊る(自宅など) Dancing In Private (at Home etc)	9	36
自主的な映像制作・配信 Independent Audio-visual production/Distribution	4	29
セラピー Therapy	4	11
モデル Modelling	1	5

国内 Japan
国外 International

(Butoh Research 2018 国内&国外 | Japan & International)

!

活動の形態については、「公演への出演」が最も多く、次いで「ワークショップ・レッスン講師」が挙がっていることも国内と国外で違いが見られなかった。国外においても、自身で舞踏を実践するのみならず、他者に教えている人が多く存在しているということが確認された。その他に、「セラピー」を挙げる人が国内外ともに一定数存在することも舞踏のあり方の一つとして興味深い。また、公演に出演することだけが舞踏の実践であるとは言えないため、「(自宅などで)プライベートで踊る」「自主的な映像製作・配信」という選択肢を2018年度より新たに加えた。舞踏のアーカイヴを行う上では、舞踏が今後より多様な活動形態へと派生していく可能性も視野に入れるべきであると考える。

Regarding types of activities, there was no difference between Japan and abroad where “Performance Appearances” were the most common activity, followed by “Workshop/Lesson Instruction”. This confirms that many people outside of Japan are not only practicing but also teaching Butoh. It is also interesting that “Therapy” is thought of as a form of Butoh by people both in Japan and internationally. Additionally, as being part of a performance is not the only way to practice Butoh, both “Dancing in private (at home etc.)” and “Independent Audio-visual production/Distribution” were added as possible responses to the 2018 survey. As well as archiving Butoh, we should consider the possibilities of Butoh diversifying into different forms in the future.

公演・パフォーマンス会場
Performance Venues

2017年にアンケート対象者が踊った場所(国内)
Where did you dance in 2017? (Japan)

京都 | Kyoto(12)
UrBANGUILD、京都芸術劇場 春秋座 studio21、有鄰館、京都大学西部講堂、春秋山荘、アトリエ劇研、元・立誠小学校、京都芸術センター、a.room、東福寺、京都国際マンガミュージアム、京都舞踏館
UrBANGUILD, Kyoto Art Theater Shunjuza studio21, Yurinkan Museum, Kyoto University Seibu Kodo, Syunju Sanso, Atelier Gekken, Old Rissei Elementary School, Kyoto Art Center, a.room, Tofuku-ji, Kyoto International Manga Museum, KYOTO BUTOH-KAN

兵庫 | Hyogo(6)
神戸アートビレッジセンター、神戸市立灘区民ホール、DANCE BOX、フレンテホール、神戸港船上(観光船ファンタジー号)、AI・HALL(伊丹市立演劇ホール)
Kobe Art Village Center, Nada Ward Community Hall, DANCE BOX, Frente Hall, On board Kobe Seabus Fantasy, AI-HALL (Itami Municipal Theater Hall)

富山 | Toyama(1)
黒部市国際文化センター コラーレ
Kurobe City International Cultural Center Colare

福岡 | Fukuoka(7)
北九州芸術劇場、GALLERY SOAP、枝光本町商店街アイアンシアター、ミリカローデン那珂川、舞踏青龍會アトリエ、イタリア会館、チープサイド
Kitakyushu Performing Arts Center, GALLERY SOAP, Edamitsu Honmachi Shotengai Irontheater, Mirica Roden Nakagawa, Butoh Seiryu-kai Atelier, Centro Italiano di Fukuoka, Cheap side

石川 | Ishikawa(1)
金沢市民芸術村
Kanazawa Citizen's Art Center

鳥取 | Tottori(1)
鳥の劇場
BIRD Theatre

滋賀 | Shiga(1)
滋賀県立芸術劇場 びわ湖ホール
Biwako Hall Center for the Performing Arts, Shiga

岡山 | Okayama(3)
上之町會舘、ルネスホール、奈義町現代美術館
Kaminocho Kaikan, Renaiss Hall, Nagi-cho Museum of Contemporary Art

熊本 | Kumamoto(2)
熊本市現代美術館、新聞博物館
Contemporary Art Museum Kumamoto, Shinbun Museum

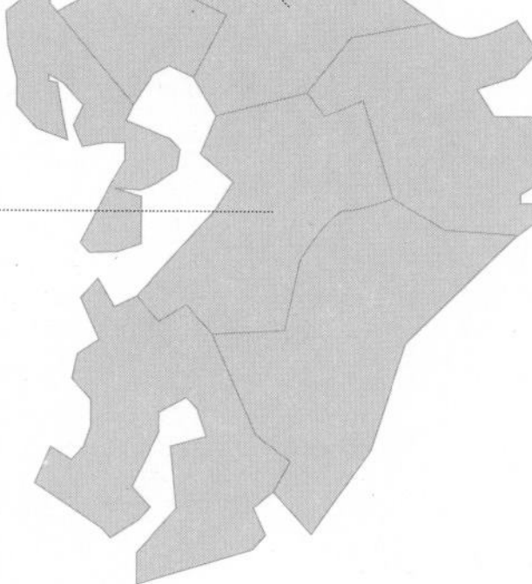

三重 | Mie(1)
Théâtre de Belleville
Théâtre de Belleville

大阪 | Osaka(3)
茨木市クリエイトセンターホール、枚岡神社、空堀商店街界隈
Ibaraki City Civic General Center (Create Center) Hall, Hiraoka Shrine, Karahori Shopping Street

愛知 | Aichi(5)
穂の国とよはし芸術劇場プラット、中日劇場、パティオ池鯉鮒(知立市文化会館)、真清田神社、大府夏まつり
Toyohashi Arts Theatre PLAT, Chunichi Theatre, Chiryu Cultural Center (Patio Chiryu), Masumida Shrine, Obu Summer Festival

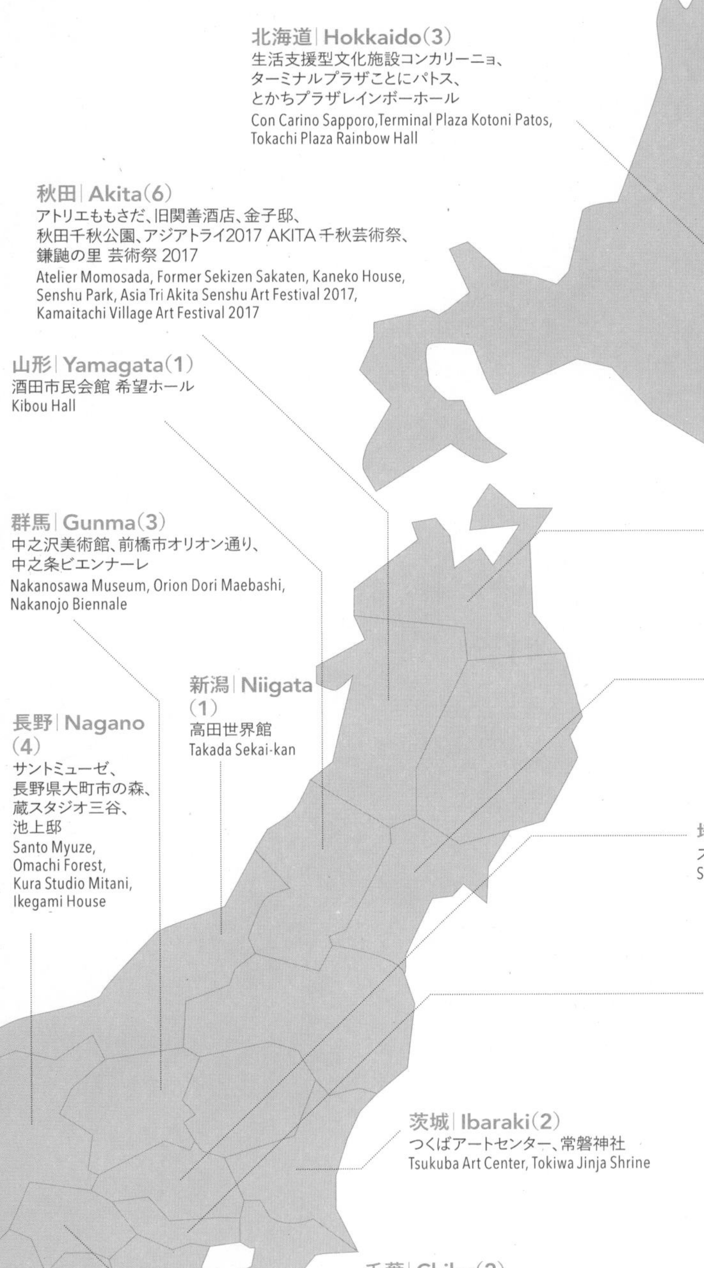

北海道 | Hokkaido(3)
生活支援型文化施設コンカリーニョ、ターミナルプラザことにパトス、とかちプラザレインボーホール
Con Carino Sapporo,Terminal Plaza Kotoni Patos, Tokachi Plaza Rainbow Hall

秋田 | Akita(6)
アトリエももさだ、旧関善酒店、金子邸、秋田千秋公園、アジアトライ2017 AKITA 千秋芸術祭、鎌鼬の里 芸術祭 2017
Atelier Momosada, Former Sekizen Sakaten, Kaneko House, Senshu Park, Asia Tri Akita Senshu Art Festival 2017, Kamaitachi Village Art Festival 2017

山形 | Yamagata(1)
酒田市民会館 希望ホール
Kibou Hall

群馬 | Gunma(3)
中之沢美術館、前橋市オリオン通り、中之条ビエンナーレ
Nakanosawa Museum, Orion Dori Maebashi, Nakanojo Biennale

新潟 | Niigata(1)
高田世界館
Takada Sekai-kan

長野 | Nagano(4)
サントミューゼ、長野県大町市の森、蔵スタジオ三谷、池上邸
Santo Myuze, Omachi Forest, Kura Studio Mitani, Ikegami House

青森 | Aomori(7)
八戸市南郷文化ホール、青森県立美術館、三沢市公会堂、淋代海岸、三沢市商店街、弘前大学、鳴海要記念陶房館
Hachinoheshi Nango Community Hall, Aomori Museum of Art, Misawa Civic Center,Sabishiro Beach, Misawa Shopping Street, Hirosaki University, Narumi Kaname Memorial Museum

宮城 | Miyagi(4)
せんだい演劇工房10-Box、佐々木美術館&人形館、蔵王わん!ワン!ランド、山ノ神神社
Sendai Theater Workshop 10-BOX, Sasaki Art & Doll Museum, ZAO Wan! Wan! Land, Kogotasan Shrine

埼玉 | Saitama(2)
スタジオ・バミ、富士見市文化会館・キラリふじみ
Studio-BAMI, Kirari Fujimi

東京 | Tokyo(68)
中野テルプシコール、こまばアゴラ劇場、神楽坂セッションハウス、アートスペース .kiten、明治座、新歌舞伎座、座・高円寺、SPACE 雑遊、金王八幡宮、東京藝術大学、なかのZERO、七針、ストライプハウスギャラリー、スペシャルカラーズ、アルティカセブン、東京芸術劇場、南池袋公園、メディアージュ、五反田の家、新宿ジャム、江古田フライングティーポット、美学校、アトリエ第Q芸術、豊洲シビックセンターホール、Yellow Vision、濃淡の間、楽道庵、高円寺Grain、日暮里 d- 倉庫、武蔵野市民文化会館、新木場のオフィス、ギャラリー南製作所、上野公園、調布市せんがわ劇場、浅草東洋館、日本大学体育館、ザムザ阿佐谷、シアターX、スタジオサイプレス、ギャラリーやどかり、寺田倉庫、CLUB LINER、世田谷パブリックシアター、井の頭公園、隅田公園、錦糸町駅前、VACANT、多摩六都科学館、東京ビッグサイト、学校法人片柳学園、ギャラリー鴻、Shibuya O-EAST、妙善寺、新国立劇場、阿佐谷天、天使館、RAFT、gift_lab、豊島屋酒造、早稲田大学、新宿ゴールデン街、代々木公園、Art Center Ongoing、スパイラルガーデン、SCOOL、なってるハウス、両国BEAR、サブテレニアン
Nakano Terpsichore, Komaba Agora Theater, Session House, Artspace .kiten, Meijiza, Shin Kabuki-za, Za-Koenji Theatre, SPACE zatsuyu, Konno Hachimangu Shrine, Tokyo University of the Arts, Nakano ZERO, Nanahari, STRIPED HOUSE GALLERY, Special Colors, Artica 7, Tokyo Metropolitan Theatre, Minami-Ikebukuro Park, Mediage, Gotanda House, Shinjuku Jam, Flying Tea Pot, Bigakko, Atelier Q, Toyosu Civic Centre Hall, Yellow Vision, Noutan Art Space, RakudoAn, Grain Koenji, d-Soko Nippori, Musashino Civic Cultural Hall, Office in Shin-Kiba, Gallery Minami Seisakusho, Ueno Park, Sengawa Theater, Asakusa Toyokan, Nihon University gymnasium, Zamuza Asagaya, Theatre X, Studio Cypress, Gallery Yadokari, Warehouse TERRADA, CLUB LINER, Setagaya Public Theatre, Inokashira Park, Sumida Park, Kinshicho Station, VACANT, Tama Rokuto Science Center, Tokyo Big Sight, Katayanagi Institute, Tokyo University of Technology Kamata Campus Gallery, Shibuya O-EAST, Myozenji Temple, New National Theater Tokyo, Asagaya-ten, Tenshikan, RAFT, gift_lab, Toshimayasyuzou, Waseda University, Shinjuku Golden Gai, Yoyogi Park, Art Center Ongoing, Spiral Garden, Scool, Knuttel House, Ryogoku Bear, Subterranean

茨城 | Ibaraki(2)
つくばアートセンター、常磐神社
Tsukuba Art Center, Tokiwa Jinja Shrine

千葉 | Chiba(2)
千葉県養老川全流域の境内や路上二十箇所、月出工舎
Along the banks of Yoro river in Chiba and 20 street locations, ARS TSUKIDE

神奈川 | Kanagawa(12)
横浜能楽堂、横浜赤レンガ倉庫1号館、若葉町ウォーフ、慶応義塾大学日吉来往舎、逗子海岸、藤沢公民館、大野一雄舞踏研究所、象の鼻カフェ、横浜にぎわい座・のげシャーレ、BankART、KAAT、Archiship Library & Cafe
Yokohama Noh Theater, Yokohama Red Brick Warehouse 1,WAKABACHO WHARF, Keio University Hiyoshi Campus,Zushi Beach, Fujisawa Community Center,Kazuo Ohno Dance Studio, Zounohana Cafe, Yokohama Nigiwai-za (Small Hall), BankART, Kanagawa Arts Theatre, Archiship Library & Cafe

静岡 | Shizuoka(1)
沼津ラクーン
Numazu Rakuun

山梨 | Yamanashi(3)
山梨県のとある蔵、甲府桜座、清春芸術村
A warehouse in Yamanashi, Sakuraza, Kiyoharu Art Colony

公演の集客
Audience Numbers

一公演（複数ステージ含める）にて達成された集客の規模を教えてください。
How many people attended each of your performances? (Total for multiple stagings)

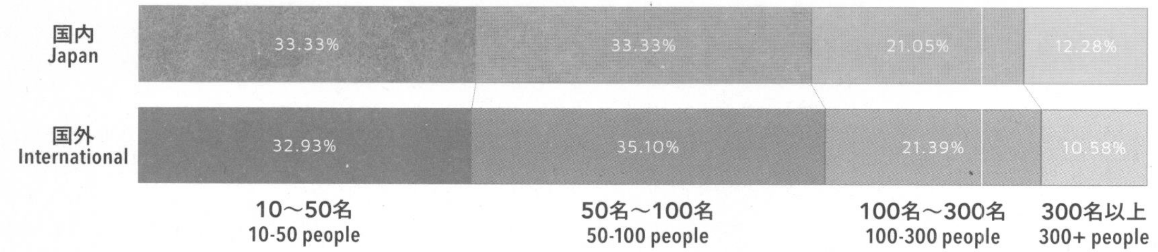

(Butoh Research 2018 国内&国外 | Japan & International)

What was the average price of your tickets?
公演チケットの平均的な価格を教えてください。

	国内 Japan	国外 International
無料 | free	8.21%	24.39%
1,500円未満（15ドル未満）| 1,500yen (under $15)	5.47%	34.63%
1,500円以上〜3,000円未満（15-30ドル）| 1,500-3,000yen ($15-30)	49.31%	31.32%
3,000円以上〜5,000円未満（30-50ドル）| 3,000-5,000yen ($30-50)	15.06%	1.8%
5,000円以上（50ドル以上）| Over 5,000yen ($50+)	NO DATA	0.6%

(Butoh Research 2018 国内&国外 | Japan & International)

!

集客規模については、国内外ともに100名以下の回答が多い（国内：約67% 国外：約68%）。また、チケットの平均価格は、国内では「1500円以上〜3000円未満」が約49%を占める。国外では、「無料」の回答が比較的多く見られる。公的な補助制度等が背景にあるのか、それとも趣味的に行なっているのかは定かではないが、何れにせよ、国内だけでなく国外においても、大規模な集客には至っていない状況を窺い知ることができる。

The most common responses regarding audience numbers were under 100 both in Japan and abroad (Japan: about 67%, International: about 68%). In Japan, ticket prices between "1,500-3,000yen ($15-30)" accounted for about 49% of responses, while most international performances were "Free". It is not clear whether these were funded by other sources or performed as a hobby, but it can be seen regardless that not many large audiences were attracted either in Japan or abroad.

集客のターゲット
Target Audiences

集客のターゲットについて教えてください。(複数回答可)
Who were your target audiences? (Multiple answers permitted)

	国内 Japan	国外 International
アート・表現全般に興味がある観客 | Audience with a general interest in art and culture	49	253
舞踏に興味がある観客 | Audience interested in Butoh	31	137
ダンス全般に興味がある観客 | Audience interested in dance in general	24	128
ダンサーや舞踏を知らない観客 | Audience unacquainted with dance or Butoh	20	106
自身の固定ファン | Established fan-base	17	23
家族・友人・知人 | Family / Friends / Acquaintances	14	30
他ジャンルアーティスト | Artists from other fields	4	81
ダンサー・振付家 | Dancers / Choreographers	2	33
その他 | Other	1	66

(Butoh Research 2018 国内&国外 | Japan & International)

!

国内外ともに、「アート・芸術全般に興味がある観客」がターゲットの最上位に挙がった。舞踏またはダンスの愛好者層に留まらず、広義のアートとして享受してもらいたいという期待があるのではないだろうか。生の舞台だけでなく、写真や映像といったメディアを通して広がってきた舞踏の特徴とも関係し得る、興味深い点である。より積極的にアート愛好者層にアピールする形で、舞踏が進化態を形成していく可能性も感じさせる。

Both in Japan and internationally, "Audience with a general interest art and culture" was the top target audience. It seems there is some expectation that Butoh may be enjoyed by the wider art community and not only by Butoh or dancer lovers. This may relate to Butoh's characteristic as a form that reaches people through photography and video, not just live performances. It also shows the potential that Butoh has to evolve and appeal to more arts lovers.

集客の工夫
Attracting Audience

!

2017年度版アンケートにおいて、「どのような集客の工夫に手応えを感ましたか?」の質問に対して最も多かった回答は、「SNSでの告知」であった。各自が行なっている工夫をさらに引き出すことができないかと考え、2018年度版アンケートでは回答を記述式に切り替えたところ、「地道な宣伝」「企画コンセプトの面白さ」「他ジャンルアーティストとのコラボレーション」などが挙げられたものの、他ジャンルの表現にはない「舞踏らしさ」を集客の方法に結びつける回答はほぼ見受けられなかった(「舞踏の言語化」が1件)。

In 2017, the most common answer to the survey question "What do you feel attracted the best audience?" was "Social Media". Wondering what individual responses to this question would look like, in the 2018 survey we switched to open responses, and received answers such as "responsible advertising", "interesting original concepts", and "collaborating with artists from other genres", but did not find so many Butoh-specific expressions such as "Butoh-ness" (just one mentioned "the language of Butoh").

経済状況
Economic Breakdown

2018年中の舞踏家・ダンサーとしての活動における収入および支出を教えてください。
How much did you make as a Butoh artist or dancer in 2018?

収入 Income	国内 Japan	国外 International
無し | None	21.91%	29.21%
10万円(1,000ドル)未満 | Under 100,000yen ($1,000)	28.76%	28.61%
10万円(1,000ドル)以上 | Over 100,000yen ($1,000)	26.02%	23.49%
100万円(10,000ドル)以上 | Over 1,000,000yen ($10,000)	10.95%	8.13%
300万円(30,000ドル)以上 | Over 3,000,000yen ($30,000)	2.73%	3.91%
無回答 | No response	0%	6.62%

支出 Expenses	国内 Japan	国外 International
無し | None	13.69%	15.96%
10万円(1,000ドル)未満 | Under 100,000yen ($1,000)	38.35%	40.66%
10万円(1,000ドル)以上 | Over 100,000yen ($1,000)	31.5%	28,01%
100万円(10,000ドル)以上 | Over 1,000,000yen ($10,000)	4.1%	6.02%
300万円(30,000ドル)以上 | Over 3,000,000yen ($30,000)	2.7%	2.4%
無回答 | No response	0%	6.92%

Butoh Research 2018
国内&国外 | Japan & International

舞踏との関わり方
Involvement in Butoh

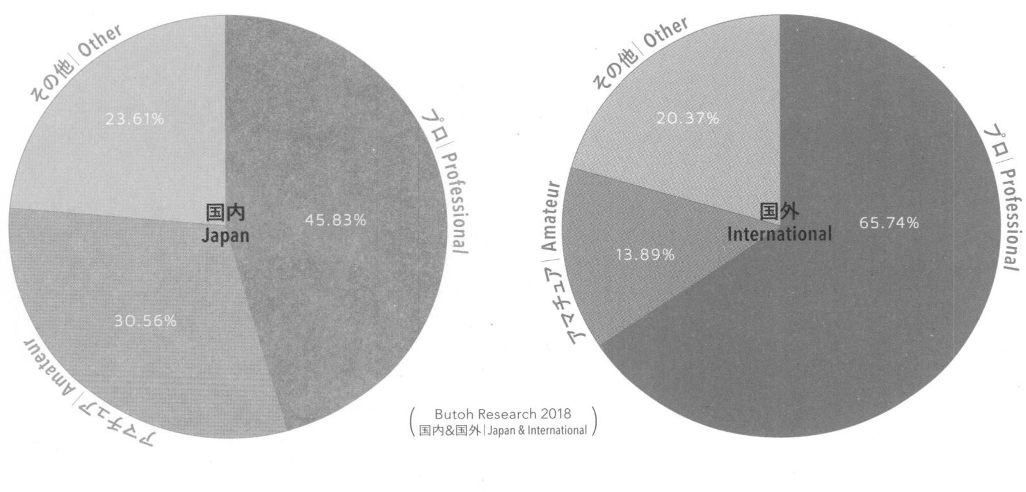

国内外ともに、「収入なし」と「10万円未満の収入」が過半数を占める(国内:約51% 国外: 約58%)。100万円以上の収入を得ている回答者は国内で約14%、国外ではわずか約12%で、舞踏の公演活動の収益化の難しさを窺い知ることができる。支出に関しても同様に、「支出なし」と「10万円未満の支出」が多い。これに反して、回答者のプロアマの比率を見ると、プロは決して少数であるとは言えない(国内:約46% 国外:約66%)。趣味的な活動をしている人が多いと考えるよりも、ある程度の支出が生じるであろう興行よりもワークショップやレッスンで収入を得ているプロの存在が考えられる。エデュケーションやアウトリーチの活動は、舞踏の普及には欠かせない。その一方で、コストがかかることが制作・上演におけるリスクや障壁として大きくなってくれば、舞踏の舞台作品が質量ともに減少していく可能性もある。

Both in Japan and internationally, the majority of responses regarding income was "None" or "Under 100,000yen ($1,000)" (Japan: about 51%, International: about 58%). Only about 14% of respondents earn more than 1 million yen ($10,000) in Japan and about 12% outside of Japan, indicating the difficulties in monetising Butoh performances. Many also responded "None" or "Under 100,000yen ($1,000)" for expenditures. Having said that, it is not as though the proportion of professionals is small compared to amateurs (Japan: about 46%, International: about 66%). Rather than assuming that many people are doing Butoh as a hobby, it may be that there are professionals who earn more money in workshops and lessons than in expensive performances. Education and outreach activities are essential for the spread of Butoh. But if the costs of putting on a performance are so high they create a barrier, it may greatly decrease the number of Butoh performances.

集客達成度と経済満足度
Audience Targets & Economic Satisfaction

集客の達成度はいかがでしたか。
Did you achieve your target audience numbers?

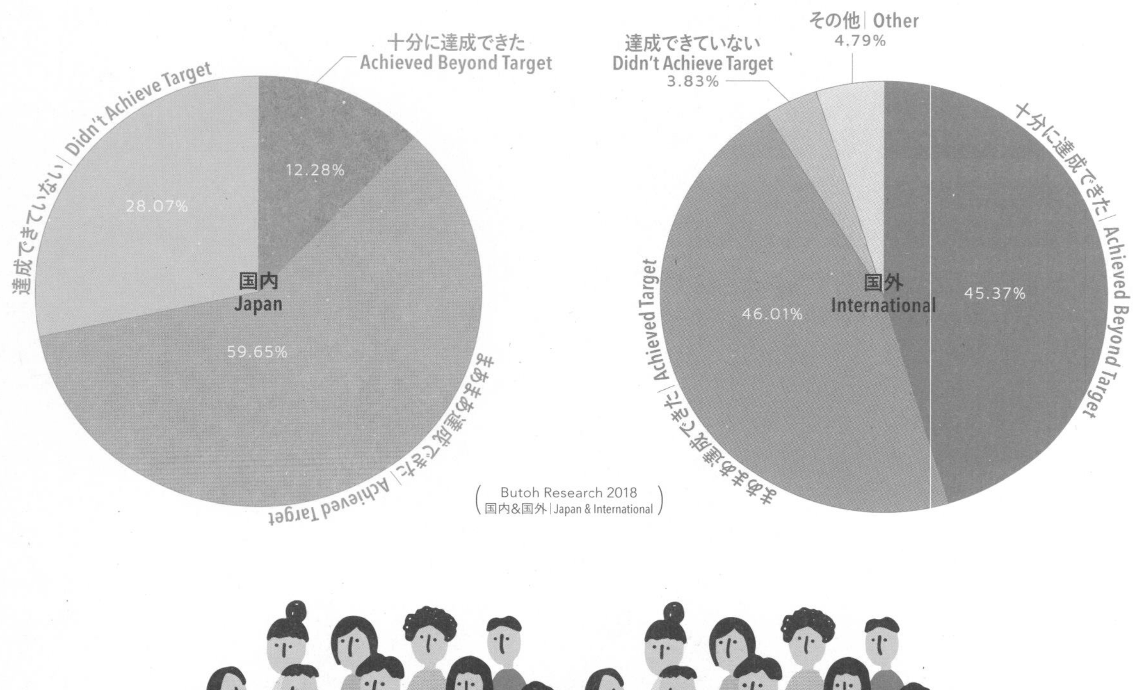

ターゲットした層への集客の達成度を見ると、国内外ともに「まあまあ達成できた」「十分に達成できた」が大きな割合を占める（国内：約72% 国外：約91%）。しかし、通年の経済状況に関しては「まったく満足していない」「それほど満足していない」が半数以上を占めており（国内：約78% 国外：約53%）、特に国内の舞踏家の満足度は著しく低い。集客が出来ているにもかかわらず、経済的な満足に結びつかないということは、舞台公演そのものが興行として成立していない、あるいは単体で成立しても安定した収入に至るほどの頻度で行うことが出来ない等の状況が推測できる。

また、2018年版アンケートより、「状況を改善するために必要なことは何ですか?」という質問を加えた。回答は様々であったが、「小規模な公演を対象とする助成制度の充実化」「舞踏家としての質の向上」「観客の層を広げるための表現の工夫」「ネットワークの拡大」「活動の計画性」「インターネットでの配信」などの回答が国内外問わず挙げられた。また、「人々は舞踏を『暗黒』や『恐怖』といったネガティブなイメージを持ちやすい。舞踏を見たことが無い人に向けて、ダンサーは今の舞踏が何かを示して、宣伝することに努力しなければいけないと思う。」といった舞踏固有の課題と結びつけた回答もあった。

2018年中の舞踏家・ダンサーとしての経済状況に満足していますか。
How satisfied were you with your income as a Butoh artist or dancer in 2018?

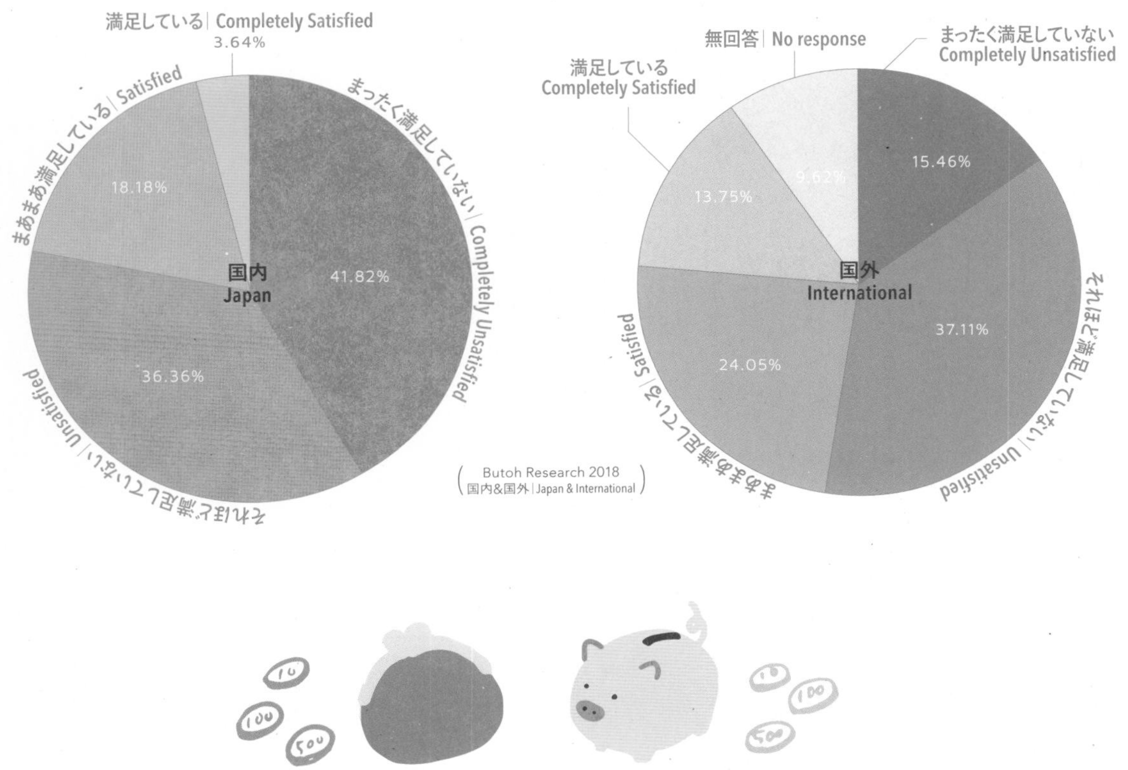

A high percentage of both Japanese and international respondents said that they either "Achieved Beyond" or "Achieved" their audience targets (Japan: about 72%, International: about 91%). However, over half responded that they were either "Completely Unsatisfied" or "Unsatisfied" with their annual income (Japan: about 78%, International: about 53%), with a particularly low satisfaction rate among Butoh dancers in Japan. Despite attracting audience, the fact that this isn't reflected in economic satisfaction rates implies that performances are either not well-established enough in the industry, or that if they are, they are not regular enough to provide a stable income.

In the 2018 survey we added the question "What is needed to improve this situation?". There were various responses, with answers such as "an enhancement of subsidies for small-scale performances", "better quality Butoh dancers", "a mode of expression that attracts a wider audience", "network expansion", "action plans" and "Internet distribution" from both Japan and overseas. We also had Butoh-specific answers such as "People tend to have a negative image of Butoh, such as 'darkness' or 'fear.' I think dancers have to make an effort to show and advertise what Butoh is today to those who have never seen it."

ケイトリン・コーカー

外国人研究者が日本で13年間みてきた舞踏活動の状況
— BUTOH RESEARCH 2017の調査結果を巡って

BUTOH RESEARCH 2017の調査結果の感想を述べる前に、筆者自身の立場を簡単に説明します。筆者は、2006年に来日し、現在まで日本で舞踏を人類学的に研究してきました。人類学的な研究というのは、舞踏家の下に行き、お話しを伺い、身を以て舞踏を踊ろうとしつつ稽古や舞台を観察することです。筆者は、特に、土方巽の弟子による舞踏実践に注目し、2019年に『暗黒舞踏の身体経験—アフェクトと生成の人類学』という書籍を出版しました。

13年間の中で最も大きな変化といえば大切な舞踏家を失ったことです。大野一雄氏(2010年他界)、室伏鴻氏(2015年他界)、和栗由紀夫氏(2017年他界)はかけがえのない存在でした。

変わらないのは、活動継続の困難さ、舞踏の需要不足、舞踏の定義付けの不可能性です。BUTOH RESEARCH 2017の調査結果を参考にしつつ、この3つに関する感想を述べます。

まず、舞踏では生活費を稼げないため、活動の継続は困難です。では、この事実が変わらないなら、舞踏はいかに1950年代末から続いてこられたのでしょうか。

舞踏の初期からおそらく90年代半ばまでは、踊り手がキャバレーやストリップ劇場でダンサーとして働き、その給料が集団のマネージャーに直接支払われており、それにより集団生活と舞踏活動が支えられていました。踊り手は否応なく派遣されていましたが、その一方でキャバレーへの出演は踊り手の体を鍛え、舞台経験の蓄積にもつながりました。当時は素朴な食事や雑魚寝といった生活だったそうですが、全身全霊を舞踏に注ぐことができました。

90年代までには、ほとんどのキャバレーが消滅し、前述の生活もなくなりました。今では、多くの舞踏家が活動を支えるために様々なパートの仕事をしているのが現状でしょう。今日の経済情勢では、バイトやパートの給料が低く、生活と活動を維持するために正社員より多くの時間を費やして働かざるをえないことは珍しくありません。また、正社員なら、活動よりも仕事を優先することが期待されます。舞踏やダンスは職業ではなく、趣味として見なされることが多く、それが問題の一つです。その結果、40.37%(2017年度国内調査結果)が収入に関して「まったく満足していない」と回答したと考えられます。

これは需要の問題につながります。舞踏は、鑑賞者に常連が多く年齢層が高いため、一般人や若者へのアピールが弱いようです。土方巽の時代のように若者を熱狂せる活気や原動力が不足しているとはいうものの、時代のニーズに応えていないわけでもないと思います。土方巽は、前衛的なクラブから大衆的なデパートに至るまで、様々な場所で弟子たちを躍らせて、様々なメディアに現れました。また、麿赤兒氏や田中泯氏も役者としても活動することで名がより知られるようになったでしょう。現在の舞踏家は芸能人になるのも一つの手段ですが、他にSNSでの発信という手段があげられます。山海塾の石井則仁氏や大駱駝館の松田篤史氏のように、インスタグラムを通して舞踏の写真や動画を広められたら、舞踏の認知度そして需要が増えるでしょう。舞踏は今日どんどんと薄れていく肉体感覚にパンチを与えてくれるものであり、そのビジュアルの強さは武器です。舞踏家たちには時代の波に乗りつつ、次の波を導いてほしいです。

時代に共鳴しながらも、舞踏は矛盾を包括し、定義に抵抗するもののままで良いと思います。回答の中で総括的に論じられている舞踏は、日本的でありながら普遍的、「様式」があるものの様式を取っ払う前衛的なものであるという矛盾が見られます。不変の本質に言及する回答があると同時に、舞踏は時代によって変化していくという回答もあります。舞踏は肉体と同様に支配に従わず、勝手に生きていくものです。我々の思う、文化、民族、美学、そういったものの虚無を露わにするものです。言葉で舞踏の内実を掴もうとしても、その内実が逃げていくことも、舞踏の魅力だと思います。

ケイトリン・コーカー
1985年、カリフォルニア生まれ。2006年、サウスカロライナ大学卒業し来日、暗黒舞踏の研究を開始する。17年、京都大学大学院人間・環境学研究科博士課程修了(文化人類学博士)。立命館大学衣笠総合研究機構専門研究員を経て、現在京都大学国際高等教育院特定講師。

Caitlin Coker

Work on Butoh as viewed by a Foreign Researcher over 13 years — the 2017 BUTOH RESEARCH results

Before stating my impressions of the Butoh Research 2017 survey results, let me first explain my own position. I came to Japan in 2006, and have been studying Butoh from an anthropological perspective. When I say anthropological, I mean I study Butoh artists behind the scenes, speaking to them, observing their practice and performances while also dancing myself. This year, 2019, I published a book focusing on the practice of the students of Tatsumi Hijikata titled *A Physical Experience of Ankoku Butoh: The Anthropology of Affect and Creation.*

The biggest change in the last 13 years has been the loss of important Butoh artists such as Kazuo Ohno (d. 2010), Ko Murobushi (d. 2015), and Yukio Waguri (d. 2017), who were truly irreplaceable.

Things that haven't changed are the difficulties of making a living as a Butoh artist, lack of demand for Butoh and the impossibility of defining Butoh. I would like to comment on these three points while referencing the Butoh Research 2017 results.

First, continuing to perform is difficult if one cannot earn a living through Butoh. But if this fact has not changed, how has Butoh survived since the late 1950s?

From the beginning of Butoh to probably around the mid-1990s, dancers worked in cabaret and strip clubs, and the money earned from this was given directly to Butoh group managers, providing income both for the group and their activities. Although not a lifestyle of choice, these cabaret performances strengthened the bodies of the dancers, and gave them stage experience. They lived on simple meals and slept in cramped spaces, but they were able to put their entire lives into Butoh.

By the 1990s most of the cabarets were shut down, and this lifestyle disappeared. These days many Butoh artists do various kinds of part time work to sustain themselves. In today's economic situation part time salaries are low, and it is not unusual to have to work longer hours than regular workers in order to sustain this life. In addition, workers are expected to prioritize work over their other activities. It is therefore common for Butoh and dance to be seen not as a profession but a hobby, and this is a problem. As a result, 40.37% (2017 Japan survey) of respondents say they are "completely unsatisfied" with their salaries.

This connects to the issue of demand. Butoh appears to have little appeal to the general public and young people, because the audiences tend to be the same and of an older generation. Although there is a lack of drive and enthusiasm among the youth compared to Tatsumi Hijikata's era, I don't think this means it does not meet today's needs. Tatsumi Hijikata made his students dance in a variety of places, from avant-garde clubs to popular department stores, and he appeared in various media. Likewise, the names Akaji Maro and Min Tanaka are well known due to their careers as screen actors. Today's Butoh artists could become entertainers, or they could use social media. If we spread more pictures and videos of Butoh on Instagram, like Sankai Juku's Norihito Ishii or Dairakudakan's Atsushi Matsuda, this would create an awareness and demand for Butoh. Butoh gives a punch to the fading bodily sensations of today, and the strength of that visual is a weapon. I would like to see dancers guide the wave of tomorrow while riding the wave of today.

Butoh resonates with its times and is full of contradictions, and I think it is fine for it to resist definition. We can see these contradictions from the survey responses - it is Japanese while being universal, an avant-garde 'style' that throws aside all styles. While an unchanging essence is often mentioned, there is also talk of Butoh changing with the times. Butoh is not about controlling the body, but the body living on its own accord. It exposes the voids we conceive of as culture, human, or art. I think that how the secrets of Butoh escaping our grasp even as we try to put them into words is part of what makes it Butoh.

Caitlin Coker

Born in California, 1985. Graduated from the University of South Carolina in 2006 and began studying Ankoku Butoh. Completed a PhD in Cultural Anthropology at Kyoto University in 2017. Worked as a researcher at the Kinugasa Research Organisation at Ritsumeikan University, and now as a lecturer at Kyoto University Graduate School of Human and Environmental Studies.

舞踏に興味を持ったきっかけ
Reasons for Starting Butoh

あなたが舞踏をはじめたきっかけを教えてください。(複数回答可)
What was the reason you started Butoh? (Multiple answers permitted)

項目 / Item	国内 Japan	国外 International
舞踏ワークショップ・舞踏の作品制作への参加 Participated in a Butoh workshop or production	17	213
生の舞踏公演を鑑賞して Attended a live Butoh performance	18	168
他ジャンルのダンスからの興味の移行 Developed an interest via other genres of dance	17	103
写真・映像・チラシ・ポスター・雑誌・インターネット等のメディアを通して舞踏を見て Saw Butoh in photographs, film, flyers, posters, magazines, on the Internet etc.	11	101
演劇や映画などの隣接領域の芸術からの興味の移行 Developed an interest via other artistic disciplines such as theatre or film	13	72
家族・知人・教員等からの勧め Recommended by family, acquaintances, teachers etc.	7	48
その他 Other	9	45

(Butoh Research 2018 国内&国外 | Japan & International)

2017年度における、「舞踏を始めたきっかけを教えてください」の質問に対する記述回答を以下の6つのカテゴリーに分類することができた。

〔A〕生の舞踏公演を鑑賞して
〔B〕演劇や映画などの隣接領域の芸術からの興味の移行
〔C〕写真・映像・チラシ・ポスター・雑誌・インターネット等のメディアを通して舞踏を見て
〔D〕家族・知人・教員等からの勧め
〔E〕舞踏ワークショップ・舞踏の作品制作への参加
〔F〕その他

〔A〕生の舞踏公演を鑑賞したことや〔E〕舞踏ワークショップ、舞踏の作品制作への参加など、舞踏に直接的に触れた経験を挙げる回答は多く見られた一方で、〔C〕写真や映像などのメディアを通して見たことや、チラシ、ポスターなどの印刷物から舞踏に出会ったという回答も同程度に多く見られた。舞台上の出来事だけでなく、記録媒体を通してもその魅力が伝播する、ということは舞踏の持つインパクト、あるいは今後も有効なポテンシャルなのかもしれない。また、〔B〕隣接領域の芸術から舞踏を知ったという回答も複数あり、複数のジャンルを横断・越境するような初期の活動の影響を窺うことができた。

上記の6つのカテゴリーはそのまま、2018年度版の回答選択肢として反映した。国外では、「舞踏ワークショップ・舞踏の作品制作への参加」(213件)が「生の舞台公演を鑑賞して」(168件)よりも多い。舞台作品に触れるよりも、エデュケーションあるいはアウトリーチの過程で舞踏を知る機会が多い状況を読み取ることができる。また、国外アンケートでは、「舞踏ワークショップ・舞踏の作品制作への参加」「生の舞台公演を鑑賞して」の具体名の内訳がそれぞれ以下の通りであった。

In the 2017 survey there were 6 choices in response to the question "What was the reason you started Butoh?":

(A) Attended a live Butoh performance
(B) Developed an interest via other artistic disciplines such as theatre or film
(C) Saw Butoh in photographs, film, flyers, posters, magazines, on the Internet etc.
(D) Recommended by family, acquaintances, teachers etc
(E) Participated in a Butoh workshop or production
(F) Other

Many respondents chose direct experiences of Butoh, such as (A) Attended a live Butoh performance or (E) Participated in a Butoh workshop or production, and about the same number of respondents chose (C) Saw Butoh in photographs, film, flyers, posters, magazines, on the Internet etc. The fact that Butoh can attract people through recorded mediums and not just through live performances is one of its strengths, and may be a potential for its future. Additionally, a number of respondents said that they (B) Developed an interest via other artistic disciplines, which shows us how the influence of the early days of Butoh has spread across multiple genres.

These six response options were the same for the 2018 survey. Internationally, "Participated in a Butoh workshop or production" (213) accounted for more than "Attended a live Butoh performance" (168). This shows more people learning about Butoh through education and outreach programmes than through performances.

In the overseas survey we also asked those who responded "Participated in a Butoh workshop or production" or "Attended a live Butoh performance" for the names of the dancers involved, which were as follows:

舞踏をはじめたきっかけ – 参加した舞踏ワークショップやプロダクション
Reasons for Starting Butoh – Butoh Workshops and Productions

Name	Count
竹之内淳志 Atsushi Takenouchi	38
大野慶人 Yoshito Ohno	26
吉岡由美子 Yumiko Yoshioka	24
和栗由紀夫 Yukio Waguri	21
中嶋 夏 Natsu Nakajima	17
遠藤公義 Tadashi Endo	17
桂勘 Kan Katsura	17
室伏 鴻 Ko Murobushi	15
哈爾賓派 Harupin-ha	12
大野一雄 Kazuo Ohno	12
笠井 叡 Akira Kasai	11
Diego Piñon	11
岩名雅記 Masaki Iwana	10
工藤丈輝 Taketeru Kudo	9
カルロッタ池田 Carlotta Ikeda	8
大野一雄&慶人 Kazuo & Yoshito Ohno	8
富永真紀子 Makiko Tominaga	8
山海塾 Sankai Juku	8
ジョン・ラーグ Joan Laage	7
ケン五月 Ken Mai	7
SU-EN	6
カセキユウコ Yuko Kaseki	6
麿 赤兒 Akaji Maro	5
財津暁平 Gyohei Zaitsu	5
関 美奈子 Minako Seki	5
正朔 Seisaku	5
蟬丸 Semimaru	5
古関すまこ Sumako Koseki	5
福原哲郎 Tetsuro Fukuhara	5
Vangeline	5
長岡ゆり Yuri Nagaoka	5
大駱駝艦 Dairakudakan	4
Eugenia Vargas	4
Motimaru	4
Valentin Tszin	4
元藤燁子 Akiko Motofuji	3
吉本大輔 Daisuke Yoshimoto	3
Gustavo Collini	3
土方 巽 Tatsumi Hijikata	3
Kea Tonetti	3
若松萌野 Moeno Wakamatsu	3
藤條虫丸 Mushimaru Fujieda	3
岩下 徹 Toru Iwashita	3
鶴山欣也 Kinya Tsuruyama	3
向 雲太郎 Kumotaro Mukai	3

舞踏をはじめたきっかけ – 鑑賞した生の舞踏公演
Reasons for Starting Butoh – Butoh Performances

Name	Count	Name	Count	Name	Count	Name	Count
山海塾 Sankai Juku	32	岩名雅記 Masaki Iwana	10	Natalia Cuéllar	3	今 貂子 Ima Tenko	2
大野一雄 Kazuo Ohno	24	遠藤公義 Tadashi Endo	10	山崎広太 Kouta Yamazaki	3	ジョン・ラーグ Joan Laage	2
室伏 鴻 Ko Murobushi	18	カルロッタ池田 Carlotta Ikeda	9	川口隆夫 Takao Kawaguchi	3	向 雲太郎 Kumotaro Mukai	2
竹之内淳志 Atsushi Takenouchi	17	富永真紀子 Makiko Tominaga	9	Vangeline	3	Marie-Gabrielle Rotie	2
大駱駝艦 Dairakudakan	13	和栗由紀夫 Yukio Waguri	8	芦川羊子 Yoko Ashikawa	3	Maruska Ronchi	2
中嶋 夏 Natsu Nakajima	13	桂勘 Kan Katsura	7	アリアドーネの會 Ariadone Company	2	Maya Dunsky	2
田中 泯 Min Tanaka	12	エイコ&コマ Eiko & Koma	6	白虎社 Byakkosha	2	関 美奈子 Minako Seki	5
大野慶人 Yoshito Ohno	12	土方 巽 Tatsumi Hijikata	6	吉本大輔 Daisuke Yoshimoto	2	SU-EN	2
笠井 叡 Akira Kasai	11	麿 赤兒 Akaji Maro	5	Diego Piñon	2	田中トシ Toshi Tanaka	2
吉岡由美子 Yumiko Yoshioka	11	カセキユウコ Yuko Kaseki	5	Eugenia Vargas	2	Valentin Tszin	2
哈爾賓派 Harupin-ha	10	ケン五月 Ken Mai	4	財津暁平 Gyohei Zaitsu	2	天児牛大 Ushio Amagatsu	2
大野一雄&慶人 Kazuo & Yoshito Ohno	10	工藤丈輝 Taketeru Kudo	4	白桃房 Hakutobo	2		

!

大野一雄や大野慶人、室伏鴻、中嶋夏、山海塾といった名前に加えて、国外に拠点を移し、長年に渡って活動を継続しながら各地で影響を与えてきた何名かの舞踏家の名前が浮かび上がった。とりわけ「舞踏ワークショップ・舞踏の作品制作への参加」の回答でトップを占めた竹之内淳志は、欧州内で知名度を得ている様子が窺える。その他には、吉岡由美子、遠藤公義（ルビ：ただし）、岩名雅記、カルロッタ池田の名前も頻出している。

In addition to names such as Kazuo Ohno, Yoshito Ohno, Ko Murobushi, Natsu Nakajima, and Sankai Juku, some names that came up were of dancers who have moved and been active abroad for many years. Atsushi Takenouchi in particular was mentioned the most for "Participated in a Butoh workshop or production", and seems to have gained recognition in Europe. Other names included Yumiko Yoshioka, Tadashi Endo, Masaki Iwana, and Carlotta Ikeda.

舞踏の定義
Defining Butoh

「あなたは舞踏をどのように説明しますか?」という質問に対する記述回答からは、その表現の多くが詩的あるいは思索的であることに加えて、総じて舞踏への強い想いや熱意を感じさせられた。2018年度国外調査で得られた332件の回答にどのようなワードが含まれているかを抽出したところ、「dance」(203回)「butoh」(125回)「body」(109回)「form」(74回)「movement」(47回)「art」(44回)に続いて、「soul」(38回)「life」(38回)「transformation」(25回)「spirit」(15回)「philosophy」(13回)「death」(13回)「existence」(10回)などの自己の内面や精神、哲学に関わる名詞が挙がっていた。動詞では、「dance」(23回)の後に続くのは「become」(19回)「feel」(15回)「transform」(14回)であった。日本国外の実践者が舞踏をどのように捉えているかにおいて、精神世界や哲学への志向性、ならびに「Transformation＝変化すること・変貌すること」と関連づける回答が少なからずあった。

同質問に対する、2017・2018年度日本国内調査で得られた回答198件に含まれる単語の抽出では、「身体」(50回)「表現」(48回)「ダンス」(45回)「日本」(37回)「踊り」(36回)「舞踏」(33回)「舞踊」(15回)「白塗り」(14回)「動き」(14回)「前衛」(13回)が挙がっており、国内では比較的客観的な説明を志向する傾向があるように見られた。

とはいえ、舞踏の輪郭をあぶり出すという目的に照らし合わせるならば、回答を定量化することよりも、その熱量と多様さを直接提示することが最もふさわしい。2017・2018年度に国内外から寄せられた467件の回答を、個人情報と紐付かない範囲で本書カバーに全掲載している。(2017国内・2018国内・2018国外 掲載順不同)

In response to the question "How would you describe Butoh?" many gave poetic or speculative answers, emphasising strong ideas and enthusiasm for Butoh. From the 332 responses in the 2018 overseas survey, we found "dance" (203 times), "Butoh" (125 times), "body" (109 times), "form" (74 times), "movement" (47 times), "art" (44 times), followed by "soul" (38 times), "life" (38 times), "transformation" (25 times), "spirit" (15 times), "philosophy" (13 times), "death" (13 times), "existence" (10 times), and other nouns relating to the inner, mental, and philosophical aspects of the self. For verbs, "dance" (23 times) was followed by "become" (19 times), "feel" (15 times) and "transform" (14 times). Regarding how practitioners outside of Japan perceive Butoh, a considerable number relate it to the spiritual world, philosophy and "transformations".

In response to the same question, the most common words among the 198 responses to the 2017 and 2018 Japan surveys included "body" (50 times), "expression" (48 times), "dance" (45 times), "Japan" (37 times), "dance: odori" (36 times), "Butoh" (33 times), "dance: buyō" (15 times), "white paint" (14 times), "movement" (14 times), and "avant-garde" (13 times). There seems to be a tendency for comparatively objective descriptions in Japan.

Having said that, the purpose here is to present a general overview of Butoh, and so rather than looking at this quantifiably, it is more appropriate to use this information simply to present the diversity and strengths of feeling. On the cover of this book we have printed all 467 responses to this puestion from the 2017 and 2018 surveys from both Japan and abroad. (Randomised order, from the 2017 Japan survey / 2018 Japan survey / 2018 International survey).

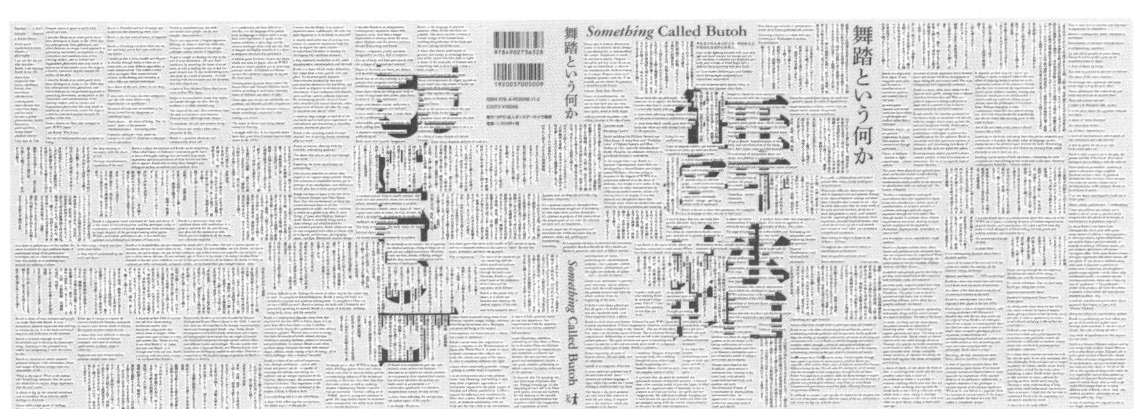

記憶に残っている舞踏作品

Inspirational Butoh Works

国内の回答結果 | Responses from Japan — 2017&2018

（註）確認ができた作品名のみを掲載 | Only titles that could be confirmed are published.

大野一雄 34件
Kazuo Ohno

『花』
『ラ・アルヘンチーナ頌』
『死海』
『わたしのお母さん』
『花鳥風月』
『睡蓮』
『宇宙の花』
『無』
『御殿、空を飛ぶ』
映画『書かれた顔』

山海塾 16件
Sankai Juku

『金柑少年』
『海の賑わい 陸(オカ)の静寂—めぐり』
『かがみの隠喩の彼方へ—かげみ』
『降りくるもののなかで—とばり』
『歴史いぜんの記憶—うむすな』
『遥か彼方からの—ひびき』
『卵を立てることから—卵熱』

大駱駝艦 13件
Dairakudakan

『風さかしま』
『完全なる人人』
『海印の馬』
『羅生門』
『貧棒な人』
『皇大睾丸』

土方 巽 12件
Tatsumi Hijikata

『疱瘡譚』
『ひとがた』
『東北歌舞伎計画』
『四季のための二十七晩』
『静かな家』
『土方巽と日本人—肉体の叛乱』

大野慶人 12件
Yoshito Ohno

『花と鳥』

笠井 叡 9件
Akira Kasai

『セラフィータ』
『我が黙示録』
吉岡実追悼『聖あんま断腸詩編』
『丘の麓』

上杉満代 5件
Mitsuyo Uesugi

『ベイビーメランコリア—夢六夜—』
『M』

室伏 鴻 4件
Ko Murobushi

『quick silver』

首くくり栲象 3件
Kubikukuri-Takuzou

『庭劇場』

中嶋 夏 3件
Natsu Nakajima

『根も葉もなく、、、夢と廃棄』
『瓦礫と包帯』

和栗由紀夫 3件
Yukio Waguri

『病める舞姫』

石井満隆 2件
Mitsutaka Ishii

『自在』

白桃房 2件
Hakutobo

『日本の乳房』

田中 泯 2件
Min Tanaka

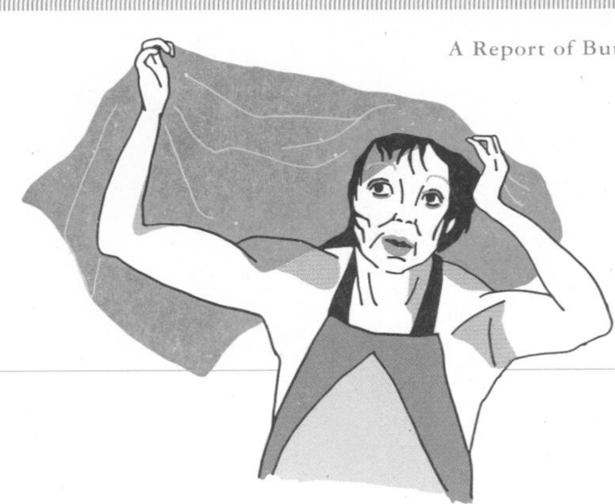

芦川羊子 1件
Yoko Ashikawa
『鯨線上の奥方』

天児牛大 1件
Ushio Amagatsu
大野一雄 百歳の年 ガラ公演『百花繚乱』での『HIBIKI』より抜粋ソロパフォーマンス

工藤丈輝 1件
Taketeru Kudo
『荒漠器』

五井 輝 1件
Teru Goi
『神居』

小林嵯峨 1件
Kobayashi Saga
『マ・グ・サ・レ』

島崎 徹 1件
Toru Shimazaki
『Here we are!』

高井富子 1件
Tomiko Takai
『まんだら屋敷』

玉野黄市 1件
Koichi Tamano
『自然の子供』

ダンス・ラヴ・マシーン 1件
Dance-Love-Machine
『狐のコン』

ティツィアナ・ロンゴ 1件
Tiziana Longo
『MUT』

成瀬信彦 1件
Nobuhiko Naruse
『マ・グ・サ・レ』

筆宝ふみえ 1件
Fumie Hippo
舞踏舎天鶏の公演『女中たち』

堀内博子 1件
Hiroko Horiuchi
『変容と秘儀・I』

南 阿豆 1件
Azu Minami
『Scar Tissue IV ～消えない傷跡～』

宮下省死 1件
Shoji Miyashita
『マ・グ・サ・レ』

大岩英夫 1件
Hideo Oiwa

大森政秀 1件
Masahide Omori

川口隆夫 1件
Takao Kawaguchi

黒沢美香 1件
Mika Kurosawa

ケン五月 1件
Ken Mai

財津暁平 1件
Gyohei Zaitsu

境野ひろみ 1件
Hiromi Sakaino

相良ゆみ 1件
Yumi Sagara

田仲ハル 1件
Hal Tanaka

根来裕子 1件
Yuko Negoro

長谷川宝子 1件
Takako Hasegawa

ピナ・バウシュ 1件
Pina Bausch

北方舞踏派 1件
Hoppo Butoh-ha

松原東洋 1件
Toyo Matsubara

睦美・寧呂 1件
Mutsumi - Neiro

元藤燁子 1件
Akiko Motofuji

雪 雄子 1件
Yuko Yuki

吉本大輔 1件
Daisuke Yoshimoto

記憶に残っている舞踏作品
Inspirational Butoh Works

国外の回答結果 | International Responses — 2018

（註）確認ができた作品名のみを掲載 | Only titles that could be confirmed are published.

大野一雄 96件
Kazuo Ohno

Admiring La Argentina

My Mother

Film *The Written Face*

The Dead Sea

Ka Cho Fu Getsu

Water Lilies

Palace Soars Across the Sky

The Dead Sea

室伏 鴻 56件
Ko Murobushi

Edge

quick silver

Le Centaur et L'Animal

EN

Handsome Blue Sky

The Crazy Cloud Collection

Inframince 1

山海塾 51件
Sankai Juku

UMUSUNA- Memories before History

MEGURI - Teeming Sea, Tranquil Land

KAGEMI - Beyond the Metaphors of Mirrors

KINKAN SHONEN

TOBARI - As If in An Inexhaustible Flux

UNETSU - The Egg Stands out of Curiosity

大野慶人 41件
Yoshito Ohno

Flower and Bird

Kuu

Water Lilies

Ka Cho Fu Getsu

土方 巽 34件
Tatsumi Hijikata

Film *Himiko*

A Girl

Summer Storm

Story of smallpox

Tatsumi Hijikata and Japanese People

The Masseur

Film *The Navel and the A-Bomb*

竹之内淳志 28件
Atsushi Takenouchi

Thousand drops, thousand flowers

EMBRACE

SKIN

大駱駝艦 27件
Dairakudakan

CRAZY CAMEL

Film *The Naked Summer*

Sumera Daikogan

Secrets of Mankind

Sea-Dappled Horse

The Book of the Dead

吉岡由美子 24件
Yumiko Yoshioka

100 Light Years of Solitude

Before the Dawn

TWO

i-ki

笠井 叡 19件
Akira Kasai

Pollen Revolution

Seraphita

Butoh America

I dance the Japanese Constitution

カルロッタ池田 19件
Carlotta Ikeda

Waiting

Utt

Zarathoustra-Variations

Haru no Saiten

遠藤公義 17件
Tadashi Endo

MA

FUKUSHIMA MON AMOUR

MABOROSHI

IKIRU - HOMMAGE Á PINA BAUSCH

カセキユウコ 17件
Yuko Kaseki

SHOOT JEEZ MY GOSH

Unspelled

KUDAN

Ame to Ame

中嶋 夏 12件
Natsu Nakajima

Like Smoke Like Ash

Garden

工藤丈輝 11件
Taketeru Kudo

El amor al terror

A Vessel of Ruins

田中 泯 10件
Min Tanaka

『空の型』(Shape of the Sky)

和栗由紀夫 8件
Yukio Waguri

Journey of the Spirit

Vangeline 6件

Butoh Beethoven

吉本大輔 5件
Daisuke Yoshimoto

Eros and Thanatos

Ruins of the Body

財津暁平 5件
Gyohei Zaitsu

Une fleur sans nom

ジョン・ラーグ 5件
Joan Laage

Black Widow

Three Little Pierrots

石本華江 5件
Kae Ishimoto

Inventario de mi vida

桂勘 5件
Kan Katsura

Time Machine

Curious Fish

ケン五月 5件
Ken Mai

Requiem of Flowers

玉野黄市・弘子 5件
Koichi & Hiroko Tamano

Aoi Hana

Imre Thormann 3件

Enduring Freedom

富永真紀子 3件
Makiko Tominaga

In Silence

関 美奈子 3件
Minako Seki

TWO

川口隆夫 3件
Takao Kawaguchi

About Kazuo Ohno

伊藤キム 2件
Kim Itoh

Dead and Alive—Body on the Borderline

国外の回答結果 | International Responses — 2018

（註）確認ができた作品名のみを掲載 | Only titles that could be confirmed are published.

SU-EN 2件

Scrap Bodies

Sylwia Hanff 2件

The gardens have left their trees

Adam Koan 1件

Eucharist / Viscera

Alexander Wenzlik 1件

Sirene

B-Floor Theatre 1件

San Dan Ka

Emilie Sugai 1件

A leveza da flor

Frauke 1件

Three bodies

Joao Butoh 1件

Homage To Mr.O

秦 かのこ 1件
Kanoko Hata

Beauty of Nature

向 雲太郎 1件
Kumotaro Mukai

Two Suns

金 満里 1件
Kim Manri

Cosmos of Blessings

Maureen Fleming 1件

WILDFLOWERS, A Feminine Genesis

吉田光雄 1件
Mitsuo Yoshida

『ココロミノヨル』(Kokorominoyoru)

原田伸雄 1件
Harada Nobuo

Ethereal red river

Paul Michael Henry 1件

Love for the Dead Bag

白井 剛 1件
Tsuyoshi Shirai

Node / The Old Man of the Desert

川本裕子 1件
Yuko Kawamoto

Quiet House

転形劇場 1件
Tenkei Gekijo

The Water Station

岩名雅記 12件
Masaki Iwana

芦川羊子 6件
Yoko Ashikawa

今 貂子 5件
Ima Tenko

麿 赤兒 4件
Akaji Maro

白虎社 4件
ByakkoSha

長内真理 4件
Mari Osanai

上杉満代 4件
Mitsuyo Uesugi

友惠しづねと白桃房 4件
TOMOE SHIZUNE and HAKUTOBO

白桃房 3件
Hakutobo

Maya Dunsky 3件

Michael Sakamoto 3件

若松萌野 3件
Moeno Wakamatsu

Natalia Cuéllar 3件

正朔 3件
Seisaku

Diego Piñon 2件

Lobsang Palacios 2件

Maruska Ronchi 2件

Melissa Lohman 2件

福原哲郎 2件
Tetsuro Fukuhara

天児牛大 2件
Ushio Amagatsu

ゆみうみうまれ 2件
Yumi Umiumare

元藤燁子 1件
Akiko Motofuji

Alan Sutherland 1件

Ambra G. Bergamasco 1件

Anastazia Louise Aranaga 1件

古川あんず 1件
Anzu Furukawa

アリアドーネの會 1件
Ariadone Company

azumi O E 1件

Calé Miranda 1件

DAIPANbutoh Collective 1件

Denise Fujiwara 1件

DEREVO 1件

エイコ&コマ 1件
Eiko & Koma

Esparta Martínez 1件

Gustavo Collini 1件

Habillé d' eau 1件

玉野弘子 1件
Hiroko Tamano

西山弘志 1件
Hiroshi Nishiyama

Hiroshi Sakurai 1件

Holly Chernobyl 1件

北方舞踏派 1件
Hoppo Butoh-ha

胡高阳 1件
Hu Gao Yang

櫻井郁也 1件
Sakurai Ikuya

金亀伊織 1件
Iori Kinki

保坂一平 1件
Ippei Hosaka

Jacki Job 1件

Kage Mulvilai 1件

国外の回答結果｜International Responses — 2018

（註）確認ができた作品名のみを掲載｜Only titles that could be confirmed are published.

Katrina Wolfe 1件

Kitt Johnson 1件

LEIMAY 1件

Lena Ang 1件

Lucie Betz 1件

Macarena Ortuzar 1件

Margherita Tisato 1件

Marie-Gabrielle Rotie 1件

Megan Janet White 1件

藤條虫丸 1件
Mushimaru Fujieda

石井則仁 1件
Norihito Ishii

OddDance 1件

Oguri 1件

Rhea Volij 1件

Roland Walter 1件

勅使川原三郎 1件
Saburo Teshigawara

小林嵯峨 1件
Kobayashi Saga

大西小夜子 1件
Sayoko Onishi

Sheri Brown 1件

Stephanie Lanckton 1件

サブボディ共振塾ヒマラヤ 1件
Subbody Resohance Butoh Himalaya

古関すまこ 1件
Sumako Koseki

滝田高之 1件
Takayuki Takita

石出卓也 1件
Takuya Ishide

五井 輝 1件
Teru Goi

Tiago Ianuck 1件

ティツィアナ・ロンゴ 1件
Tiziana Longo

とりふね舞踏舎 1件
Torifune Butoh Sha

岩下 徹 1件
Toru Iwashita

Wannapa P-Eubanks 1件

木村 由 1件
Yu Kimura

鈴木ユキオ 1件
Yukio Suzuki

Yuko Ota 1件

Zen Zen Zo 1件

舞踏を実践することの喜び
The Joys of Butoh

2018年度版アンケートより、「舞踏をやっていて『満足』や『喜び』を感じることがあれば、どのようなことか教えて下さい。」という設問を新たに加えた。経済的満足度が著しく低いにも関わらず、舞踏を続けていることの理由を調べたかった。記述式なので回答内容は多岐に渡るが、演劇やダンスといった舞台芸術全般に共通する「観客に伝わる、分かち合える」という方向性の回答もある一方で、自己の内面探求、空間との一体化、制度からの解放、自然・宇宙との交信に喜びを感じるといった回答も見られた。なお、本書に掲載されている「舞踏スクリーンショット2019」では「あなたにとって舞踏の魅力は何ですか?」という質問を行っており、回答の具体例はこちらも参照されたい。

A new question we asked in the 2018 survey was "If you derive a sense of satisfaction or joy in performing Butoh, could you describe what it is?". We wanted to find out why people continue to dance Butoh despite the low economic satisfaction. As we invited open responses we had many answers, but one common perspective was that, as with theatre, dance and other performing arts, it can be "shared and communicated with the audience", while others mentioned exploring the inner self, becoming one with the space, liberation and the joy of communicating with nature and the universe. As such, in "A Snapshot of Butoh 2019" which appears as a chapter in this book, we asked the question "What attracted you to Butoh?". Please refer to this section for the responses.

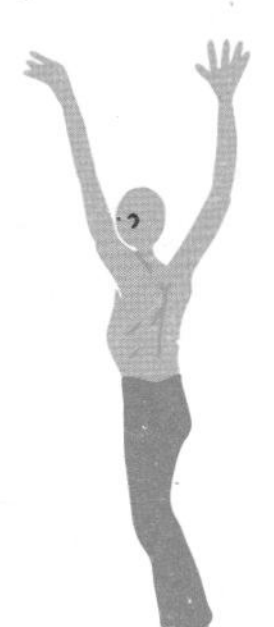

舞踏の継承について
The Inheritance of Butoh

実践者がそれぞれ舞踏の継承についてどのような考えを持っているかを具体的に明らかにしたいという意図で、2018年度版アンケートより、「舞踏というジャンルが今後も継承されるために必要だと思うことがあれば教えて下さい。」という設問を新たに加えた。ここでも、一般的に考えられる継承方法とは異なる、舞踏固有の解決策あるいは回答の傾向が発見できないかと考え、選択式ではなく記述での回答を求めた。
映像、写真、テキストなどの外形的な記録の必要性を肯定する意見もあるが、それ以上に、舞踏は個々の内面性(「魂」「心」「精神」「意識/無意識」「内部」「深い」などのキーワード)や創造力に依拠する、あるいは徒弟制度や対人関係を通じてのみ受け継がれるという意見が日本国外でとりわけ多く見られたことは興味深い。国内外ともに、伝統芸能等の継承方法として一般的に想起される「型」の必要性を主張する回答は少なかった。
後述の「舞踏スクリーンショット2019」では、「身体芸術である舞踏は、どのようにしたら残すことができるでしょうか?あるいは残すことができないでしょうか?」という質問に置き換え、仮に舞踏の継承が不可能と考えるケースにおいても、その理由を少しでも浮き彫りにできないかと試みた。

With the intention of clarifying what practitioners think in terms of the inheritance of Butoh for future generations, in the 2018 survey we asked "What, if anything, do you think is necessary for the genre of Butoh to continue in the future?". Again, in the hopes of moving away from general preservation methods and discovering a Butoh-specific method or trend among the answers, we invited open responses to this question.
Although there were responses affirming the need for videos, photographs and text, we also received interesting opinions, especially from outside Japan, suggesting that Butoh is individual (keywords: "soul", "heart", "spirit", "conscious/unconscious", "inner", "deep" etc.), depends on creativity, or can only be inherited through apprenticeships or interpersonal relationships. We did not receive many responses from Japan or overseas arguing the need for a "kata", a common method in preserving traditional performing arts. In "A Snapshot of Butoh 2019", we replaced this with the question "As a performative art inherently involving the physical body, how can Butoh be preserved? Or, is this even possible?". By doing so we hoped to get some detailed answers even in the cases where it was felt that preserving Butoh may be impossible.

マーゴ・オリボー

2000年、パリの中心にエスパス・ベルタン・ポワレという小さなスペースがオープン。幾度目かのパリでの舞踏ブームと重なり、オープン数ヶ月後には会場に入りきれないほどの観客が集まり、瞬く間に舞踏の会場として有名に。オープン当時たまたまパリに居た私は、そのブームに飲み込まれるようにベルタン・ポワレのスタッフになりました。踊り手と関わるなかで、舞踏の照明家と言われるようになり、更には大学院生として、パリの舞踏ネットワークの研究も始めています。

調査結果を見ると、活動歴が20年以上の方がけっこういらっしゃいますが、その中で、日本出身ではない踊り手の割合がどの程度なのか、興味のあるところですね。今では考えられないことですが、2000年代には、「日本人以外には舞踏は踊れない」、「日本人の舞踏しか見たくない」、ということが普通に言われていました。ベルタン・ポワレの舞踏フェスティバル(毎年1ヶ月に亘り開催)も、2006年にジョン・ラーグが参加するまでは、日本の文化としての舞踏を紹介する場にとどまっていたように思います。そのような状況の中で、Butô Clipという、公募のショートプログラムを、私の企画として2010年より隔年でオーガナイズしています(現在はA la Butôと改名)。公募の上で選考をするという形をとることで、参加の枠を広げるとともに、Butôの解釈を提言するという試行錯誤を、Butôのスタイルがどんどん変化するなかで、悪戦苦闘しながら続けています。

変化するスタイルという意味では、ローナ・ラウエイとマルレーヌ・ヨプステル。二人とも踊るだけではなく、フェスティバルのオーガナイズをするなど、ヨーロッパでは、幅広く活躍している踊り手ですが、彼女たちのスタイルは、おおよそ一般的な舞踏のイーメジとは遠く、明るく力強くて、舞踏の前衛的な力を再確認させてくれます。

ベルタン・ポワレでは、舞踏フェスティバル20周年記念プログラムを企画中ですが、オープンした2000年当時からは、舞踏をめぐる状況が、随分と変わりました。当時は、土方巽や大野一雄の踊りを映像で観ることはほとんど不可能でしたが、今はネット上に映像が溢れかえっていますよね。いくつかの舞踏の本も仏訳されており、以前はワークショップの場での伝達でしか習得できなかった舞踏というものを、それぞれが独自に研究できるようになっている様に思います。その結果として、当然解釈は拡大し、スタイルにも幅ができています。スタイルのない舞踏が生まれてきている、とも言えそうです。

フランスでは、舞踏は形が大事なのではない、ということがよく語られます。そのことが、多くの人を魅了し新たなスタイルの探求につながっているように思います。何を持って舞踏と呼ぶのかはつねに議論の対象で、その議論そのものが、フランスにおける舞踏ネットワークの基盤をなしているようにさえ思います。

口コミネットワークとも言える情報伝達のシステムが、はっきりと存在していて、情報が国を超えて回っています。「舞踏に興味を持ったきっかけのワークショップは何ですか」という問いの返答に、竹之内淳志の名前が多く出ますが、彼の成功はこの口コミネットワークでの成功であると思います。その中では、舞踏家としての系譜や経歴よりも、友人が語る体験談や、一緒に参加しよう、という誘いの方が力を持つのです。

観客やワークショップ生の判断の基準は、個人の名前。ここでは舞踏というラベルはあまり機能しません。SNS上で見かける、魅力的な写真をアップしている踊り手の情報には反応するけれど、聞いたことのない舞踏家の情報には目が止まらない、そんなことが起きているように思いますね。もう、舞踏というラベルで、集客できる時代ではないのかもしれません。そのことが、自由な表現につながり、世界のあちこちで、舞踏という名のもとに、新しい観客を魅惑する、ようになることを願っています。

マーゴ・オリボー
京都芸術大学美術科卒業後、アトリエ劇研スタッフルーム所属を経て、1998年に渡仏。フリーの照明家として、舞踏やダンスを中心にアヴィニヨン演劇祭等で活動。2000年より、エスパス・ベルタン・ポワレのテクニカルスタッフ、企画運営にも参加。2018年よりパリ第8大学芸術学修士課程在籍。

Margot Olliveaux

In the year 2000, Espace Culturel Bertin Poirée, a small space in the heart of Paris was opened. Coinciding with the Paris Butoh-boom, the venue was regularly selling out within the first few months, and quickly became known as a Butoh venue. I just so happened to be in Paris at the time and, caught up in the boom, became a staff member at Bertin Poirée. I became known as a lighting technician among the dancers, and now I also study the Parisian Butoh network as a graduate student.

Looking at the survey results, there have been many responses from people who have been doing Butoh for over 20 years, but it is the percentage of those not from Japan that I find particularly interesting. Although it's unthinkable now, in the 2000s it was common to hear "no-one other than Japanese people can dance Butoh", or "I don't want to see Butoh by non-Japanese people". Even the *Festival Espace Culturel Bertin Poirée* (held for one month every year), was originally considered only an introduction to Japanese culture until Joan Laage's participation in 2006. It was in such conditions that I began organising an open-call short biennial program *Butô Clip* in 2010 (now *A la Butô*). By using an open call and selection process, we widened the circle of participants and continue to fight to propose reinterpretations of Butoh through trial and error amidst an ever-changing Butoh 'style'.

Lorna Lawrie and Jöbstl Marlène both have very different styles of performance. They are not only dancers, but do a wide range of things such as organising festivals in Europe, and their style is very different from the general Butoh 'image'; it is bright, strong, and reaffirms the avant-garde strength of Butoh.

Although at Bertin Poirée we are now planning the 20th anniversary of our Butoh festival since we opened in 2000, our approach to Butoh has changed substantially. At the time it was almost impossible to see films of Tatsumi Hijikata and Kazuo Ohno, but now the Internet is overflowing with footage. Where in the past the only knowledge of Butoh could be gained through workshops, there are now French translations of books, and it has become possible to study it through many methods. As a result, interpretations and styles have expanded. It could even said that a Butoh without a style is emerging.

In France, it is often said that form is not important in Butoh. I think this is what fascinated a lot of people, and drew them to try and find new styles. What makes Butoh 'Butoh' is the source of much discussion, and it is these discussions themselves that make the foundation of the Butoh network in France.

The system of passing on information through word of mouth is very well ingrained, and this is how information moves on beyond countries. In response to the question "What workshops triggered your interest in Butoh?", Atsushi Takenouchi's name gets mentioned a lot. However I think his success is based on the success of word of mouth. I think friends talking about their experiences and encouraging others to join them is a stronger force than the class or career of the Butoh artist.

The opinions of your audience and students become your reputation. In this regard, the 'Butoh' label means very little. Although people may be interested in information regarding dancers with distinctive photographs on social media, I don't think people are interested in Butoh artists they have never heard of. It may be that we are no longer in an era in which the label 'Butoh' draws audiences. I hope this encourages a freer form of expression, in which the name Butoh can become a starting point from which new audiences are inspired all over the world.

Margot Olliveaux

Graduated from Kyoto City University of the Arts and worked at Atelier Gekken before moving to France in 1998. Works as a freelance Butoh and dance lighting technician at Festival d'Avignon. Working at Espace Culturel Bertin Poirée since 2000, including production. Enrolled in a Masters of Arts degree at the University of Paris 8 since 2018.

記録公開への関心とその方法
On Documentation

公演の記録を公開することに関心がありますか。
Are you interested in allowing public access to your performance documentation?

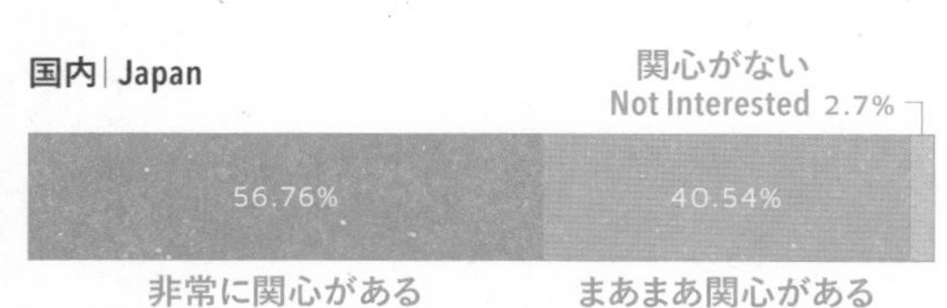

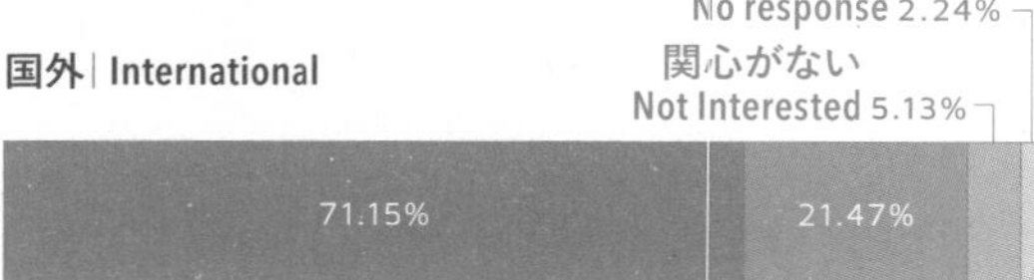

(Butoh Research 2018 国内&国外 | Japan & International)

記録資料として何を残すことに意義があると思いますか。(複数回答可)
What forms of documentation do you think are most important? (Multiple answers permitted)

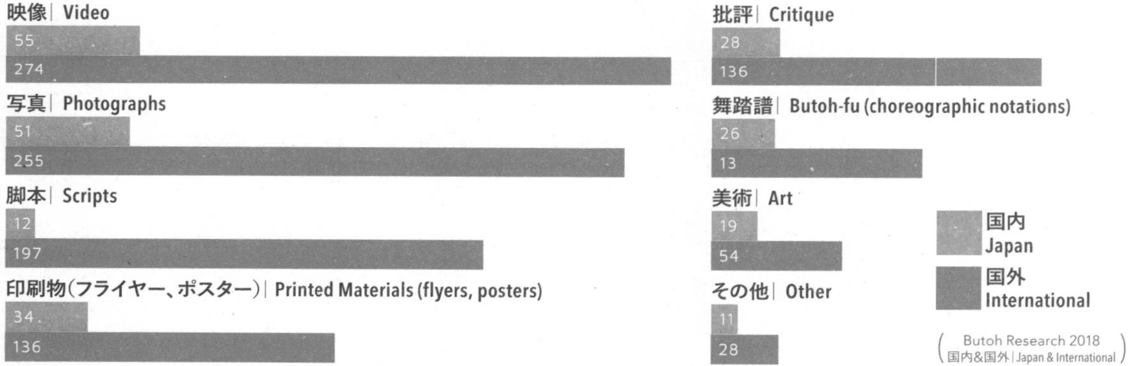

(Butoh Research 2018 国内&国外 | Japan & International)

!

最後に、公演記録を公開することへの関心の度合いを調べた。国内外ともに、「非常に関心がある」「まあまあ関心がある」が大きな割合を占めた(国内:約97% 国外:約93%)。「記録資料として何を残すことが意義があると思いますか?」の質問に対しては、国内外ともに「映像」と「写真」が上位を占めた。

舞踏は、身体を用いた活動ではあるものの、外形的な振付や様式的な特徴だけでは定義しづらいため、表層的な記録・保存だけで本質を捉えることは困難であるのかもしれない。舞踏をアーカイヴするということは、その他の身体を使ったパフォーマンスと共通する部分があるのか、あるいは全く独自の方法を用いるべきなのか、それはいかなる方法なのか。この点をより詳細に掘り下げることを今後の課題としていきたい。

Finally, we wanted to see the level of interest in publicising performance documentation. Both in Japan and overseas, "Definitely Interested" and "Somewhat Interested" accounted for a large percentage (Japan: about 97%, International: about 93%). In response to the question, "What forms of documentation do you think are the most important?", "Video" and "Photographs" came out top both in Japan and overseas.

While being a body-based art form, Butoh is difficult to define simply with choreography stylistic features, making its essence potentially difficult to capture with only the use of recorded and preserved materials. Are there any similarities between Butoh and other performing arts? Does it need an entirely new form of archiving? If so, what is it? We hope to consider these points in more detail in the future.

まとめ：成果／アンケートを経ての展開
Summary: Results / Post-Survey Plans

実践者を対象にしたアンケート調査を通じて、「舞踏が世界に広がっている」という現況と、実践者の活動実態の一端を可視化できたことは大きな成果である。また、活動実態だけでなく、舞踏に対する価値観の多様性や、各地において影響力をもって伝道者的役割を果たす者たちの存在が確認できた。記述式の回答では、ときに実践者の人生観や哲学とも結びついた舞踏に対する多様な解釈とととともに、総じて舞踏への熱意が強く表れており、時代と国境を超えて人々を惹きつけうる舞踏のポテンシャルと、発展可能性を改めて感じることができた。国内外ともに、舞踏をめぐる活動の経済状況は厳しい様子ではあるが、多くの実践者にとって、舞踏が各人の生と分かち難く結びつき、その表現や生活に大きな影響を及ぼしていることが窺い知れた。舞踏についての解釈を言語化し、広く共有することは、対外的な説明に有用であるのみならず、舞踏を探求する実践者間の交流促進にもつながることが期待される。また、これまでは実践者に対する調査を実施してきたが、舞踏に期待することについて、制作者や鑑賞者を対象とした調査を行うことも今後検討したい。舞踏がより世の中に浸透していくにはどのような方法があるのか、異なる複数の視点からの考察が必要であろう。

本調査を通じて、過去の資料を収集整理するのみならず、今まさに行われている活動を記録し、共有する重要性を改めて認識した。そこで2019年度は、2017・2018年度の回答者を対象に新たなアンケートを配布し、「舞踏スクリーンショット2019」と題して本書に完全掲載することにした。

- アンケート対象者：2017・2018年度アンケート回答者
- 実施時期：2019年11月5日〜26日
- 調査方法：メールにてアンケートフォームを送付
- 回収結果：114件（うち日本語回答57件、英語回答56件、スペイン語回答1件）

「舞踏スクリーンショット 2019」では、自身の活動の発端、舞踏との関わり方・舞踏を続けることのモチベーション、そしてどのように舞踏を残していくべきと考えるかを尋ねる3つの質問を設け、さらに現在の自身の活動を示す写真の提供を依頼した。その回答からは、実践者それぞれの活動に影響を与えている源泉の存在、極めて多様な過去と現在の接続が見出せる。これらは、舞踏という現象の「今」を部分的ではあるにせよ捉え、切り取ったアーカイヴともみなしうるだろう。

リサーチの方法論は、常に反省的な再考と刷新が求められるが、そのような試行錯誤の過程を通じて、新しいコンテンツや人的ネットワーク、ひいてはアーカイヴそのものが生まれ、形を成し、「舞踏という何か」の輪郭もまた朧げながら明らかになっていくのではないだろうか。そしてその中にこそ、舞踏のさらなる可能性が秘められていると考えている。

Through these surveys, we have been able to successfully visualise "Butoh spreading around the world" along with some of the practitioners' activities. We have also been able to see the diversity of Butoh's significance, and confirm the existence of people carrying its influence to a variety of places. The descriptive responses have shown us a range of Butoh interpretations, sometimes including the practitioners' views of life and philosophies, along with a generally strong enthusiasm for Butoh, giving us a sense once again of Butoh's ability attract people beyond eras and borders, and its potential for development. Despite economically difficult situations both in Japan and abroad, for many practitioners Butoh is inseparably connected to life, and greatly influencing their expressions and lifestyles.

The verbalisation and widespread interpretations of Butoh is not only useful for perfunctory definitions, it also promotes exchange between practitioners exploring Butoh. Although so far we have focussed our research on practitioners, we would also like to conduct a survey on both creators and viewers expectations of Butoh. It will be necessary to consider multiple perspectives in order to find a method for Butoh to permeate the world more fully.

This research has revealed the importance of not only collecting and organising past materials but also recording and sharing work that is currently taking place. We therefore decided for 2019, to distribute a new survey to the respondents from 2017 and 2018, and fully publish the responses in this book with the title "A Snapshot of Butoh 2019".

- Survey Target Audience: Respondents from the 2017/2018 surveys
- Survey Period: 5 ~ 26 November 2019
- Survey Method: Survey form by e-mail
- Number of Responses: 114 (including 57 in Japanese, 56 in English, and 1 in Spanish)

In "A Snapshot of Butoh 2019" we asked respondents to answer three questions on their reasons for starting Butoh, motivations for continuing, and thoughts on how to preserve it, along with a photograph showing their current activities. The responses revealed sources of influence on each practitioner's activities, as well as a wide variety of past and present connections. Through them we can capture some of the "current" state of Butoh, which can now be considered part of the archive.

Research methodologies require constant reflection and renewal. Through such trial and error processes, new content and human connections, or in other words the archive itself is born, takes shape, and an outline of "Something called Butoh" becomes clearer even in its ambiguity. Perhaps within that, more potentials of Butoh could be hidden.

アンケート質問項目(2018)

回答者の属性

性別、年齢、活動年数、活動拠点地、所属団体、舞踏との関わり方(プロフェッショナル/アマチュア)、ウェブサイト(SNS可)

1. 2018年1月〜12月の活動状況について

Q1-1 2018年の活動の主な形態について、3つまで選んで下さい。

Q1-2 2018年に、あなたが踊った場所について教えて下さい。(複数記入可、都市や劇場名をご記入下さい)

Q1-3 一公演(複数ステージ含める)にて達成されたおおよその集客規模について、該当するものにチェックして下さい。

Q1-4 公演チケットの平均的な価格について、該当するものにチェックして下さい。

Q1-5 集客のターゲットは特にどのような種類の人々でしたか?3つまで選択して下さい。

Q1-6 1-5の質問を達成するなかで、どのような集客の工夫が手応えを感じましたか?

Q1-7 1-5の質問に対して、2018年における達成度はいかがでしたか?

2. 2018年1月〜12月の経済状況について

Q2-1 2018年中の舞踏家/ダンサーとしての活動におけるおおよその収入に関して、該当するものにチェックして下さい。

Q2-2 2018年中の舞踏家/ダンサーとしての活動にかかったおおよその支出に関して、該当するものにチェックして下さい。

Q2-3 2018年中の舞踏家/ダンサーとしての経済状況に満足していますか?

Q2-4 2-3の質問で「それほど満足していない」「まったく満足していない」とご回答頂いた方にお尋ね致します。状況を改善するために必要と思われることがあれば、教えて下さい。

3. 舞踏に対する価値観について

Q3-1 あなたが舞踏をはじめたきっかけを教えて下さい。(複数選択可)

Q3-2 あなたは舞踏をどのように説明しますか?

Q3-3 これまで観た舞踏公演の中で一番印象に残っているものを教えて下さい。

Q3-4 舞踏をやっていて「満足」や「喜び」を感じることがあれば、どのようなことか教えて下さい。

Q3-5 舞踏というジャンルが今後も継承されるために必要だと思うことがあれば教えて下さい。

4. 公演の記録について

Q4-1 公演の記録を公開することに関心がありますか?

Q4-2 4-1の質問で「興味がある」「まあまあ興味がある」とお答えいただいた方に質問です。記録資料として何を残すことが意義があると思いますか?(複数回答可)

Q4-3 4-1の質問で「関心がない」とお答え頂いた方に質問です。公開したくない理由を教えて下さい。

Q4-4 公演記録・資料のアーカイヴに関する調査のために、今後個別にご連絡を差し上げることは可能ですか?

Survey Questions (2018)

Respondents' Attributes

Gender, Age, Years of Activity, Base of Activities, Affiliated Organisation, Butoh Involvement (Professional/Amateur), Website (and Social Media)

1. Activities between January and December 2018

Q1-1 Please select three activities from the box below to describe your main activities in 2018.

Q1-2 Please fill in where you danced in 2018(e.g. name of theater or event space; name of city).

Q1-3 Please tick the corresponding attendance for each performance, including for repeat performances.

Q1-4 Please tick the corresponding admission charge for the average performance ticket. Please calculate your answer into US$.

Q1-5 What is the particular target audience you are trying to reach? Please select up to three from the categories listed below:

Q1-6 With reference to Q1-5, how did you feel was the response to your efforts to attract an audience?

Q1-7 With reference to Q1-5, how do you estimate your level of accomplishment in 2018.

2. Economic Situation between January and December 2018

Q2-1 Please tick the applicable income bracket regarding your approximate income for your activities as a Butoh performer / dancer during 2018.

Q2-2 Please tick the corresponding bracket for approximate expenses related to your activities as a Butoh performer / dancer during 2018.

Q2-3 Are you satisfied with your economic situation as a Butoh performer / dancer during 2018?

Q2-4 With reference to those who answered "I'm not so satisfied" or "I'm not at all satisfied" in Q2-3, please indicate what you think is necessary to improve your financial situation.

3. Sense of Values concerning Butoh

Q3-1 What inspired you to become interested in Butoh. (Multiple answers possible)

Q3-2 How would you describe Butoh to others?

Q3-3 What are the most impressive Butoh performances you have seen, to date?

Q3-4 If you derive a sense of satisfaction or joy in performing Butoh, could you describe what it is?

Q3-5 How important do you think for passing on the Butoh genre to the performers of the future?

4. Documenting and Archiving Performances

Q4-1 Are you interested in allowing the public access to your documentation (audio-visual, written, etc.) about your performance/s?

Q4-2 For those who answered "I am very interested" or "Somewhat interested" in Q4-1, what type of documentation do you think is meaningful for public access? (Multiple answers possible)

Q4-3 For those who answered "I am not interested" in Q4-1, could you please indicate the reason/s you do not wish to allow the public access to them?

Q4-4 With regard to enhancing the present survey, would it be possible to contact you individually concerning archival records and materials?

凡例

肩書き｜活動拠点｜所属団体｜活動年数

アルファベット順。姓名表記は原文まま。

Reference

Occupation	Base	Affiliation	Years of Activity

Alphabetical order. Names written as provided.

A Snapshot of Butoh 2019

舞踏スクリーンショット2019

Q1 あなたが舞踏をはじめたきっかけを教えて下さい。

Q2 あなたにとって舞踏の魅力は何ですか？

Q3 世界的に、様々な分野で貴重な文化に関する記録を保存し、広く共有していこうというアーカイヴの取り組みが進んでいます。身体芸術である舞踏は、どのようにしたら残すことができるでしょうか？

Q1 Please tell us how you became involved with Butoh?

Q2 What attracted you to Butoh?

Q3 On a global level, the creation of archives are making important inroads into the consolidation and sharing of precious cultural records in various artistic fields. As a performative art inherently involving the physical body, how can Butoh be preserved? Or, is this even possible?

Q1 あなたが舞踏をはじめたきっかけを教えて下さい。
Q2 あなたにとって舞踏の魅力は何ですか？
Q3 身体芸術である舞踏は、どのようにしたら残すことができるでしょうか？

Mariam Ala-Rashi

Cultural Anthropologist for Dance and Performance Studies | China, Mongolia, Japan | 15 years

ダンス・パフォーマンス研究の文化人類学者 | 中国・モンゴル・日本 | 15年

Q1 Reason for Starting Butoh
My first encounter with Butoh was in 2008 when studying Dance and Dance Education in Germany. It has always been an art form I wanted to explore in Japan, and in 2017 I was finally able to take my first class with Yoshito Ohno in Tokyo, Japan.

Q2 Attraction to Butoh
Coming from a background in ballet and Middle Eastern dance I was intrigued to discover new emotional worlds that are culturally, historically and politically charged and which confronted one's self in the most brutal as well as subtle way.

Q3 On Archiving
Everything is ever-evolving and each artist adds a personal nuance to this art form. However, passing it on in a holistic way from one generation to the next is probably the best way of knowing, evolving and preserving.

Q1 舞踏をはじめたきっかけ
舞踏に初めて出会ったのは、2008年にドイツでダンスとダンス教育について学んでいた時です。舞踏は常に私が日本で学びたかった芸術形式の一つでした。2017年に東京で、大野慶人のクラスを初めて受けることができました。

Q2 舞踏の魅力
それまでバレエと中東ダンスの教育を受けてきた私は、文化的に、歴史的に、そして政治的にも刺激を帯びた、新しい感情世界を発見することに興味を持ちました。それは繊細でありながらも、最も容赦ない方法で、自分自身と向き合わせてくれました。

Q3 アーカイヴについて
舞踏家たちは、常に進化しているこの芸術形式に、それぞれの個人的なニュアンスを加えています。しかし、全体論的な方法で次の世代へと伝承していくことが、おそらく舞踏を知るために、進化させるために、そして後世に残していくためには最善の方法だと思います。

Researching Chinese contortionism in East Asia, with participant observation

https://jp.linkedin.com/in/mariam-ala-rashi-ab6b13190

Guyphytsy Aldalai

Dancer, Choreographer | Guadalajara (Mexico) | Festival MARES (Director) | 10 years

ダンサー・振付家 | グアダラハラ（メキシコ） | Festival MARES（主宰） | 10年

A Piece of Red Cloth, collaboration with Weina Li Ph. Kai Wai Wong

www.guyphytsy.com
www.encuentromares.com

Q1 Reason for Starting Butoh
I was part of a theater company that worked under the laboratory method of Jerzy Grotowski as well with the work of Eugenio Barba. During the training, the investigation, and the research with this group I learned about butoh and we also practice butoh exercises as part of our routine.

Q2 Attraction to Butoh
The possibility of “be” and its potential state. Be movement, not make movement. Be silence, not make silence. Being able to explore and investigate states of beings of all kinds, through and with the body. The act of a constant poiesis and a big desire, a seed growing inside.

Q3 On Archiving
Writing is an important media that goes along with the research that involves the body, having personal archives, notes and essays can contribute and have an impact on a large scale. Among butoh activities, like festivals, having conferences or talks with experts from diverse fields, from literature, science, and philosophy, can help to feed these studies and grow the archive.

Q1 舞踏をはじめたきっかけ
私は、イェジー・グロトフスキの実験劇場から派生し、エウジェニオ・バルバの作品などを上演する劇団に所属していました。この団体と一緒に行なっていた稽古や調査や研究の中で、舞踏について知り、日々のエクササイズとして舞踏の稽古を行なっていました。

Q2 舞踏の魅力
「なる」ことの可能性と、その潜在的な状態。動きを作るのではなく、動きになること。静けさを作るのではなく、静けさになること。身体を通じて、そして身体とともに、あらゆる種類の存在に変貌する状態を探求すること。常に生成する行為があり、大きな欲望の種が自身の内側で育っていくこと。

Q3 アーカイヴについて
書物は、身体に関わるリサーチに付随する重要な媒体です。個人的活動のアーカイヴ、ノートやエッセーは広範囲にインパクトを与え得るでしょう。舞踏フェスティバルのような機会で、文学、科学、そして哲学などの様々な学問領域の専門家による会議やトークがあると、研究に寄与するだけでなく、アーカイヴを育てることになると思います。

凡例 肩書き | 活動拠点 | 所属団体 | 活動年数
Reference Occupation | Base | Affiliation | Years of Activity

有科珠々 | Juju Alishina

コレオグラファー・ダンサー | パリ（フランス） | NUBA | 38年

Choreographer, Dancer | Paris (France) | NUBA | 38 years

Photo: Hans Kleijn

Q1 舞踏をはじめたきっかけ
日本で演劇を実践していた十代の頃、言語に囚われない身体表現を集中的にやりたいと思い、専門的な訓練を行っている京都の白虎社に入団したのが舞踏を始めたきっかけです。

Q2 舞踏の魅力
舞踏と私が志向していた踊りには共通点が多く、方向性が合っていました。古典舞踊よりも自由度が高く、日本の美学が凝縮され独創性に満ち先鋭的である点に惹かれました。

Q3 アーカイヴについて
可能です。創始者の作品や、その死後に舞踏を続けてきた人々がその体験と思想を加えた作品をアーカイヴ化することは、世界の様々の国で舞踏に触発されて踊っている人々の道標となるでしょう。

Q1 Reason for Starting Butoh
As a teenager practising theatre in Japan, I wanted to find a method of body expression that didn't rely on words, and so I joined Byakkosha in Kyoto, who were giving some professional training.

Q2 Attraction to Butoh
Butoh had a lot in common with the dance that I was aiming for. It was freer than traditional dance, and I was attracted to the way Japanese aesthetics were condensed into radical imagination.

Q3 On Archiving
It's possible. The works of the founders, and the works of people who acquired their experience and ideas after their deaths can be archived, and guide people all over the world whose dance is inspired by Butoh.

http://www.dansenuba.fr/

アオキ裕キ | Yuuki Aoki

振付家・ダンサー | 東京（日本） | 新人Hソケリッサ！ | 13年

Choreographer, Dancer | Tokyo (Japan) | Sokerissa! | 13 years

駅伝芸術祭リターンズ
Photo: Sakanaka Takafumi

http://sokerissa.net/

Q1 舞踏をはじめたきっかけ
当初はメディアなどに主流である流行の踊りに傾倒し、ニューヨーク留学中に同時多発テロに遭遇、そこでの衝撃が自身の根底を問うきっかけとなり舞踏に出会いました。

Q2 舞踏の魅力
自由を得る手段、完成していないこと

Q3 アーカイヴについて
変容すること、偏りがちなイメージを無くすこと。思考中心社会においての身体芸術の有用性の浸透、若者への興味獲得へ向け、誰もが繰り返し触れられるアプローチなど、長期的な視点での取組みを目指す。

Q1 Reason for Starting Butoh
I was initially drawn to mainstream dance styles popular in the media, but then experienced terrorism while studying abroad in New York, which caused me to question my roots and brought me to Butoh.

Q2 Attraction to Butoh
That it's a way to gain freedom, and is unfinished

Q3 On Archiving
Keep it transforming, and lose biased imagery. Aim for long-term approaches: focus on the usefulness of body-based artforms in a reason-centered society, how to gain the interest of the youth, and ways we may interact with it again and again.

Q1 Please tell us how you became involved with Butoh?
Q2 What attracted you to Butoh?
Q3 As a performative art inherently involving the physical body, how can Butoh be preserved? Or, is this even possible?

Q1 あなたが舞踏をはじめたきっかけを教えて下さい。
Q2 あなたにとって舞踏の魅力は何ですか？
Q3 身体芸術である舞踏は、どのようにしたら残すことができるでしょうか？

浅井信好 | Nobuyoshi Asai

舞踏家・振付家・芸術監督 | 愛知（日本）| ダンスハウス黄金4422 | 20年

Butoh Dancer, Choreographer, Artistic Director | Aichi (Japan) | Dance House Kogane 4422 | 20 years

ソロ作品 "REI" の公演写真

https://nobuyoshiasai.com

Q1 舞踏をはじめたきっかけ

2003年に世田谷パブリックシアターにて山海塾の「うつり」を鑑賞したことがきっかけ。

Q2 舞踏の魅力

表現形態として、精神だけではなく、身体に対しても内的な対話を行いながら、拡張していく舞踏は西洋の舞踊形式と異なり、日本の文化や風土、歴史と強く結びついていることが魅力である。

Q3 アーカイヴについて

創成期より舞踏は変化し続け、それぞれの舞踏家や振付家が独自の舞踏哲学を持っていることによって拡張していく利点はあるが、「舞踏とは何なのか」「舞踏という踊りの基本動作とは」と言った明確な基礎が定義されないことで本質を失った状態で継承されていくことを危惧する。

Q1 Reason for Starting Butoh

I had an appreciation for Sankai Juku's *Utsuri*, which I saw at Setagaya Public Theatre in 2003.

Q2 Attraction to Butoh

As a form of expression, there is not only a spiritual, but a physical dialogue with the inner self which is inherently different from Western dance forms, and strongly connected to Japanese culture, nature and history.

Q3 On Archiving

Since the beginning Butoh has always been changing, and while there are advantages for Butoh dancers and choreographers who understand its philosophy to broaden their horizons, I am concerned that without a clearly defined basis of asking "What is Butoh?", "What movements make Butoh?", its essence will be lost.

Dominique Baron-Bonarjee

Visual Artist, Dancer, Researcher | International | Goldsmiths University Art Department | 10 years

ビジュアルアーティスト・ダンサー・リサーチャー | 世界各地 | Goldsmiths University Art Department | 10年

Photo: K. Hayashi

www.dominiquebb.com

Q1 Reason for Starting Butoh

Butoh came to me, through my questions about identity and embodiment. My first experiences were in the UK and France. In 2012 I received a dance scholarship to visit Japan. Over four years there, I met a range of practitioners who continue to influence my dance research and technique.

Q2 Attraction to Butoh

I was initially attracted to the aesthetic of Butoh. Gradually I discovered the rich historical context of Butoh, as a post-war performance art form, and this really cemented my interest. It's proved to be an inspiration in thinking about the environmental, economic and political changes happening in the world today.

Q3 On Archiving

My own research demonstrated to me how slippery Butoh is as a form, being hard to trace according to a single lineage. As a practitioner-researcher, I'm involved in developing new methods for sharing complex embodied knowledge. These types of artworks require a different modality of preservation: practice-based academic research has the potential to de/re-create the archival format.

Q1 舞踏をはじめたきっかけ

アイデンティティーと身体性への問いを通じて、舞踏と出会いました。私が初めて舞踏を経験したのはイギリスとフランスでした。2012年にダンスの奨学金を得て、日本を訪れました。そこでの4年間で、私のダンスの研究と技術に影響を与え続ける、様々な舞踏の実践者と出会いました。

Q2 舞踏の魅力

私はまず最初に、舞踏の美学に魅了されました。徐々に、舞踏の持つ豊かな歴史背景を発見し、興味を真剣に向けるようになりました。今では、今日この世界で起きている環境、経済、政治の変化の数々について考える上でのインスピレーションとなっています。

Q3 アーカイヴについて

私自身の研究の中で理解した限りでは、型としての舞踏はつかみ所がなく、単一の系統から辿ることが困難です。実践者であり、研究者でもある身として、私は複合的な知識を具現化し共有するための新しいメソッドを開発することに携わっています。この種の創造的作業は、舞踏を後世に残すための、これまでとは異なる様式を必要とします。すなわち、アーカイヴのフォーマットを刷新する可能性を持つ、実践に基づいた学問的研究と言えるでしょう。

Anna Barth

Freelance Dancer, Choreographer | Berlin (Germany) | DanceArt Lab Berlin (Artistic Director), Exploratorium Berlin, Kazuo Ohno Dance Studio | 27 years

フリーランスダンサー・振付家 | ベルリン（ドイツ） | DanceArt Lab Berlin（主宰）・Exploratorium Berlin・大野一雄舞踏研究所 | 27年

FOLDING ≈ UNFOLDING with Marcelo Aguirre (DanceArt Lab, Berlin) Video still: Ingo Schneider

www.annabarth.de

Q1 Reason for Starting Butoh
Meeting Kazuo Ohno, dancing *La Argentina* at the Akademie der Künste in Berlin in 1989.

Q2 Attraction to Butoh
Resonance, Widening, amplification of my approach towards what dance can be.

Q3 On Archiving
Dance is an ephemeral art. It's real power lies in live-performance. Nevertheless the documentation of my dance has become important to me.I am not quite sure why, but it might translate something to people who are interested in dance, now + in future.

Q1 舞踏をはじめたきっかけ
1989年にベルリン芸術アカデミーで「ラ・アルヘンチーナ頌」を踊る大野一雄と出会いました。

Q2 舞踏の魅力
ダンスの可能性に対する私のアプローチに共鳴し、その幅を広げ、拡張するもの。

Q3 アーカイヴについて
ダンスは儚い表現です。その本当の力はライヴのパフォーマンスにあります。しかし、自分のダンスを記録することが、私にとっても大切になってきました。どうしてなのかは分かりませんが、ダンスに興味を持つ人々に、今そしていつか未来に、何かを伝えることができるかもしれないからです。

Mireille Bergeron and Gérard-Charles Valente

Actress | Montreal (Canada) | Union des Artistes | 15 years

女優 | モントリオール（カナダ） | Union des Artistes | 15年

Mireille Bergeron playing Rio Rim

Q1 Reason for Starting Butoh
The mix of approaches, Jerzy Grotowski, Carbone 14, the movie *Les Enfants du Paradis* and also contemporary dance, has given us a spirit of free creation that has resulted in a form that we have been able to name only after seeing Kazuo Ohno perform in Montreal, in *La Argentina*.

Q2 Attraction to Butoh
Butoh is a particular introspection and channeling of emotions: a ritual is created to unfold, through the silence of beings, the range of emotions that lead to beauty and light.
It's a way of feeling and breathing.

Q3 On Archiving
The question is how to create a memory. By talking about it, communicating and putting forward the icons that embody this form of expression without definition.
Minimally, we need to create an annual international event deployed on the WEB with some associated physical locations in three countries that could vary from year to year and create a university research chair.

Q1 舞踏をはじめたきっかけ
イェジー・グロトフスキ、Carbone 14、映画「天井桟敷の人々」やコンテンポラリーダンスなどの表現方法をまぜることが、自由な創造精神を私たちに与えてくれました。そして、モントリオールでの大野一雄の「ラ・アルヘンチーナ頌」公演を観て初めて、私たちはその形を名付けることができるようになりました。

Q2 舞踏の魅力
舞踏は自分の内側を見つめ、感情を他の形に転化することだと思います。存在の静けさ、美と光へと繋がる感情を通じて、儀式がその姿を顕します。感じるため、呼吸をするための一つの方法だと思います。

Q3 アーカイヴについて
どのように人々の記憶に残すかということが問題だと思います。話し合うことで、この舞踏という定義を持たない表現形式を具現化するアイコンについて人に伝えたり勧めたりすることができるのです。最低限、年ごとに異なる3つの国々の実際のロケーションを使って、毎年国際的なイベントを起こし、それをウェブで展開しながら、大学でもリサーチの講座を立ち上げるべきです。

Q1 あなたが舞踏をはじめたきっかけを教えて下さい。
Q2 あなたにとって舞踏の魅力は何ですか？
Q3 身体芸術である舞踏は、どのようにしたら残すことができるでしょうか？

Karolina Bieszczad-Roley

Artistic Director, Producer, Dr | Oslo (Norway) | 20 years

芸術監督・プロデューサー・博士｜オスロ（ノルウェー）｜20年

The image is a compilation of 3 images from last year's project *Multiverse*, holographic performance with Yoshito Ohno, Saga Kobayashi and Daisuke Yoshimoto (Tårnet Kulturarena, Oslo) November 2018.

www.butoh-encounters.com

Q1 Reason for Starting Butoh
I first came across Butoh when living in Australia in 2000. After returning to Poland, I did my MA in Butoh dance. Then I moved to London, UK where I did my PhD in Butoh dance photography. Since 2017 I run a creative platform called Butoh Encounters.

Q2 Attraction to Butoh
I previously studied mainly "classical" theatre and when I came across Butoh, I felt I could not understand it and that is why I liked it. I have been researching Butoh for the past 18 years and I hope I will never fully understand it.

Q3 On Archiving
It depends what we mean by "archives". Any documenting activity changes the original art in some way. Especially live performances that are based on an embodied experience. But I believe there is great value in "marking the path" to the original art, by collecting documents that give us a window into understanding what this art might have been like.

Q1 舞踏をはじめたきっかけ
私が舞踏に出会ったのは、2000年にオーストラリアに住んでいた時です。ポーランドに戻った後、舞踏の修士号を得ました。それからロンドンに移り、舞踏における写真学の博士号を取得しました。2017年以降は、Butoh Encountersというクリエイティブ・プラットフォームを運営しています。

Q2 舞踏の魅力
以前は主に「クラシカル」な演劇を学んでいました。舞踏に出会った時にそれが理解できず、それが故に私は舞踏を好きになってしまいました。これまでの18年間、舞踏を研究し続けてきましたが、その全てを理解することはこれからも決してないと見込んでいます。

Q3 アーカイヴについて
「アーカイヴ」と言う時にそれが何を意味しているかに依ると思います。どのような記録活動も、元となる芸術を何かしら変化させてしまうものです。しかし、その芸術がどのようなものであったかを私たちに垣間見せてくれる記録物を収集することによって「道に印を残す」ことにも大きな価値があると信じています。

Dr Lynne Bradley

Physical Theatre Director | Brisbane (Australia) | Zen Zen Zo Physical Theatre | 28 years

フィジカルシアター演出家｜ブリスベン（オーストラリア）｜Zen Zen Zo Physical Theatre｜28年

GAIA, a co-production between Zen Zen Zo Physical Theatre (Australia) & Dairakudakan (Japan)

www.zenzenzo.com

Q1 Reason for Starting Butoh
I saw a performance by Dairakudakan (*Kaiin no Uma*) which changed my life. After that I studied Butoh with Katsura Kan, and later Maro Akaji, who has been my teacher ever since. My company Zen Zen Zo Physical Theatre collaborates with Dairakudakan in Japan and Australia. I am a leading Butoh teacher in Australia, and regularly direct Butoh-inspired productions.

Q2 Attraction to Butoh
I love that Butoh holds traditional and contemporary Japanese culture in balance, that it's rooted in Japanese culture yet intrinsically universal. That it celebrates the body in all its beauty and ugliness. It is anti-rational, yet profoundly meaningful. It is full of juxtaposition and contradiction, which makes it endless fascinating!

Q3 On Archiving
Continue to collect photos and videos. Whilst Butoh is a live performance form, digital records go a long way to preserving its history. Funding more books (in English) would enable more scholarship around Butoh to be accessible for non Japanese audiences (where this is much interest in Butoh).

Q1 舞踏をはじめたきっかけ
大駱駝艦の公演「海印の馬」を観て、私の人生が変わりました。その後、桂勘の下で舞踏を学んだ後に、以降私の師となる麿赤兒に教えを受けました。私のカンパニーZen Zen Zo Physical Theatreは、日本とオーストラリアで、大駱駝艦と共同で作品の製作を行なっています。オーストラリアで私は舞踏を率先して指導しながら、舞踏に影響を受けた作品の創作を定期的に行なっています。

Q2 舞踏の魅力
舞踏が伝統的かつ同時代的な日本文化をバランスよく保っていること、そして日本文化にルーツを持ちながらも、その本質が普遍的なところが大好きです。そして、身体の持つ美しさと醜さの全てを祝福するところ。舞踏は非論理的でありながら、深遠な意味を持っています。様々な事象の対置と矛盾に溢れており、そのことが際限なく魅力的です！

Q3 アーカイヴについて
写真と映像を収集し続けることです。舞踏はライブパフォーマンスの形を取っていますが、デジタルの記録はその歴史を保存するのに大いに役立ちます。（英語の）書籍に対する資金支援がより増えると、舞踏界隈の学問が（舞踏への関心がより高い）日本以外の観客に届きやすくなると思います。

Claude-Marie Caron

Movement Teacher | Montreal (Canada) | 42 years

ムーヴメント指導者 | モントリオール (カナダ) | 42年

Demon (鬼), (Vehicule Art, Montreal, Canada) 1982.
Photo: Michel Dubreuil.

Q1 Reason for Starting Butoh
In the early seventies, I entered conscious moving with Tai Chi Chuan and still do it. Few years later, I began performing and heard about Min Tanaka. In the eighties I saw Kazuo Ohno, Muteki Sha and attended a workshop by Natsu Nakajima. After that, the path was confirmed.

Q2 Attraction to Butoh
I was attracted to the dark, minimalist, slowness where the body finds its true nature. Letting the hidden come out with or without laughter and scream. It is sadness and tragedy, love and gentleness. It is from the bones, the scary consciousness opening doors, crossing bridges between worlds.

Q3 On Archiving
For preservation, Archives (Writings, photos, videos) are essential as legacy, as a map. Preservation in the territory, the dance as living action will pass from one generation to the other only through bodily experience in some kind of apprenticeship. or deep quest. Butoh will live because there will always be explorers uncovering the immaterial treasures of dance.

Q1 舞踏をはじめたきっかけ
1970年代初頭に太極拳をはじめ意識的に身体を動かすようになり、今でもまだ続けています。その数年後にパフォーマンスを始めた時に、田中泯のことを噂に聞きました。80年代に大野一雄と霧笛舎の公演を観て、中嶋夏のワークショップに参加しました。それから、私の進むべき道が決まりました。

Q2 舞踏の魅力
身体がその真の性質を顕す、暗く、ミニマルで、ゆっくりとした動きに惹かれました。笑いや叫びの有無に関係なく、隠されたものを曝け出すこと。それは、悲しみや悲劇、あるいは愛や優しさの姿です。骨から生まれる舞踏は、恐る恐るドアを開く意識、異なる世界の間にかかる橋なのです。

Q3 アーカイヴについて
舞踏を残す為に、アーカイヴ（書き物、写真、映像）は地図として、あるいはレガシーとして、必須のものです。何かしら徒弟教育のような関係上の身体的経験を通じてのみ、ダンスという生き物は一つの世代から次の世代へと伝えられることが可能です。あるいは、粘り強く追求することによっても、あり得るでしょう。ダンスを探求する人々はいつも、非物質的な宝物の数々を見つけ出すので、舞踏は生き残っていくと思います。

Carlos Iván Cruz Islas

Degree in Dramatic Arts | Latin America | TEATRO CUERPO SOCIAL | 17 years

演劇学士 | ラテンアメリカ | TEATRO CUERPO SOCIAL | 17年

Q1 Reason for Starting Butoh
I am an orphan of the body, born without transcendent encounters, a dirty image between mirrors. Guided along the path of the criminal in my memory, I cry into the night, searching for an abandoned skin that will shelter my soul. I am the apprentice that left my body in the shadows of darkness.

Q2 Attraction to Butoh
It's a flower of emptiness. Ecstasy, a contemplation of the invisible universe where we can glimpse our presence in the immensity of vast infinity, as vagabonds of the universe. Our ancestors understood bare feet, surrendered themselves to natural forces with wisdom, offering up their bodies to free the spirit, and move the soul. Where do we come from, where will we go? Butoh inhabits all abandoned spaces.

Q3 On Archiving
Butoh grows and shrinks in the bodies of the others, the shadows growing up through roots, raking up the ancestors buried in the wombs of our being, and waking the dead that live within us. Exhuming memories from the depths of our shadows. An absolute demand for suicide, to offer up presence in return for essence. To disappear, until you can feel the illusion that we are dancing together united. Butoh is transformation, resistance, and refuses to be colonised by the skin of capitalism. Meat that reveals itself to brutal conquest, to exploitations, enslavement and contempoary plunder. The Japanese body holds dialogues with bodies of the world through Butoh, erasure, and the shadows in the eyes of the blind.

(originally written in Spanish)

Q1 舞踏をはじめたきっかけ
私は肉体の孤児だ。遭遇の超越も知らず、鏡の間の醜い像から生まれた。私の記憶の犯罪者の顔に誘われて、夜にむせび泣きながら、旅をする、魂に隠れ家を与える打ち捨てられた皮膚を探しながら。私は影の暗闇の中に肉体を置き去りにした学徒である。

Q2 舞踏の魅力
それは虚無の花。不可視の宇宙を見つめる恍惚、その広大な無限の中に、宇宙をさまよう私たちの存在を目に捉えることを得る。古の人々は裸足の民を知りながら、叡智を持つ自然の力に身を委ねる、聖霊を解き放ち、魂を黙らせるために、肉体を差し出す。私たちはどこから来たのだろう、どこへ行くのだろう。舞踏は打ち捨てられた空間のひとつひとつに棲息する。

Q3 アーカイヴについて
舞踏は他者の肉体の中に成長し、衰退する。影は自らの根から生え、私たちの存在の子宮に埋められた先人たちを発掘する、私たちの中に住む死者を呼び覚ましながら。影の奥底の記憶を掘り起こす。私という人間の自死に対する絶対的な要求は、本質へと帰するために存在を捧げるのだ。消滅し、結ばれてあることの幻想のなかで共に踊ったことを感じることができるまで。舞踏とは変貌、抵抗、資本主義の皮によって植民化されることを拒絶すること。残忍な征服に対して、搾取と奴隷制、現代の剥奪に対して立ち上げる肉。日本の肉体は、舞踏、消去、盲人の眼差しの中の影を通じて世界の肉体と対話する。

WWW.TEATROCUERPOSOCIAL.BLOGSPOT.COM

Q1 あなたが舞踏をはじめたきっかけを教えて下さい。
Q2 あなたにとって舞踏の魅力は何ですか?
Q3 身体芸術である舞踏は、どのようにしたら残すことができるでしょうか?

雫境 DAKEI

聾(ろう)の舞踏家・ダンサー|東京(日本)|濃淡(主宰)|22年

Deaf Butoh Dancer, Dancer | Tokyo (Japan) | NOUTAN (Artistic Director) | 22 years

Photo: Rokka Ando

https://noutan-in-a-line.jimdosite.com/
https://www.facebook.com/shizuku.dakei
https://www.facebook.com/dakeinoutanshizuku/

Q1 舞踏をはじめたきっかけ
日本ろう者劇団に在籍した時、先輩のユニットグループの旗揚げ公演に参加した。参加者の中に舞踏家がいて、「スキンヘッドだから」ということで舞踏公演の出演に誘われた。

Q2 舞踏の魅力
ひとつは、私は耳が聞こえないので、音楽に対して「憧れ」のようなものとして捉えている。音ではない、視覚的な「音楽」としての身体表現の可能性を大いに孕んでいる。

Q3 アーカイヴについて
舞台公演の撮影、またワークショップの風景を撮影した動画を残すことで、どのように動いたかを観察できるのではないでしょうか。そのためにコスパの良い、専門動画撮影の団体を立ち上げるとどうでしょうか?

Q1 Reason for Starting Butoh
I was part of the Japanese Theatre of the Deaf when I participated in a senpai's performance. Among us was a Butoh dancer, and I was invited to be in a Butoh performance for "being a skinhead".

Q2 Attraction to Butoh
As a deaf person, I see it as something that catches the "longing" I have for music. I greatly appreciate the possibilities of a non-auditory, visual "music".

Q3 On Archiving
By filming performances and archiving videos that capture the atmosphere of workshops, I think it is possible to study movements. Could some funding be organised to put together a professional filming group for this purpose?

Mizu Desierto

Performing Artist | Portland (USA) | Water in the Desert (Artistic Director) | 23 years

パフォーミングアーティスト|ポートランド(アメリカ合衆国)|Water in the Desert(主宰)|23年

Matriarch, solo performance.
Photo: Miana Jun

https://www.witd.org/

Q1 Reason for Starting Butoh
After the death of my father at a young age, Butoh found me. Now for exactly half of my lifetime, I have been in a dynamic relationship to the art and its artists. While I do not consider myself a purely Butoh creator, it has deeply influenced my life.

Q2 Attraction to Butoh
From an early age, Butoh proposed to me a pathway to investigate the mystery of existence through the body. It first presented itself as an essential embodied art rebellion of the violent trajectories of humanity and over time has become an act of healing, both on and off the stage.

Q3 On Archiving
I believe that Butoh belongs to the dancers who were part of the original movement and should be preserved as such through the archives of photos, films and dance notation. I also believe in an essence of Butoh that is beyond any particular cultural identification or definition and will always exist outside of any attempts towards preservation, containment or codification.

Q1 舞踏をはじめたきっかけ
若い頃に父を亡くした後、舞踏が私を見つけてくれました。今ではちょうど人生の半分に渡って、舞踏や、舞踏家とのダイナミックな関係を保っています。自分自身は純粋な舞踏家とは言えませんが、舞踏は私の生き方に深い影響を与えています。

Q2 舞踏の魅力
最初の頃から、舞踏は私に、身体を通して人間存在の不可思議さを掘り下げるための道を与えてくれていました。当初、舞踏は人間性の暴力的な軌跡を具現化した重要な芸術の抵抗だったのが、時を経て、舞台の中でも外でも、治癒行為の一つとなりました。

Q3 アーカイヴについて
舞踏は、その動きの原型の大部分を生み出したダンサーに帰属しており、写真や映像や舞踏譜のようなアーカイヴを通して残されるべきだと思います。また、あらゆる文化的認識や定義を超えて、舞踏を保存、分類、またはコード化しようとする全ての試みの外側に存在し続けるのが舞踏の本質だと信じています。

凡例 肩書き|活動拠点|所属団体|活動年数
Reference Occupation | Base | Affiliation | Years of Activity

Maya Dunsky

Multidisciplinary Artist, Butoh Dancer, Choreographer, Painter | Israel | 36 years

マルチディシプリナリーアーティスト・舞踏家・振付家・画家 | イスラエル | 36年

With Hands Outstretched, solo performance.2018

www.mayadunsky.com/

Q1 Reason for Starting Butoh
In 1983 I saw Sankai Juku group and Ariadone group in Israel. Since then I held the vision to study Butoh in Japan and found my way to Ohno Kazuo, the great master, spiritual father of Butoh, by whom I had the privilege to study for more than 2 years.

Q2 Attraction to Butoh
I intuitively felt that Butoh would liberate me from wrong perceptions about what dance is and could lead me to find authentic of being and presence as an essence.

Q3 On Archiving
It is necessary to create a vivid archive which reflects global scenes of Butoh as an international yet unique expression, with its different manifestations. There is not much value for Butoh as a physical form of dance to be imitated, without deep research of the meaning of spiritual creative dance /being.

Q1 舞踏をはじめたきっかけ
1983年にイスラエルで山海塾とアリアドーネの會を観ました。それから、日本で舞踏を学ぶ夢を持ち、偉大なる師、そして舞踏の父である、大野一雄に遂に出会うことができました。幸運にも彼の下で2年以上、舞踏を学ぶことができました。

Q2 舞踏の魅力
私は直感的に、舞踏は私をダンスに対する誤った認識から解放し、人としての本当の在り方へと導いてくれると感じました。

Q3 アーカイヴについて
国際的でありながら特異な表現でもある舞踏のグローバルなシーンを反映する活力のあるアーカイヴは、異なる複数の意思表明を伴って構築することが必要です。精神的かつ創造的な、踊ること／存在することの意味を深く研究しないで、身体的な形式だけを模倣するのであれば、舞踏にはそれほどの価値はありません。

Edoheart

Poet, Music Producer, Visual Artist, Singer, Communications Strategist, and Performer | New York (USA) , Lagos (Nigeria) | 12 years

詩人・音楽プロデューサー・ヴィジュアルアーティスト・歌手・コミュニケーション専門家・パフォーマー | ニューヨーク（アメリカ合衆国）・ラゴス（ナイジェリア） | 12年

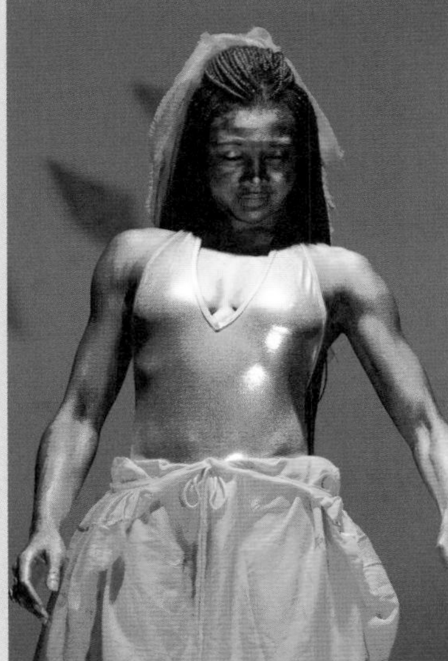

Korea Experimental Arts Festival, 2008.
Photo: Young-il Kwon

https://edoheart.org

Q1 Reason for Starting Butoh
In 2000 or 2001, I saw an advertisement for a butoh dance performance at the University of Michigan where I was a student - probably Dairakudakan. It was very striking. When I moved to New York, I undertook intensive study with Yukio Waguri.

Q2 Attraction to Butoh
I saw in butoh, the power to become and inhabit language; the possibility of becoming or doing anything imaginable; a place to grasp the traumas I and others live; an opportunity to unite my love of poetry, visual arts, music, and performance; something truthful, something hopeful, humbling and freeing.

Q3 On Archiving
Butoh has preserved an ancient performative art. We need only witness indigenous African performance to see butoh. A butoh body is a vehicle for performing language. So let us investigate language. My people, the Edo of Nigeria, and the Japanese share the same word for water or rain: ame. We can preserve butoh by crediting the lineages of performative languages.

Q1 舞踏をはじめたきっかけ
2000年あるいは2001年に、私が学生として在籍していたミシガン大学で舞踏公演の宣伝を見ました。多分、大駱駝艦だったと思います。とても衝撃的でした。その後ニューヨークに移り住んだ時に、和栗由紀夫の集中講座を受けました。

Q2 舞踏の魅力
舞踏の中に、言語に化身する力、言語に棲みつく力を感じました。想像できるものは何にでも変貌し、あらゆることを実現できる可能性。私や他者が抱えるトラウマを理解する場所。詩、ビジュアルアート、音楽やパフォーマンスに対する私の愛を統合できる機会。真実の何か。あるいは希望に満ちた、人を謙虚にさせ、人に自由を与える何か。

Q3 アーカイヴについて
舞踏は古代のパフォーミングアーツを受け継いできました。アフリカの土着的パフォーマンスの中にも、舞踏を見つけることができます。舞踏的身体は、言語を表現するための媒体です。ですから、その言語を皆で探求していきましょう。私の友人であるナイジェリアのエド州民は、水や雨のことを日本人と同じ言葉、「Ame」と言います。このような諸言語の系統を認めることで、舞踏を後世に残すことができると思います。

Q1 Please tell us how you became involved with Butoh?
Q2 What attracted you to Butoh?
Q3 As a performative art inherently involving the physical body, how can Butoh be preserved? Or, is this even possible?

Q1 あなたが舞踏をはじめたきっかけを教えて下さい。
Q2 あなたにとって舞踏の魅力は何ですか？
Q3 身体芸術である舞踏は、どのようにしたら残すことができるでしょうか？

遠藤公義 | Tadashi Endo

振付家・ダンサー | ゲッティンゲン（ドイツ）| 30年

Choreographer, Dancer | Göttingen (Germany) | 30 years

Tadashi Endo's solo FUKUSHIMA MON AMOUR by Marciej Rusinek

www.butoh-ma.de

Q1 舞踏をはじめたきっかけ
1972年芝居仲間根津甚八と土方巽「疱瘡譚」を観た事と1989年大野一雄との出会い。

Q2 舞踏の魅力
舞踏の舞台には何かいつも自然現象が起きている感覚と、大野一雄そして大野慶人という稀に見る貴重な人間の存在。

Q3 アーカイヴについて
舞踏は日本で起きた文化革命であり未だその過渡期にあり、能や歌舞伎のような伝統芸能としては保存されていかないだろうし、保存されるべきでもない。しかし土方巽、大野一雄の残した形跡は、世界中の人間にリサイクリングされていくと思う。

Q1 Reason for Starting Butoh
Seeing Tatsumi Hijikata's *Hosotan* with Jinpachi Nezu in 1972, and meeting Kazuo Ohno in 1989.

Q2 Attraction to Butoh
Butoh performances always feel like the occurrence of a natural phenomenon. Also, the existence of unique individuals like Kazuo Ohno and Yoshito Ohno.

Q3 On Archiving
Butoh is a cultural revolution of Japan, which exists in a place of transition. It most likely cannot, and should not, be preserved as a cultural tradition like Noh or Kabuki. However, I believe that the remaining traces left by Tatsumi Hijikata and Kazuo Ohno will go on being recycled by people all over the world.

榎木ふく | Fuku Enoki

舞踏家 | 東京（日本）| 小林嵯峨＋鷲・NOSURI | 12年

Butoh Dancer | Tokyo (Japan) | Kobayashi Saga + NOSURI | 12 years

私のエチカ*Vol.2*参加作品。タイトル『身を置くことから』
Photo: Makoto Onozuka ©Onozuka

Twitter: @enokifuku

Q1 舞踏をはじめたきっかけ
演劇活動をしていて身体へのアプローチが不十分だと感じた時に、知人から土方巽の存在を知らされました。初めて目にしたものは、映像では映画『卑弥呼』。衝撃を受けた舞踏家は師・小林嵯峨です。

Q2 舞踏の魅力
深い所でのコミュニケーションが図れる事です。

Q3 アーカイヴについて
辞めないことでしょうか？

Q1 Reason for Starting Butoh
While working in theatre but feeling it lacked in physicality, I heard about Tatsumi Hijikata through an acquaintance. The first thing I saw was the film *Himiko*. The Butoh dancer that struck me most was my master Saga Kobayashi.

Q2 Attraction to Butoh
The transpiring of deep communication.

Q3 On Archiving
Perhaps it is to not stop?

凡例 | 肩書き | 活動拠点 | 所属団体 | 活動年数

Reference | Occupation | Base | Affiliation | Years of Activity

Iván Daniel Espinosa

Choreographer, Multimedia Artist | Seattle (USA) | 6 years

振付家・マルチメディアアーティスト | シアトル（アメリカ合衆国） | 6年

Messengers Divinos, performance & sound installation (Seattle Butoh Festival) 2018
© CAREY 2018

www.ivanespinosa.org

Q1 Reason for Starting Butoh

After first encountering the art of Butoh at a Japanese film festival, I soon became interested in the physical practice during my first Butoh workshop in Seattle. Since then, I have been choreographing both stage performances and outdoor, site-specific performances that actively explore concepts from Butoh exercises and practices.

Q2 Attraction to Butoh

From the beginning I've been fascinated with how Butoh challenges our perceptions of space and time. This altered space – where boundaries of time, identity, and language blur – can offer us the possibility of redefining our world(s). I'm particularly interested in applying this to our engagements with the earth and nature.

Q3 On Archiving

Film preservation of seminal performances, along with video archiving of contemporary developments, is an effective manner of preserving Butoh. In addition, one of the most vital ways of preserving the SOMATIC PRACTICE of Butoh is through teaching. Just as martial artists have preserved their forms by teaching them worldwide, Butoh artists need to pass on the practice to new generations.

Q1 舞踏をはじめたきっかけ

日本映画祭で初めて舞踏に出会った後、シアトルで初めて受けた舞踏ワークショップで行なった身体の稽古に興味を持ち始めました。それから、舞台での公演と屋外でのサイトスペシフィックパフォーマンスの両方の振付けを行いながら、舞踏のエクササイズと稽古から得たコンセプトを探求しています。

Q2 舞踏の魅力

当初より、舞踏が私たちの空間と時間の知覚の仕方に疑いを投げかけていることに魅了されています。時間やアイデンティティー、言語の境界を曖昧にする、舞踏によって変化させられた空間は、私たちの世界を再定義する可能性を与えてくれます。またこのことを、私たちの地球と自然に対する関わり方にも応用できるのではないかと、関心を持っています。

Q3 アーカイヴについて

同時代の発展を映像でアーカイヴすることと併せて、独創性に富む公演映像の保存は、舞踏を後世に残す上で効果的な方法だと思います。それに加えて、舞踏の身体技法を残す上でもっとも重要な方法は、教えることです。武術家が世界中でその型を教え広めているのと同じように、舞踏家も新しい世代へと、その技術を受け渡していかなければいけません。

Damiano Fina

Performer | Italy | 5 years

パフォーマー | イタリア | 5年

The Alchemical Body, 2017.
Photo: Fabrizio Panozzo.

www.damianofina.it/en

Q1 Reason for Starting Butoh

During an artistic residency in Portugal I was advised to meet the butoh dance of Atsushi Takenouchi, who would soon become my first butoh master.

Q2 Attraction to Butoh

The first time I met butoh dance, I felt at home. It was as if my whole organism had suddenly been inhabited by the spirit of dance.

Q3 On Archiving

I believe that the peculiarity of butoh dance is to dig into the arts of the human organism by leading the dance back to its rituality. In this sense, I consider butoh dance to be cross-cultural. The creation of archives is useful to share and map the development of this dance in the world, being able to study its distinctive aspects and common elements at the same time.

Q1 舞踏をはじめたきっかけ

ポルトガルでのアーティスト・イン・レジデンスの間、竹之内淳志という舞踏家に会うことを勧められ、彼はすぐに私の最初の舞踏の師となりました。

Q2 舞踏の魅力

初めて舞踏に出会った時に、私は故郷にいるような心地がしました。それはまるで、私という有機体の全てに、踊りの精が突然に住みついてしまったような感覚でした。

Q3 アーカイヴについて

舞踏の特異性は、ダンスを儀式的なものに回帰させることで、人体という芸術に深く入り込むことだと思います。この意味において、舞踏は様々な文化を横断するものだと考えています。アーカイヴを構築することは、舞踏の特徴的な側面と普遍的要素を同時に研究することを可能にするがゆえに、世界中の舞踏の発展を分かち合い、可視化することに役立つと思います。

精神のリレー 2019

A Spiritual Relay 2019

石井則仁
Norihito Ishii

Photo: Makiko Kumagai

私が舞踏の師として仰ぐ人は、天児牛大です。
2019年の時点で研修期間も含め約11年、山海塾のもとで活動してきました。

引き継いできていること、引き継いでいきたいことは、大きく分けていうと“表現者（ダンサー）としての精神性”と“アーティスト（作者）としての精神性”です。

まず、天児さんの踊りは物凄く細かい。
舞踏は、自分の内側の世界と外側の世界が、人だけでなく動物や物、様々な感情や環境に変化・変容し、表現・表出していくものです。それは私の言葉で言うとファンタジーであり夢でもあります。
天児さんの何が細かいかというと、自分の内面と外面の設定がシンプルに強く、繊細且つ明確にある。それは動きの流れがミリ単位で決まっていて、間の取り方も全て決まっている。そして意識の持ち方と感情の振れ幅が深い。だからこそ、強大な集中力を生み出し、お客さんを魅了できる存在になるのだと、山海塾に所属した当初から思っています。表現がどうあるべきかということに対して、職人なのです。そしてそこにはちゃんとした身体技術もあります。
表現者として上記のことを引き継いでいきたいと思っています。上記のことを徹底しているからこそエネルギーが生まれ、3階席からでも観客は集中力が途切れることなく魅入ってしまうのだと思います。

天児さんは稽古から本番直前まで、とにかく客観視します。作品としてのコンセプチュアルな部分を貫き通しながら、客観的に各シーンが集中力を持って見ていられるものであるかをチェックします。

The person that I aspire to as a Butoh teacher is Ushio Amagatsu.
As I write this in 2019, I have already been working with Sankai Juku for about eleven years, including the initial training phase.

What I have acquired and that which I would like to carry forward can be broadly divided into “spirituality — as someone who expresses himself as a dancer”, and “spirituality — as an artist or a creator.”

First and foremost, Amagatsu's dance is tremendously intricate. Butoh is a process through which one's inner world and one's outer world change, transform, express and manifest themselves not only on a human but also on animal and material, emotional and environmental levels. It is both a fantasy and a dream.
What makes Amagatsu's dance so intricate is that his inner and outer configurations are at once simple, strong, delicate, and clear. In practice, this entails that a dancer's movement flow is determined to every last millimeter, and that all time intervals are structured. Moreover, there's a great depth to his way of engaging consciousness and the range of emotions at his disposal. Given how he forges such great concentration, I felt from the outset of my time with Sankai Juku that he could create an arresting stage presence for audiences. In terms of what form expression should take, Amagatsu is a true craftsman. This also involves mastering the technique needed. As someone who express myself through my body, I would like to carry forward all those qualities I outlined already. I believe that by availing of the thoroughness described above I will be able to generate such energy that even audience members seated on the third floor will become completely entranced.

In any case, from the time of rehearsals right up until the actual performance, Amagatsu scrutinizes everything objectively. As well as working on the conceptual aspect of the

石井則仁

17歳からストリートダンスを踊り始め、様々なコンテストにて入賞。メディアなどでの活躍後、活動場所を舞台空間へ。様々なダンスカンパニーの国内外の公演に参加する傍ら、蜷川幸雄や宮本亜門の演劇作品にも出演。2010年より舞踏カンパニー山海塾に在籍。ソウル国際振付フェスティバルでJury prize（2013年）、SCFアワード（2015年）を受賞。国内だけでなく海外でも精力的に活動している。

Norihito Ishii

Norihito Ishii started performing street dance at the age of seventeen and won various contests. After being initially active in the media world, he shifted focus to the world of the stage. While participating in various dance company performances both in Japan and overseas, he also appeared in theatrical works by Yukio Ninagawa and Amon Miyamoto. In 2010, he joined the Butoh dance troupe Sankai Juku. Ishii was awarded the Jury Prize (2013) and SCF Award (2015) at the Seoul International Choreography Festival. He is currently active in Japan as well as overseas.

照明・音楽・美術がある空間の中で、各シーンや作品全体、踊りをどう見せるかデザインしています。
山海塾に入ってから私は、山海塾の作品をシルク・ド・ソレイユやバレエ作品のように思うようになりました。舞台の近くで見ても感情や動きの細かさを楽しめ、観客席の後ろ側で見ても全体の構造やデザインとしても楽しめるからです。

天児さんは多くの文化を学ぶ中で視覚的なデザインなども取り込み、作品に活かしていると思っています。
照明をどう当てたら闇の谷間が出来ないか、どの素材で美術を作って、どれぐらいの重さでどう吊ったらいいかなど、多岐に渡って知識を持ち、踊りやデザインだけでなく、照明や音楽・音響、舞台美術の素材やそのデザインまで、多くのことを知っています。

舞台芸術は総合芸術です。天児さんの背中を追い、自身が作品を作る際はこの姿勢を引き継いでいます。

昔、天児さんに言われた言葉が舞台に向かう時にいつも反芻します。
「疑問を常に追求しなさい」と。

piece, he focuses objectively, checking how each individual scene is to be seen.
In terms of stage lighting, music, and décor, he designs how to present the dance in each individual scene and in the whole work.
Since joining Sankai Juku, I have come to think that the troupe's pieces somewhat resemble the Cirque du Soleil or some balletic works. Not only can those sitting close to the stage can enjoy the emotion and fine movements but also those audience members at the back of the venue can appreciate the work's overall structure and design.

I think that thanks to the process of researching various cultures, Amagatsu has also incorporated visual designs in the Sankai Juku's works.
He also possesses a wide range of know-how: how to use stage lighting to avoid to creating a valley of darkness, what materials to use for the decor, how much weight to hang, and so forth. He is very knowledgeable about music and lighting, sound design, and materials to be used for designing the decor.

The performing arts are synthetic by nature. I will follow in Amagatsu's footsteps and continue his approach whenever I embark on creating my own works.

I still think over what Amagatsu used to say to us whenever we would step out on stage:
"Constantly explore your doubts."

天児牛大 | Ushio Amagatsu (1949-)

1975年、山海塾を創設。80年より海外公演を開始し、フランスと日本を主な拠点に2年に1度ほどのペースで新作を発表。82年以降の17作品はすべてパリ市立劇場の共同制作となる。ヨーロッパのみならず、北米、中南米、アジア、オセアニアなど、これまでに48カ国のべ700都市以上でツアーを行う。97年からはオペラの演出も手がける。

Founded Sankai Juku in 1975. Began performing overseas in 1980, and subsequently presents a new piece every two years. All works since 1982 have been co-produced by the Théâtre de la Ville (Paris). Toured more than 700 cities in 48 countries, not only in Europe but also in North America, Latin America, Asia and Oceania. Directs operas since 1997 in addition.

Q1 あなたが舞踏をはじめたきっかけを教えて下さい。
Q2 あなたにとって舞踏の魅力は何ですか？
Q3 身体芸術である舞踏は、どのようにしたら残すことができるでしょうか？

藤谷由美 | Yumi Fujitani

振付・演出家※ | パリ（フランス）| 35年

Choreographer, Director* | Paris (France) | 35 years

カルロッタ池田と室伏 鴻へのオマージュ作品Elles『形としての舞踏』をやってみた作品
Photo: Gourreau Jean-Marie

※パフォーマー、舞踏というと先入観が強いので避けます。色々な作品に役者としても参加します。でも完全に舞踏家でしょう。

*There is prejudice in using words such as Performer or Butoh Dancer so I avoid these. I also work as an actor. But what I do is Butoh.

Q1 舞踏をはじめたきっかけ

状況劇場公演前に配られたチラシでカルロッタ池田と室伏鴻主催の福井県でのアリアドーネの會のワークショップに参加。白虎社も配っていたが行かなかった。

Q2 舞踏の魅力

どんなテクニックも通用しないところ。『何でもあり』な自由さと危険さ。全てナッシング、一から出直しで向かって行ける潔さと厳しさ。そしてあくまでも胡散臭く、バカバカしく、出鱈目。*諸先輩への尊敬を込めて…

Q3 アーカイヴについて

舞踏が舞踏そのものとして残る事と、舞踏を内在しながら他のジャンルへと移行していく事、他の分野からの舞踏へのアプローチ、この三つの点で舞踏が続いていく事については私はなんの危惧も持っていません。東西問わずに誰かがしつこく公演をやり、誰かがしつこくワークショップを続けていくでしょう。
これは舞踏である、舞踏でないという境がとても難しいし、素人とプロの見分けも難しい。そもそもその境が無いからこれだけ多くの人に愛されているのだと思います。見る側の熟練と広い深い知識そして愛が必要だと思います。スタイルとしての舞踏ではなく真面目にコツコツと続けている舞踏家に光をといったところでしょうか？

Q1 Reason for Starting Butoh

I was given a flyer for a workshop with Ariadone Campany's Carlotta Ikeda and Ko Murobushi in Fukui when I went to see a theatre performance. They were also distributing for Byakkosha but I didn't go.

Q2 Attraction to Butoh

That there are no common techniques. The freedom and danger of 'anything goes'. Everything is Nothing, the sincerity and severity of having to face all from the beginning. And the awkward, ridiculous, nonsensicalness of it. *With respect to mentors...

Q3 On Archiving

I have no fear regarding Butoh's continuation in terms of it being preserved as itself, it being used as a base to transform into another genre, or it being approached from other fields. In both the East and West, I'm sure there will always be someone persistently creating performances and running workshops. It is very difficult to define the boundary between what is Butoh and what isn't, as is distinguishing amateurs and from professionals. I think it's precisely because there are no such boundaries that it is loved by so many. I think skillful watching, deep knowledge and love are most important. Perhaps we need to shine a brighter light on Butoh dancers who continue dancing with focus rather than a Butoh 'style'?

Yael Gaathon

Choreographer, Dancer | Aarhus (Denmark) | Blue Cliff (Artistic Director) | 30 years

振付家・ダンサー | オーフス（デンマーク）| Blue Cliff（主宰）| 30年

Shinpai Shinaide - Don't Worry About Us, 2018

www.bluecliff.org

Q1 Reason for Starting Butoh

I was working as an actress with Itim Theatre Ensemble, one of the biggest experimental theatre group in Israel. The director Rina Yerushalmi, decided to hire Yori Ran, who studied with Kazuo Ohno, to train the actors in Butoh. This training influenced our way of moving and talking on stage.

Q2 Attraction to Butoh

In Butoh I found many of things I was craving for as a performer: the connection between mind, body and movement; the dedication; the focus; the connection to the spirit; the awareness which is beyond time and space. Butoh gives me the tools to express the deepest parts of myself.

Q3 On Archiving

Documentation of the performing arts is always problematic. It will never give us the full experience of the original performance, just as a painting of an apple will never give us the same experience as eating an apple. Archives, verbal or visual, can help us understand ideas and thoughts, it can give us inspiration and point us in the right direction.

Q1 舞踏をはじめたきっかけ

私はイスラエルで最も大きな実験演劇グループの一つ、Itim Theatre Ensembleに女優として所属していました。俳優たちに舞踏の稽古をさせるために、ディレクターのRina Yerushalmiが、大野一雄の下で学んでいたYori Ranを採用することに決めました。この稽古が、ステージ上の私たちの動きや話し方に影響を与えました。

Q2 舞踏の魅力

私は舞踏の中に、パフォーマーとして渇望していた多くのことを発見しました。精神と身体、そしてムーヴメントとの繋がり。献身すること。フォーカス。魂との繋がり。時空を超えた意識。舞踏は、自分自身の最も深い部分を表現するツールを与えてくれます。

Q3 アーカイヴについて

パフォーミングアートを記録することは常に問題を孕んでいます。りんごの絵が、りんごを食べることと同じ経験を与えてくれないのと全く同じように、舞踏の記録は、オリジナルのパフォーマンスを完全な形で体験させてくれることはないでしょう。言語的なものであれ、視覚的なものであれアーカイヴはアイデアや思想の理解を助け、インスピレーションを与え、私たちを正しい方向へと導くことが可能です。

Adrien Gaumé aka SIDELANER

Facilitator | Europe | 9 years

ファシリテーター | 欧州 | 9年

Once upon a Butoh Delight (PANCH, Basel)

Q1 Reason for Starting Butoh
From the first session, without resistance. A visceral sensation led me to prefer to meet most of the masters working in Europe who realized my aspiration to live as a nomad. I travel as a poet and create with this generous toolbox. It seems to me possible to meet me gradually.

Q2 Attraction to Butoh
The salient intuition of making me available for buried questions, mine and those, more or less visible, surrounding. Then behind the phenomenological and maieutical aspect, the joy of sharing and continuing to discover potentialities for oneself and within ephemeral collectives. A refreshing socio-political significance.

Q3 On Archiving
Initially, I was concerned about the poor quality of video documentation when it existed, and then I accepted that it was deficient. In a general way the kinesthetical experience is so strident and sometimes dizzying that one could almost postulate that it is giving him thanks for being elusive. Blessed is the soul that escapes.

Q1 舞踏をはじめたきっかけ
初めてのセッションから、抵抗なく(舞踏にのめり込みました)。ある種の本能的な感覚から、欧州で活動するほぼ全ての舞踏家との出会いを求め始めました。彼らは私が放浪者として生きる願望を実現させてくれました。私は詩人として旅をしながら、舞踏という、たくさんの表現ツールが入った箱を携えて創作を行なっています。少しづつ、私は本当の自分自身に近づいているような気がしています。

Q2 舞踏の魅力
舞踏のお陰で、自分自身と、自分を取り巻く現実的なこと、非現実的なことに対する深い疑問を持つことができます。また、現象学的かつ理論的な側面の背後に、つかのまの集まりの中で自分自身のポテンシャルを共有し、発見し続けることの喜びを感じます。舞踏は、これまでにない新しい社会政治学です。

Q3 アーカイヴについて
当初、映像記録を行なっていた頃は、その質の低さを心配していましたが、その後、不十分なものだと受け入れるようになりました。一般的に、運動感覚上の経験はとても不快で、時にはめまいがするようなことなので、人は舞踏の捉えどころのなさに対して感謝さえすることができるのです。遁走する魂に幸あれ。

https://bodytellinglab.wixsite.com/bodytellinglab

Lucie Grégoire

Choreographer, Dancer, Teacher | Montreal (Canada) | 40 years

振付家・ダンサー・教師 | モントリオール(カナダ) | 40年

Q1 Reason for Starting Butoh
In 1985, I did a workshop in Japan with Min Tanaka, Tatsumi Hijikata and Kazuo Ohno. In 2003, I met Yoshito Ohno in his studio in Yokohama and we co-created three one-hour dance pieces during a ten years collaboration: *Eye* (2004), *Flower* (2008) and *In Between* (2011).

Q2 Attraction to Butoh
The connection with the inner world and the metamorphoses of the body and mind.

Q3 On Archiving
It is very important to preserve Butoh. Yoshito Ohno himself is the only living archive in this world. When he will die, a large part of the butoh archive will disappear with him.

Q1 舞踏をはじめたきっかけ
1985年に日本で、田中泯、土方巽、そして大野一雄のワークショップに参加しました。2003年に、大野慶人に横浜の彼のスタジオで出会い、『Eye』(2004)、『Flower』(2008)、『In Between』(2011)というそれぞれ1時間ほどの作品3つを10年にわたる彼との共同創作のなかで創りました。

Q2 舞踏の魅力
内的世界との繋がりと、身体と精神のメタモルフォーゼ。

Q3 アーカイヴについて
舞踏を残すことはとても重要です。大野慶人は、彼自身が舞踏の生きるアーカイヴです。彼が亡くなってしまう時には、舞踏アーカイヴの大部分が彼と共にこの世界から失われてしまうでしょう。

Flower with Yoshito Ohno (Agora de la danse, Montreal Canada) 2008. Photo: Michael Slobodian

www.luciegregoiredanse.ca

Q1 あなたが舞踏をはじめたきっかけを教えて下さい。
Q2 あなたにとって舞踏の魅力は何ですか？
Q3 身体芸術である舞踏は、どのようにしたら残すことができるでしょうか？

Andrés Gutiérrez

Director, Choreographer, Actor | Bayku Company | 20 years

演出家・振付家・俳優 | Bayku Company | 20年

Taken in a dressing room before Function (Medellin, Colombia)

www.bayku.cl

Q1 Reason for Starting Butoh
In the late 90s Chile began to have a new stream of arts. I went to an audition for something I didn't know what it was and in the end it ended up being my way of life. A way of life that has led me to present butoh for Latin America.

Q2 Attraction to Butoh
Feel the constant movement from the inside transforming into dance, of how resistance training later becomes poetry. Feel the body bloom as if it were a flower. Walking hand in hand with who was already dead from a manifesto honoring him in dance.

Q3 On Archiving
Take this language to different places where this language was not shown. Make a brotherhood with all the groups and artistic exponents of butoh worldwide. It would be a good instance to open the doors in Japan so that we can present our art of him that we do with the Bayku company in Chile and Latin America.

Q1 舞踏をはじめたきっかけ
1990年代の後半に、チリでは新しいアートの流れが生まれました。自分でも何だかよく分からなかったオーディションに出向き、結局はそれが私の生きる道になりました。南米の人々に舞踏を広めるという生き方に辿り着いたのです。

Q2 舞踏の魅力
自分の内側に生じる絶え間ない動きが踊りに変化して、筋力トレーニングが詩となるのを感じ取ること。花のように、身体が開いていくのを感じること。既に死んでしまっている者と、手を取り合って一緒に歩み、踊りの中でその死者を讃えること。

Q3 アーカイヴについて
舞踏がまだ紹介されていない様々な場所に、この言語を持っていくこと。全世界の舞踏の実践者や舞踏グループを全て、兄弟のように互いに親しくさせること。例えば、チリと南米でBayku Companyが表現している舞踏の形を日本でも紹介出来るよう、日本の人々が門戸を開いてくれるのは良い例となることでしょう。

Sylwia Hanff

パフォーマー・演出家 | ポーランド | Limen Butoh Theatre（主宰）・Butohpolis Festival（芸術監督）| 24年

Performer, Director | Poland | Limen Butoh Theatre (Director), Butohpolis Festival (Artistic Director) | 24 years

8 Deserts, solo.
Photo: Arkadiusz Rączka

www.limenbutoh.net

Q1 Reason for Starting Butoh
Butoh has always been there... inside of me. I started my artistic journey as physical theatre performer and professional mime actress. When I saw butoh dancers about 24 years ago, it was like I found my tribe. Since then Butoh has been my spiritual practice and way of living.

Q2 Attraction to Butoh
Deep relation with Spirit, Earth, Self, The Other. The honesty in experiencing both darkness and light. Butoh is for me a dance of hidden and mysterious beauty of Life and the Universe. Butoh is in my opinion a special kind of sensitivity and tenderness for the world.

Q3 On Archiving
I agree, that the creation of butoh archives is important – photography and video recordings are the only way, but not ideal. Spirit-body presence of the performer and the audience of witnesses is the essence of Butoh. This is Life. Life cannot be preserved in archives.

Q1 舞踏をはじめたきっかけ
舞踏は常にそこにありました…私の中に。私は、フィジカルシアターのパフォーマーかつプロのマイム役者として、アーティストとしてのキャリアをスタートさせました。24年前に舞踏家を観た時に、私は自分の民族性を見つけたように感じました。それからは、舞踏は私の精神的な訓練方法、そして生き方となっています。

Q2 舞踏の魅力
精神、地球、自己そして他者との深い関係。闇と光の両方を経験できる誠実さ。舞踏は私にとって、隠されたダンス、そして生命と宇宙の神秘的な美しさです。舞踏は特殊な種類の感受性と、世界に対する寛容性だと私は思っています。

Q3 アーカイヴについて
舞踏アーカイヴを創造することが肝要で、写真や映像による記録が唯一の方法だということは同意しますが、それで申し分ないとは言えません。パフォーマーの精神ー身体の存在、そして舞踏の本質を目撃する観客。それこそが生命です。生命はアーカイヴに残すことはできません。

凡例 肩書き | 活動拠点 | 所属団体 | 活動年数
Reference Occupation | Base | Affiliation | Years of Activity

原田伸雄 | Harada Nobuo

舞踏家｜小郡(日本)｜舞踏青龍會(主宰)・河合文化教育研究所(研究員)｜40年

Butoh Dancer | Ogori (Japan) | Butoh Seiryu-kai (Artistic Director), Kawai Institute for Culture and Education (Researcher) | 40 years

HARADA Nobuo「エーテルの赤い河」
Photo: Kaz Tsurudome

Q1 舞踏をはじめたきっかけ
1972年の市川雅企画「異貌の神々」シリーズ(於・青年座)中の笠井叡の「丘の麓」(客演・大野一雄)を観て舞踏の持つ劇薬のような混沌に触れ、演劇から舞踏に転身。

Q2 舞踏の魅力
舞踏は自己表現に非ず。呼吸の制御と意識の集中及び自己放擲による宇宙大の身体迷宮の旅。千変万化する身体変容の秘儀への参入こそが舞踏の醍醐味である。

Q3 アーカイヴについて
アーカイヴの広がりが、舞踏が伝統芸能化し現在への侵犯力を失ったことの証左では無いことを願う。アーカイヴの取り組みに敬意を表しつつも、私は刻々と生起し且つ消えていく舞踏の現在に黙々と身を挺するに如かず。

Q1 Reason for Starting Butoh
In 1972 I saw Akira Kasai's *Oka no Fumoto* (guest: Kazuo Ohno) as part of the *Ibou no Kamigami* series (venue: Seinen-za), and having met with Butoh's drug-like chaos, switched from theatre to Butoh.

Q2 Attraction to Butoh
Butoh is not self-expression. It is breath control and focused awareness, a letting go of the self to journey through the universe of an inner maze. The real pleasure of Butoh is entering the secrets of the ever transforming body.

Q3 On Archiving
I hope that the spread of archives is not proof that Butoh has become a traditional performing art and lost its ability to invade the present. While I respect the efforts of archiving, I devote myself to the rise and fall of Butoh's life as the present ever fades away.

G-H

Caroline Haydon

Multimedia Artist, Producer | Los Angeles (USA) | Allen Gardner Dance Theater, Safety Third Productions | 7 years

マルチメディアアーティスト・プロデューサー｜ロサンゼルス(アメリカ合衆国)｜Allen Gardner Dance Theater・Safety Third Productions｜7年

Photo: Sean Deckert.

www.carolinemhaydon.com

Q1 Reason for Starting Butoh
My introduction to Butoh came during movement and performance art studies in Salt Lake City where I was fortunate enough to train and study with Jerry Allen Gardner, a Butoh dancer and teacher who for many years trained with and danced for Yoshito Ohno and his company.

Q2 Attraction to Butoh
Butoh's innate power to shift both dancer and witness from the conscious to the subconscious initially drew me in. The multidisciplinary and multicultural nature of Butoh means the form itself is living, breathing, and changing. As a dancer in this form I find its deep sense of presence forever inspiring.

Q3 On Archiving
This question is deeply important to my current exploration of Butoh on film and in relation to various forms of documentation or capture. I think the energetic draw of Butoh allows it to remain incredibly impactful, and a practice that will always captivate. Finding ways for its entrancing presence to be archived is a goal moving through the contemporary plane.

Q1 舞踏をはじめたきっかけ
私と舞踏との出会いは、ソルトレイクシティーでムーヴメントとパフォーマンスアートを学んでいた時に、幸運にも大野慶人の下で長年稽古を続け、彼と共に踊っていた舞踏家のJerry Allen Gardnerに師事することができたことです。

Q2 舞踏の魅力
ダンサーと観客両方の意識を、無意識へとシフトさせることができる舞踏の固有の力に、私は最初に惹き込まれました。舞踏の様々な学問領域や文化を横断する性質は、その形式そのものが生きていて、呼吸をしながら、変化し続けることを意味しています。この芸術を実践するダンサーとして、舞踏が永遠にインスピレーションを与え続ける、深遠な存在であることを確信しています。

Q3 アーカイヴについて
この質問は、映画や様々な記録媒体における舞踏を研究する現在の私にとっても、とても重要なものです。舞踏が持つエネルギーの流れ、そして人々を常に魅了してやまないその稽古の方法は、信じられない程のインパクトを持つものとしてあり続けると思います。舞踏の魅惑的な存在感をアーカイヴする方法を見つけることは、今の時代に向けられた目標です。

Q1 あなたが舞踏をはじめたきっかけを教えて下さい。
Q2 あなたにとって舞踏の魅力は何ですか？
Q3 身体芸術である舞踏は、どのようにしたら残すことができるでしょうか？

Claudia Hofmann

Media Designer | Munich (Germany) | 10 years

メディアデザイナー｜ミュンヘン（ドイツ）｜10年

while the volcano is dreaming

www.tanz-ausdruck.com

Q1 Reason for Starting Butoh
The first Butoh I saw was in the German movie *Hanami* by Doris Doerrie where Tadashi Endo and Aya Irizuki danced. I was immediately touched by the special nature of the body expression. No matter what age, the expressive possibilities are very diverse and creative.

Q2 Attraction to Butoh
Light and shadow as an expression of clarity and darkness in life is one of my Butoh principles. There seems to be a universal understanding of body expression and feelings. Through dance, the individual can connect with the collective and exchange experiences. Butoh is a medium for a profound experience of being.

Q3 On Archiving
Butoh as a performative art lives off the movement with sound and music. Videos can be shared in online archives.
Alternative: Butoh remains in performances or on symposiums a transient form of expression that is stored by the viewer only in the moment of his perception and persists in the minds of the people.

Q1 舞踏をはじめたきっかけ
私は初めて観た舞踏は、Tadashi Endoと入月絢が踊ったドーリス・デリエ監督のドイツ映画『Hanami』です。その身体表現の特別な質感に、たちまち心を奪われました。何歳であれ、表現の可能性はとても多様であり、創造的であると思います。

Q2 舞踏の魅力
人生における明晰さと不明瞭さを、光と影として表現することが私にとっての舞踏の原則の一つです。身体の表現と感覚は、普遍的な理解の仕方があるように思います。ダンスを通じて個人は集団と繋がり、経験を交換することができます。舞踏は、「在る」ことを深く経験するための手段だと思います。

Q3 アーカイヴについて
パフォーマンスアートとしての舞踏は、音や音楽を伴う動きに支えられています。映像は、オンラインのアーカイヴで共有することができます。加えて、舞踏はパフォーマンスやシンポジウムの中では、観客の瞬間的な知覚の中に保存され、その心にずっと残り続ける儚い表現として存在しています。

Brigitta Horváth / SELFLESS DANCE

Dancer, Performer | France | 20 years

ダンサー・パフォーマー｜フランス｜20年

C'est l'endroit.
Photo: Marco Rotellini

www.brigittahorvath.com

Q1 Reason for Starting Butoh
Butoh was around me since I started dance and theater: the directors, choreographers I worked with used butoh elements in the training and during the creation. My clear meeting with butoh was in 2012 at Ko Murobushi's workshop in Budapest. In the same year I started to follow Masaki Iwana.

Q2 Attraction to Butoh
The possibility of being moved by, transformed into anything. Being danced by something larger than us, humans but still expressed through a human body. The potential of letting the body be danced by extracting the self out of it ("selfless dance"). The sense of a full existence.

Q3 On Archiving
I find it hard to visually record a Butoh performance in its wholeness. Still, to make photos, videos is an important work that has to be done. But watching them one should be aware that it isn't the wholeness of the dance since a Butoh performance isn't only a visual form but a physical experience (also for the audience).

Q1 舞踏をはじめたきっかけ
私がダンスや舞台を始めた頃、舞踏はいつも私の周りにありました。私が一緒に働いていた演出家や振付家が、トレーニングや創作の中で舞踏の要素を取り込んでいたからです。明確に舞踏に出会ったと言えるのは、2012年にブダペストで室伏鴻のワークショップを受けた時です。同じ年に、岩名雅記に師事し始めました。

Q2 舞踏の魅力
何かに動かされること、あらゆるものに変貌できる可能性。私たちよりも大きい何者かに踊らされること、身体を通してのみ表現される人間の姿。自我を取り去ることによって、身体を踊らせること（「無心のダンス」）。自己の存在をフルに感じ取ること。

Q3 アーカイヴについて
舞踏のパフォーマンスを、そのまま一つの全体として視覚的に記録することは難しいと思います。しかし、写真や映像を残すことは必須であり、大切な仕事です。とは言え、写真や映像を観る時に、それが舞踏の全貌ではないことを認識しなければいけません。舞踏のパフォーマンスは視覚的な形式だけではなく、（観客にとっても）身体的な経験でもあるからです。

凡例　肩書き｜活動拠点｜所属団体｜活動年数
Reference　Occupation | Base | Affiliation | Years of Activity

胡高阳 | Hu Gao Yang

Media Worker, Voice Actor, Butoh Dancer | Beijing and other cities (China), Fukuoka (Japan) | Blue Lotus Butoh, Butoh Seiryu-kai | 5 years

メディア関係者・ヴォイスアクター・舞踏家 | 北京とその他都市（中国）・福岡（日本） | Blue Lotus Butoh・舞踏青龍會 | 5年

Close-up and soloist (798 art zone, Beijing) September 2017.
Photo: Zhao Zhenhua

Facebook: @胡高阳
Instagram: @yolowo
weibo: 微博@高阳高阳
Wechat: 微信公众号：青莲舞踏

Q1 Reason for Starting Butoh
I saw the video of Mr. Kazuo Ohno earlier, I feel it's a very special dance. In 2014, I began to learn Butoh with Mr. Katsura Kan, a Butoh teacher in Kyoto, and Mr. Harada Nobuo, in Fukuoka. And back and forth in China and Japan for study and performance.

Q2 Attraction to Butoh
Butoh encourages everyone to explore themselves and explore the integration of more art forms. The Butoh dancer can be seen as an observer. During butoh dance, we may have the chance to check out the meaning of “spirit” and “movement” from huma's consciousness and unconsciousness.

Q3 On Archiving
As a dynamic body performance, besides photos and videos, text recording is very important. Record the dancer's thoughts and the audience's feelings. In the future, more Butoh organizations between cities and countries will be established to communicate with each other, perform and promote to the public, and encourage more people to experience Butoh with the help of more art institutions.

Q1 舞踏をはじめたきっかけ
以前に、大野一雄の映像を観て、とても特別なダンスだと感じました。2014年に、京都の舞踏家の桂勘と、福岡の原田伸雄のもとで舞踏を学び始めました。それからは、舞踏の稽古や公演のために中国と日本を行き来しています。

Q2 舞踏の魅力
舞踏は、全ての人に自分自身を探求し、より多くの芸術の形を統合するように促していると思います。舞踏家は、観察者と言っても良いのかもしれません。舞踏を踊る際には、「魂」や、人の意識や無意識から生じる「動き」の意味を確認するチャンスがあるかもしれないからです。

Q3 アーカイヴについて
動的な身体のパフォーマンスに際しては、写真や映像の他に、テキストの記録がとても重要です。ダンサーの考えと、観客の感情を記録しなければいけません。将来的には、より多くの舞踏団体が都市や国の中で立ち上がり、お互いにコミュニケーションを交わしながら、公演やプロモーションを行い、アート施設の支援を受けて、より沢山の人々が舞踏を体験する機会を提供することになるでしょう。

Claire Hurpeau

Dancer, Choreographer | Strasbourg (France) | 8 years

ダンサー・振付家 | ストラスブール（フランス） | 8年

Polymorphosis, solo.
Photo: Gérard Payelle

www.clairehurpeau.com

Q1 Reason for Starting Butoh
I discovered butoh in 2006 with a solo choreographed by Carlotta Ikeda. I do not remember the title, but I remember the great intensity of the dance which highly impressed me and left me with an unforgettable feeling. As soon as I got the opportunity, I took a butoh workshop.

Q2 Attraction to Butoh
This research of intensity of dance. A wish to find a greater density of the physical body. The attempt to move with the consciousness of the whole body at a time. An interest in the subject of transformation, the possibility to transform into anything to go beyond the human condition.

Q3 On Archiving
Working on butoh archives is a great way to keep track of the base and heart of butoh and its evolution. But since butoh speaks about the impermanence of all living forms, could we let it evolve and recycle ? I fear that wanting too much to preserve this form of art ossifies and reduces it, and thus, paradoxically, damages it.

Q1 舞踏をはじめたきっかけ
2006年にカルロッタ池田のソロ作品を観て、舞踏に出会いました。作品タイトルは覚えていませんが、その踊りの凄まじい強度に私はとてつもなく圧倒され、忘れがたい感覚が残りました。それから機会を得るとすぐに、舞踏のワークショップを受けました。

Q2 舞踏の魅力
ダンスの強度を求める探求。より密度の高い身体を見つけようとする願望。身体全ての意識を使って踊ろうとする試み。何かに変貌することへの関心、そして人間条件を超越するためにあらゆるものに変容できる可能性。

Q3 アーカイヴについて
舞踏のアーカイヴに取り組むことは、舞踏の根幹へと辿り、その進化を見据える為のとても優れた方法です。しかし、あらゆる生物の非永続性を主張している舞踏を進化させ、再循環させることは可能なのでしょうか?舞踏という芸術を後世に残すことを望み過ぎてしまうと、それを硬直化させ、変形させてしまい、そして逆説的に、破壊してしまうことになるのではないかと危惧しています。

Q1 あなたが舞踏をはじめたきっかけを教えて下さい。
Q2 あなたにとって舞踏の魅力は何ですか？
Q3 身体芸術である舞踏は、どのようにしたら残すことができるでしょうか？

Julie Veronirina Iarisoa

Choreographer | Antananarivo (Madagascar) | 20 years

振付家 | アンタナナリボ（マダガスカル） | 20年

Dance improvisation in out-door space (Madagascar)

https://www.facebook.com/compagnieanjorombala/

Q1 Reason for Starting Butoh
Butoh has always inspired me in my choreographic research since I discovered a photo in 2007, since then I've done research with the help of books and videos on the internet, then I had the chance to discover buto in real when I was in Japan in 2015 at the *Kazuo Ohno Dance Festival* where I saw buto performances and also took a buto class.

Q2 Attraction to Butoh
I think that butoh helps on working on the deep down of ourselves, it helps me refocus on myself and orient towards the essence of the art that I practice which is the dance, butoh works the body and the soul at the same time.

Q3 On Archiving
In my opinion it is possible to preserve butoh by continuing the transmission of its story, to continue to share it through butoh sessions, workshops, butoh performances as well as by organizing events around butoh open to general public and especially by continuing to practice it.

Q1 舞踏をはじめたきっかけ
2007年にとある写真を見つけてから、舞踏は私の振付のリサーチにおいて、常に想像力を鼓舞し続けるものです。それ以降も書籍やインターネット上の映像の力を借りてリサーチを続けていましたが、現実に舞踏に出会う機会があったのは、2015年に大野一雄フェスティバルの公演を観て、そして舞踏のクラスを受けた時です。

Q2 舞踏の魅力
舞踏は自分自身の深い部分に向き合う時に役立ちます。自分自身に焦点を定め直し、私が修練しているダンスという芸術の本質に向きあう手助けをしてくれます。舞踏は身体と魂に、同時に働きかけてくれます。

Q3 アーカイヴについて
私が思うに、舞踏のセッションやワークショップ、公演を通じてその物語を伝え、共有し続けるだけなく、一般向けの舞踏イベントをオーガナイズし、そして特に、舞踏を実践し続けることで、舞踏を後世に残すことが可能だと思います。

Paul Ibey

Choreographer, Teacher, Performer | Montreal (Canada) | 50 years

振付家・教師・パフォーマー | モントリオール（カナダ） | 50年

la volupte d'etre, solo

Q1 Reason for Starting Butoh
I became involved in butoh in the late 1970s after having worked with the physical theatre company of lindsay kemp. I left and wished to do my own work—many people directed me towards Sankai Juku and through them I met Ohno, Ikeda, Dairakudakan, Min Tanaka, Yukio Waguri, Motofuji, Tadashi Endo. I attended many classes with these masters and decided to forge my own path in butoh.

Q2 Attraction to Butoh
Butoh was another way for me to connect with the inner emotional self with the physical body as I had done through years of conventional theatre and dance.

Q3 On Archiving
I feel butoh is still a growing art—and constantly evolving. My objection to newer practitioners is that there is no connection to the heritage and the lineage—sometimes it can seem very much a surface form, without the depth and understanding of this work as they have not encountered the remaining masters of this work.

Q1 舞踏をはじめたきっかけ
1970年代後半に、リンゼイ・ケンプのフィジカルシアターのカンパニーに所属した後、舞踏に関わり始めました。カンパニーを去ったのは、自分自身で活動を行いたいと思ったからです。多くの人が山海塾を私に勧めてくれました。また、彼らを通して大野一雄やカルロッタ池田、大駱駝艦、田中泯、和栗由紀夫、元藤燁子、Tadashi Endoに出会いました。これらの師による、沢山のクラスに参加してから、舞踏の道をひた走ることを決心しました。

Q2 舞踏の魅力
舞踏は私にとって、情緒的自我と身体とを繋げるための方法です。従来の演劇やダンスの中で私がそれまで何年も行ってきたこととは異なる方法です。

Q3 アーカイヴについて
私は舞踏がまだ成長段階の芸術であり、常に進化するものだと感じています。新規の実践者に対して私が持つ違和感は、過去の遺産や歴史との繋がりが感じられないことです。時にそれは深みがなく、現存する舞踏の師の作品に触れたことが無いために舞踏を理解していないことから、とても表層的な形に見えてしまうことがあります。

凡例 肩書き | 活動拠点 | 所属団体 | 活動年数
Reference Occupation | Base | Affiliation | Years of Activity

市原昭仁 | Akihito Ichihara

舞踊家｜関東（日本）｜山海塾｜26年

Dancer | Kanto (Japan) | Sankai Juku | 26 years

度々一緒に踊っていた鳥と

https://www.facebook.com/official.akihito.ichihara/

Q1 舞踏をはじめたきっかけ
①幼少時にテレビで観た山海塾 ②高校時代からの演劇活動 ③十代後半以降の身体表現、ダンスへの傾倒 ④大駱駝艦、山海塾の諸作品観劇 ⑤海田勝氏の稽古に参加

Q2 舞踏の魅力
身体に還元されるという感覚。普遍性が抽出されるという感覚。イメージの伝達力。（私の幼少体験：見て「魚みたい」→数十年後に当事者：本当に魚の踊りだった。）

Q3 アーカイヴについて
映像は保存と伝達において優れていると思います。私も幼少時に見た映像の影響が大きいです。当事者としては、映像編集で自分のノート情報を映像に加えて、映像ノート化、テキスト化を試みたりしたことがあります。

Q1 Reason for Starting Butoh
(1) Seeing Sankai Juku on TV as a child. (2) Theatre studies in high school. (3) Interest in dance and performance in late teens and beyond. (4) Dairakudakan and Sankai Juku performances. (5) Joined Kaita Masaru's classes.

Q2 Attraction to Butoh
A sense of returning to the body. A feeling of universality being extracted. The power to transmit an image. (My childhood experience: "you look like a fish!" → Decades later: an actual fish dance.)

Q3 On Archiving
I think film is an excellent way to archive and share. The influence of the films I saw as a child were great. As a performer, I have edited videos with my own notes to try and create noted videos and texts.

Aleksandar Ilicic

Human Rights Defender | Alcantarilla (Spain) | 7 years

人権擁護者｜アルカンタリージャ（スペイン）｜7年

Dance in Alcantarilla.
Photo: Guillermo Ruiz

Q1 Reason for Starting Butoh
It was a happy coincidence. I came to know Butoh while I was researching various forms of twentieth century dance and theater for my social communication studies. I wrote a letter to Kazuo Ohno Dance Studio and then I had the chance to personally visit the place.

Q2 Attraction to Butoh
It would have to be the strong visual style of Butoh that borders on grotesque but at the same time is very sophisticated and beautiful; something very natural. For me, it was not shocking, alien or provocative; it opened my eyes to a different form of expression.

Q3 On Archiving
Yes, it can be preserved. This can be done by archiving and documenting various media that deals with Butoh. DAN (Dance Archive Network) is a good example of it! Butoh influence can be seen in choreography, theater stage directing and culture in general. It has definitely secured its place as an art-form and is here to stay for many years to come.

Q1 舞踏をはじめたきっかけ
それは幸運な出会いでした。社会コミュニケーションを学ぶ為に、様々な20世紀のダンスや演劇をリサーチしていた時に舞踏を知りました。大野一雄舞踏研究所に手紙を送り、個人的に訪れる機会を得ることができました。

Q2 舞踏の魅力
グロテスクなものに迫りながらも、同時にとても洗練され美しい舞踏の強烈なビジュアルに私は魅了されています。それはとても自然なものです。私にとっては、衝撃的なもの、あるいは異質で挑発的なものではありませんでした。これまでにない新しい表現に目を開かせてくれました。

Q3 アーカイヴについて
はい、舞踏は後世に残すことができると思います。舞踏を扱う様々なメディアを記録そしてアーカイヴすることで、可能になると思います。ダンスアーカイヴ構想（DAN）が良い例です！舞踏の影響力はダンスの振付から、演劇の演出、そして文化全般に至るまで及んでいます。舞踏は確実に一つの芸術形式としてそのポジションを確立してきたので、今後何年も残り続けていくと思います。

Q1 Please tell us how you became involved with Butoh?
Q2 What attracted you to Butoh?
Q3 As a performative art inherently involving the physical body, how can Butoh be preserved? Or, is this even possible?

精神のリレー 2019

A Spiritual Relay 2019

伊藤キム
Kim Itoh

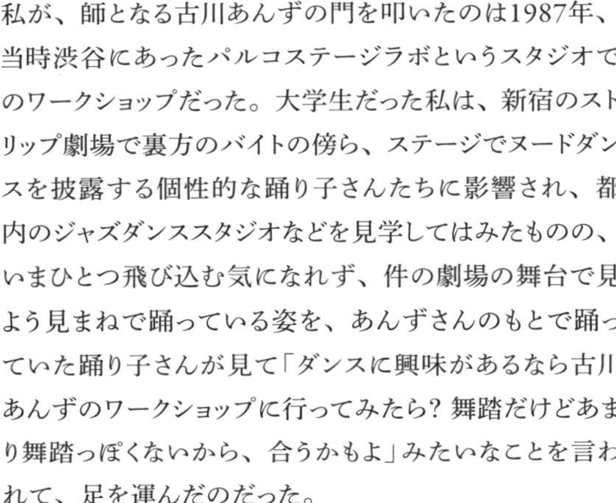

私が、師となる古川あんずの門を叩いたのは1987年、当時渋谷にあったパルコステージラボというスタジオでのワークショップだった。大学生だった私は、新宿のストリップ劇場で裏方のバイトの傍ら、ステージでヌードダンスを披露する個性的な踊り子さんたちに影響され、都内のジャズダンススタジオなどを見学してはみたものの、いまひとつ飛び込む気になれず、件の劇場の舞台で見よう見まねで踊っている姿を、あんずさんのもとで踊っていた踊り子さんが見て「ダンスに興味があるなら古川あんずのワークショップに行ってみたら? 舞踏だけどあまり舞踏っぽくないから、合うかもよ」みたいなことを言われて、足を運んだのだった。
ここでは稽古場での古川あんずの印象的な言葉を挙げてみよう。際立ったのはその明快さだった。

「両足を大きく左右に開いて立ち、重心をどちらかに移動させる。すると重心が乗っていないほうの足はフリーになって動かしやすくなる」
言われてみれば当たり前のことでも、素人の私にとっては目からウロコだった。舞踏の稽古は哲学的で難解という印象があったが、それをスッパリ裏切ってくれるようなわかりやすさだ。
「苦しんでやってたんじゃダメだよ。ダンスは楽しく!」
眉間にシワをよせて四苦八苦していても面白くない。必死で踊るのではなく楽しまなきゃ。これも求道者のような舞踏家のイメージとは違い、非常に新鮮だった。
「自分で動くのではなく、外部の力によって動かされろ」
意図・意志といったものをとにかく排除して、外部からの刺激で突き動かされることを叩き込まれた。自分で動くのは嘘だが、外からの刺激で身体が反応する(例えば熱湯に触れてビックリする)のは本物だ、という考え方。

I first asked to study under my future teacher Furukawa Anzu back in 1987 during a workshop in a studio called Parco Stage Lab in Shibuya. Back then I was a college student and was influenced by the unique dancing style of the strip dancers at a strip theater in Shinjuku where I was working part-time as a stagehand. I'd been looking around various jazz dance studios in Tokyo, but I couldn't bring myself to settle on one. I had, however, learnt a lot from observing the dancers at the Shinjuku strip theatre on stage. When one of them, who used to dance with Anzu saw me dance, she suggested: "If you're interested in dance, why don't you go to a workshop by Anzu Furukawa? It's Butoh, but not too hard core and it might even suit you." So I ended up going to her workshop. I was struck by one unforgettable thing that Anzu said in the rehearsal room. Its clarity is what stood out.

"Stand with both your legs wide open and shift your center of gravity from one side to the other. In doing so, the leg upon which you are not balancing becomes free and is easier to move."
Though what she said was mere common sense, for me, as an amateur, it really was an eye-opener. Up until that point, I somehow had the impression that practicing Butoh was both conceptual and difficult, but the way she put it made it so easy to understand.
"You shouldn't do it as though you're suffering. Dance should be fun!"
There's no fun in watching a dancer struggling, with wrinkles between their eyebrows. Rather than dance as though you were in distress, you have to enjoy it. Unlike the conventional image of a Butoh performer as a seeker of truth, Anzu's words were very refreshing.
"You shouldn't move on your own; you've got to move using external forces." What she was driving at was for me to shut-out my own intentions and desires, and let myself be driven by external stimuli. The notion that one can move spontaneously is misleading, for the body reacts to external

伊藤キム

フィジカルシアターカンパニーGERO主宰。舞踏家・古川あんずに師事。1995年「伊藤キム+輝く未来」を結成。96年フランス・バニョレ国際振付賞、02年第一回朝日舞台芸術賞・寺山修司賞、08年横浜文化賞奨励賞。05年にバックパックを背負って半年間の世界一周の旅に出る。15年、新カンパニーGEROを結成。京都造形芸術大学客員教授。かなっくホール(横浜市神奈川区)レジデンスアーティスト。

Kim Itoh

President of the Physical Theatre Company GERO. Butoh artist, student of Anzu Furukawa. Formed "Ito Kim + The Shining Future" in 1995. Winner of the International Choreographic Award in Bagnolet, France, winner of the 2002 Asahi Performing Arts Award, the Terayama Shuji Award, and the 2008 Yokohama Culture Award. In 2005 he travelled around the world as a backpacker, before forming the new GERO in 2015. Now a visiting professor at Kyoto University of Art and Design, and a resident artist at Kanakku Hall in Kanagawa.

これもしっかりと腑に落ちる言葉だった。

といった具合に、舞踏から距離をおいて遠くから客観視するようなあんずさんの考え方は、何事も冷静に見ようとする私にぴったりハマるものだった。一方で、ファンタジックで悪魔的な舞踏独特の比喩に満ちた表現や、明確な答えのない茫漠とした身体イメージを顔面めがけて投げつけるように提示されることも多く、そういうときは何もできず途方に暮れるしかないのだった。また彼女の人となりも特異で、1952年生まれで幼い頃からバレエを習い、高校時代は学生運動に参加、音大の作曲科を卒業し、大駱駝艦で舞踏を始め、子供を身ごもった大きなお腹で舞台に立つという、並外れた行動力と振れ幅の大きな生き方に私は常に圧倒されていた。
こうして彼女のもとで3年間過ごし、独立して「伊藤キム+輝く未来」を結成したのだが、それまでまったく繋がりのなかった土方巽の「私は毎晩、自分の肉体に梯子をかけて降りている」という言葉に触れたときは、まさに目から鱗が落ちるような思いだった。古川あんずに触れることで土方巽にキチンとつながっていると感じた。私が彼女から何を受け継いだかは自分では判断できないが、土方から連なる連綿とした舞踏の流れの中に伊藤キムは組み込まれているのだ、と実感した瞬間だった。

stimuli, as for example when we're jolted when we come in contact with boiling water. This, too, was persuasive advice.

As outlined above, Anzu's approach of looking objectively at Butoh from a distance really suited someone like me who wanted to take in everything calmly. I'm truly at a loss whenever she presented herself, as is often the case, as though Butoh embodied a unique fantastic and demonical metaphorical expression; it was like she was hurling a boundless physical image into one's face, without a clear answer. Another remarkable thing about Anzu was that though she was born in 1952, she studied ballet from an early age and yet joined the student movement during her high school days. She graduated from the music college's composition department and began dancing with Dairakudakan, and even reportedly appeared on stage when she was in an advanced stage of pregnancy. I was constantly astounded by her exceptional approach and her larger-than-life lifestyle.
After spending three years studying with her, I set out on my own and formed "Itoh Kim + the Shining Future." Until that point I had absolutely no link to Tatsumi Hijikata. Still, on hearing his phrase "Every evening I descend a ladder into my body," I felt as though I had been awakened to the truth. Through my contact with Anzu Furukawa, I felt as though I myself was truly connected to Tatsumi Hijikata. I can't evaluate what I have inherited from her, but it was at that juncture that I realized that Itoh Kim is firmly embedded in Hijikata's Butoh lineage.

古川あんず | Anzu Furukawa (1951-2001)

桐朋学園大学在学中、大駱駝艦に参加。1979年、大駱駝艦で出会った田村哲郎とともにダンス・ラヴ・マシーンを結成。1986年のベルリン公演をきっかけに、拠点をドイツに移す。ドイツやフィンランドの大学で教鞭を執り、古川率いるDance Butter Tokioには、多国籍のダンサーが参加するなど、数多くの後進を育てた。

Joined Dairakudakan while studying at Toho Gakuen College. There she met Tetsurō Tamura, with whom she formed Dance-Love-Machine in 1979. Moved to Germany after doing a performance in 1986. She Taught at universities in Germany and Finland, and led a multinational dance group Dance Butter Tokio, nurturing many next generation dancers.

Q1 あなたが舞踏をはじめたきっかけを教えて下さい。
Q2 あなたにとって舞踏の魅力は何ですか？
Q3 身体芸術である舞踏は、どのようにしたら残すことができるでしょうか？

今 貂子 | Ima Tenko

舞踏家・振付家｜京都（日本）｜舞踏カンパニー倚羅座・今貂子舞踏研究所｜40年

Butoh Dancer, Choreographer | Kyoto (Japan) | Butoh Company Kiraza, Ima Tenko Butoh Studio | 40 years

Photo: Hiroshi Mimura

http://imakiraza.wixsite.com/kirabutoh

Q1 舞踏をはじめたきっかけ

東方夜総会（のちの白虎社）の舞踏体験合宿に参加し、舞踏の美しさと奥深い魅力に魅せられたこと。総合芸術である舞踏に、無限の可能性を感じたため。

Q2 舞踏の魅力

存在の始原の大いなる混沌の闇とそこから導き出された光の双方を感じ、生命に肉迫していけること。踊りを通して、多くのひとと言葉を超えた対話をすることができること。

Q3 アーカイヴについて

舞踏における先人の努力の蓄積による資産は、言葉やビジュアル化できるものは記録として残せたほうがよい。言葉やビジュアルにできない部分も多いので、ひとからひとへ、直接に伝えることも大事だと思う。

Q1 Reason for Starting Butoh

I participated in the Toho night camp (later Byakkosha) Butoh experience workshop, and was shown the beauty and depth of Butoh. I felt that there were infinite possibilities in Butoh.

Q2 Attraction to Butoh

Its ability to get closer to life, by feeling both the great chaotic darkness of the origin of existence and the light that comes out of it. Its ability to communicate with a wide group of people beyond words through dance.

Q3 On Archiving

The resources accumulated from the work of our Butoh predecessors should be kept in the form of words and visuals if possible. But there is also a lot that cannot be kept as words or visuals, and it is important to pass these on directly from person to person.

石井則仁 | Norihito Ishii

舞踏家・振付演出家｜地方・海外｜山海塾｜18年

Butoh Dancer, Choreographer | Regional, overseas | Sankai Juku | 18 years

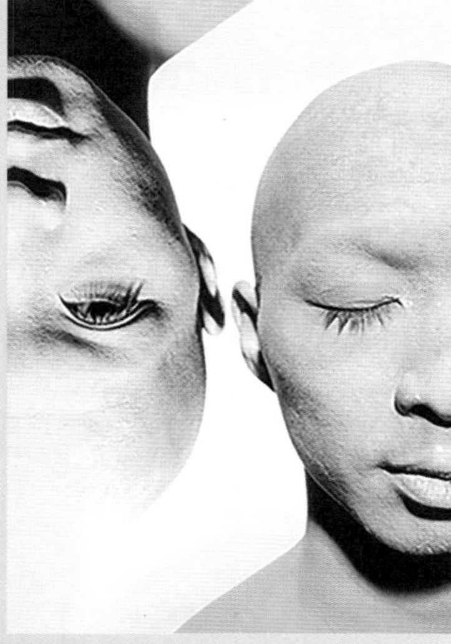

http://norihitoishii.com/index.html

Q1 舞踏をはじめたきっかけ

雑誌DDDに載っていた山海塾と大駱駝艦を見て、当時ヒップホップダンサーだった私は舞踏というものが理解できず、その後ワークショップなどに参加。西洋舞踊との違いに惹かれ学び、より飛び込むようになる。

Q2 舞踏の魅力

表現するということへの想像力・自由さ、そしてそこへの強度な集中力。

Q3 アーカイヴについて

型と振付の継承、ビデオ記録、型と振付の書記を今まで以上に残せれば伝統芸能のように残せると思います。

Q1 Reason for Starting Butoh

I saw Sankai Juku and Dairakudakan in DDD Magazine, but as a hip-hop dancer at the time I couldn't comprehend Butoh, and later participated in some workshops. Drawn by its differences to Western dance, I soon dove in.

Q2 Attraction to Butoh

The imagination and freedom of expression, and the strong focus to achieve it.

Q3 On Archiving

I think if we can preserve inherited movements and choreography, videos and documents more than we have until now, it can be preserved in a similar way to traditional performing arts.

凡例　肩書き｜活動拠点｜所属団体｜活動年数

Reference　Occupation | Base | Affiliation | Years of Activity

石本華江 Kae Ishimoto

舞踏家｜東京（日本）｜慶應義塾大学アート・センター土方巽アーカイヴ｜17年

Butoh Dancer | Tokyo (Japan) | Hijikata Tatsumi Archive - Keio University Art Center | 17 years

Q1 舞踏をはじめたきっかけ
在籍していた大学の教授より、和栗由紀夫が次回公演に向けてダンサーを探していると紹介があった。その後リハーサル時に舞踏譜という振付方法に大変興味を持ったから。

Q2 舞踏の魅力
それぞれ固有の身体に立ち戻ると同時に、身体そのものへの普遍的なアプローチができること。

Q3 アーカイヴについて
そもそも上演芸術を完全な形で残すことは不可能である。しかし公演記録や創作時のメモを残すことで、「その時その場所」に居なかった者にも「何か」を得る手がかりを与えることは可能であり、それがアーカイヴの務めであると考える。

Q1 Reason for Starting Butoh
There was an announcement at my university that Yukio Waguri was looking for a dancer for his next performance. I later became interested in the dance notation called Butoh-fu during rehearsals.

Q2 Attraction to Butoh
That one can simultaneously return to their own body, and take a universal approach to the body itself.

Q3 On Archiving
It is impossible to preserve performing arts in a perfect form. However, by recording performances and keeping creative notes, it is possible to give 'something' to those who were not there in that time and place, and I think this is the purpose of archives.

日英共同制作"Underground Archipelagos" 公演より
Photo: Aleksandr Sasha Drozd

https://ja-jp.facebook.com/kae.ishimoto

岩下 徹 Toru Iwashita

舞踊家（即興ダンス）｜京都（日本）｜山海塾｜36年

Butoh Dancer (improvised dance) | Kyoto (Japan) | Sankai Juku | 36 years

2019年5月11日（土）「徹と徹の部屋 vol.4」@東中野・ポレポレ坐
Photo: Hideto Maesawa

https://www.facebook.com/toru.iwashita.52

Q1 舞踏をはじめたきっかけ
25歳の秋、非道い抑鬱状態に陥っていた最中、生まれて初めて己が身体を丸ごと肯定的に認めることが出来た時、他の何ものにも頼らず、この身ひとつで踊ろう！と決意した。

Q2 舞踏の魅力
あらゆる様式から逃れ、〈個〉の身体感覚に立ち返り、その底知れぬ存在の深みより直接無媒介的に「表われてくるもの、押し出されてくるもの」（T.H）が、舞踏の魅力だろう。

Q3 アーカイヴについて
舞踏が交換不能の〈個〉の身体で踊られる限り、遅かれ早かれ必ず《死》がそれをこの世から消し去る。この点に於いては、舞踏は「一代限り」（T.H）。が、それは非連続の連続として他の身体のうちに胚胎し開花し得る。

Q1 Reason for Starting Butoh
Coming out of an incredibly depressed period when I was 25, I was able for the first time ever able to be entirely positive about myself, and determined to independently "dance with this one body!".

Q2 Attraction to Butoh
The most impressive thing about Butoh is the way it escapes all styles, and the self stands alone; it is "a thing that appears, a thing that exudes" (T.H.) directly from the depths of our incomprehensible existence.

Q3 On Archiving
As Butoh is a form danced by unique individuals, sooner or later Death erases these forms from this world. In this respect, Butoh is "one generation only" (T.H.). However, it can be sown and bloom in other bodies in a kind of non-continuous continuation.

Q1 Please tell us how you became involved with Butoh?
Q2 What attracted you to Butoh?
Q3 As a performative art inherently involving the physical body, how can Butoh be preserved? Or, is this even possible?

Q1 あなたが舞踏をはじめたきっかけを教えて下さい。
Q2 あなたにとって舞踏の魅力は何ですか？
Q3 身体芸術である舞踏は、どのようにしたら残すことができるでしょうか？

Françoise Jasmin

Choreographer | Paris (France) | 25 years

振付家 | パリ（フランス） | 25年

Q1 Reason for Starting Butoh
I became involved in Butoh when I realize the dance I was practicing was not what I really was inside of myself

Q2 Attraction to Butoh
Butoh is a true dance and spirit

Q3 On Archiving
The Butoh can be preserved if the practice is sincere and humble and has an objective to help humanity; to be memorized, something must be true and an interest for everybody. If not, no interest!

Q1 舞踏をはじめたきっかけ
舞踏を始めたのは、当時練習していたダンスが、私の内にある自分自身とは全く違っていたからです。

Q2 舞踏の魅力
舞踏は真のダンスであり、魂です。

Q3 アーカイヴについて
舞踏の稽古が誠実かつ謙虚であり、人間性に寄与するという目的があれば、舞踏は後世に残されていくと思います。人の記憶に残るためには、何かが真実であり、全ての人々にとっての利益とならなければいけません。そうでなければ、何の意味もありません！

be one with the nature (in Island)

www.humandance.com

Marlène Jöbstl

Artist, Teacher, Investigator | Barcelona (Spain) | 18 years

アーティスト・教師・研究者 | バルセロナ（スペイン） | 18年

My style is claiming for freedom of expression and I like to investigate a wide range of themes.
Photo: François Ollivier

https://marlenecomp.wixsite.com/jobstlmarlenebuto

Q1 Reason for Starting Butoh
I studied in a professional theatre school involving all artistic disciplines. I created my first monologue, people asked: is this theatre or dance? Shock! Artistic identity crisis. Somebody appeared: you know butoh? Sitting in the theatre, a strange body appears: I recognized myself. Butoh came to me as the answer!

Q2 Attraction to Butoh
Urgent need of freedom. No judgment of the different, of the unconventional, of the weak, of the wounded body. Every butoh dancer has his own style. Activism, provocation, no taboos, freedom. Always a deep meaning, we dance for somebody, something. Underground art, beauty, poetic, philosophy. Human values. Spirit. Expression.

Q3 On Archiving
Butoh can be « preserved » by spreading it, like nutritional seeds or necessary virus or healthy fire. It represents significant alternatives to the establishment. Butoh creates conscious bodies, aware minds, brave hearts to show, share themselves as they are. It is fundamental art. Butoh triggers the dancers as much as the audience.For me butoh is not cultural, it is human.

Q1 舞踏をはじめたきっかけ
全てのアートの手法を教える演劇のプロ養成学校で学びました。自分で最初のモノローグを作った時に、人々にこう聞かれました。「これは演劇なの、それともダンスなの？」ショックでした！アーティストとしてのアイデンティティーの危機でした。すると、ある人が現れて、「君は舞踏を知っている？」劇場で座っていると、知らない人が現れたのです。その時に、私自身を見つけました。舞踏が私に答えを持って来てくれたのです！

Q2 舞踏の魅力
自由への切迫した要求。異なるもの、慣例に従わないもの、弱いもの、傷ついたものに対して何も批判しないこと。舞踏家は皆、それぞれのスタイルを持っています。行動主義的で、挑発的、タブーが無くて、自由なのです。常に深い意味を携えて、誰かのため、あるいは何かのために踊ります。アンダーグラウンドアート、美しいもの、詩的なもの、哲学。人間的価値。精神。表現。

Q3 アーカイヴについて
栄養価の高い種子や人に必要なウィルス、または有益な火のように、舞踏はそれを広めることで「保存する」ことができるでしょう。制度に対する重要なオルタナティブを代表していると思います。舞踏は意識が張り巡らされた身体、覚醒した精神、勇気のある心を創造して、それらをありのままに他者に示し、分かち合います。舞踏は根源的な芸術です。舞踏は観客のみならず、ダンサーを奮い立たせます。私にとって、舞踏は文化的なことではく、人間そのものです。

josie j (divinebrick)

Interdisciplinary Butoh Artist | Los Angeles (USA) | Raze the Whitebox | 10 years

インターディシプリナリー舞踏家 | ロサンゼルス(アメリカ合衆国) | Raze the Whitebox | 10年

divinebrick in collaboration with Sobbing Honey (Borderlandnoise Festival, Playa de Tijuana, MX) August 2019

www.razethewhitebox.com

Q1 Reason for Starting Butoh
In 2010 Luke Joslin invited me to Tamano Sensei's class in Berkeley, Ca. Looking for a movement practice that complemented my performance art ethos, Butoh found me. Tamano Sensei's classes were very welcoming, I was never pressured to pay. Lessons continued beyond the dance studio, every action was Butoh.

Q2 Attraction to Butoh
Butoh has an inherent subversion, a purging of the colonized self. Hiroko Tamano once told me, the dancer's body is dangerous, it is awake and aware. Butoh is a reclaiming, a wild being comfortable in it's own space and skin, gracefully moving, governing itself, even at the edge of crisis.

Q3 On Archiving
Butoh is inherently elusive and will only die if contained in a rigid structure. The organic nature and elusiveness of Butoh is it's salvation. Without that it would of died in Japan. Growing and finding a home overseas was only due to its elasticity and adaptation to the dancers own personal ancestral body. Preserve the footprints not the definition.

Q1 舞踏をはじめたきっかけ
2010年にLuke Joslinから、カリフォルニア州バークレーの玉野(黄市)先生のクラスに誘われました。パフォーマンスアートの精神面を補完する動きの訓練を探していた私は、そこで舞踏に出会いました。玉野先生のクラスでは私はとても歓迎され、決して料金の支払いをせっつかれることがありませんでした。レッスンはダンススタジオの外でも続けられ、日常のあらゆる動きに関しても舞踏一色でした。

Q2 舞踏の魅力
舞踏は反制度的な力を内在しており、飼い慣らされた自己を清める作用があります。玉野弘子はかつて私に、ダンサーの身体は覚醒しているので危険だ、と教えてくれました。舞踏は、自らの空間や肌を心地よく思っていても、危機の際には優雅に動き、かつ自らを統治することもできる野生を呼び起こすものなのです。

Q3 アーカイヴについて
舞踏は本質的に掴み所がないものですので、固い構造に閉じ込められてしまうと死んでしまうでしょう。舞踏の有機的な性質と理解のしにくさは、救いでもあります。それがなければ、日本で死に絶えてしまいます。日本の外で舞踏が増え、行き所を見つけているのは、その順応性と、個々のダンサーが先祖から授かった身体性によるものです。定義では無く、その足跡を保存してくべきです。

鏡 ざゆら | Zayura Kagami

舞踏家・アーティスト | 東京(日本) | 3年

Butoh Dancer, Artist | Tokyo (Japan) | 3 years

舞踏。自分の内側、そしてすべての者に花を捧げる

http://zayura.tokyo/express/

Q1 舞踏をはじめたきっかけ
新しいダンスを探していたところ、ネット検索で暗黒舞踏というものがあるのを知り、挑戦してみたくなった。大野慶人先生の教室を見つけて、すぐに飛び込んだのがきっかけ。

Q2 舞踏の魅力
ダンスの動きや枠にとらわれず、自らとしての純粋な身体表現であるところ。自分そのものであるところ。

Q3 アーカイヴについて
動画をフルに活用し、些細なものでもすべて動画に残し、インターネットで惜しまず公開するのがいいと思う。慶人さんや他舞踏家が踊っているところ、インタビュー映像、教室の中の風景、舞台で使う小道具、練習に使う小物など。すべて動画で残す。

Q1 Reason for Starting Butoh
Whilst searching for a new dance, I came across Ankoku-Butoh in an internet search, and wanted to try it. When I found Yoshito Ohno's classes, I dove straight in.

Q2 Attraction to Butoh
Unrestricted by dance movements or choreography, it is a body expression that is true to oneself. A place where you can be yourself.

Q3 On Archiving
I think it would be good to utilize videos in full by including all the trivial details and sharing everything on the internet. Film everything. Yoshito and other Butoh artists dancing, interviews, the atmosphere of the classroom, props used onstage, items used during practice etc.

Q1 Please tell us how you became involved with Butoh?
Q2 What attracted you to Butoh?
Q3 As a performative art inherently involving the physical body, how can Butoh be preserved? Or, is this even possible?

Q1 あなたが舞踏をはじめたきっかけを教えて下さい。
Q2 あなたにとって舞踏の魅力は何ですか？
Q3 身体芸術である舞踏は、どのようにしたら残すことができるでしょうか？

Judith Kajiwara

Artistic Director | Oakland (USA) | OnenessButoh | 26 years

芸術監督 | オークランド（アメリカ合衆国） | OnenessButoh | 26年

Cellar, 2017

http://onenessbutoh.wix.com/onenessbutoh

Q1 Reason for Starting Butoh
I was searching for a dance that reflected my experiences both as a Japanese and American woman. In the late 70s I attended a performance by Koichi and Hiroko Tamano. Though it was scary, its uncanny effect deeply altered my consciousness, and I knew I had found my perfect dance.

Q2 Attraction to Butoh
Not only is it visually stunning, its ability to transform consciousness both for the audience and the practitioner is not typical of any other dance form. The physical and mental training are challenging, but the emotional and spiritual elements of being a provocative Butoh artist are even more exciting.

Q3 On Archiving
Honoring its origin is most important in preserving Butoh on the global platform. Its inception, following the bombing of Hiroshima-Nagasaki, is what makes Butoh historical, timeless and dark. My work strives to go past the dark, to recognize that, though still wounded, we are powerful beings who can heal our wounds thus bringing more love and unity into the world.

Q1 舞踏をはじめたきっかけ
私は日本人そしてアメリカ人の女性として、自分自身の経験を反映することのできるダンスを探し求めていました。1970年代後半に、玉野黄市と弘子の公演を観ました。それは恐ろしかったものの、その神秘的な効果は私の意識を深く変化させ、その時に自分にとって完璧なダンスを発見したと思いました。

Q2 舞踏の魅力
舞踏は視覚的に素晴らしいだけでなく、観客と演者の双方の意識を変化させる力があり、それは他のダンスでは見られない特徴です。舞踏のフィジカルとメンタルの訓練は難しいものですが、挑戦的な舞踏家になるための感情と精神を備えることは、それにもまして刺激的なことです。

Q3 アーカイヴについて
グローバルな規模で舞踏を残す上で最も重要なことは、その起源を敬うことだと思います。広島と長崎の原爆に続くその起源は、舞踏を歴史に残し、時代を超えて、暗黒のものとしました。私の作品は、暗黒時代を過去のものとし、私たちはいまだ傷を負いながらも、その傷を癒すことができ、より多くの愛と結束をこの世界にもたらすことができる力強い存在であると信じることに向けられています。

Josma Kalho

Psychiatrist | Paris (France) | Laboratoire de bioflexibilité | 46 years

精神科医 | パリ（フランス） | Laboratoire de bioflexibilité | 46年

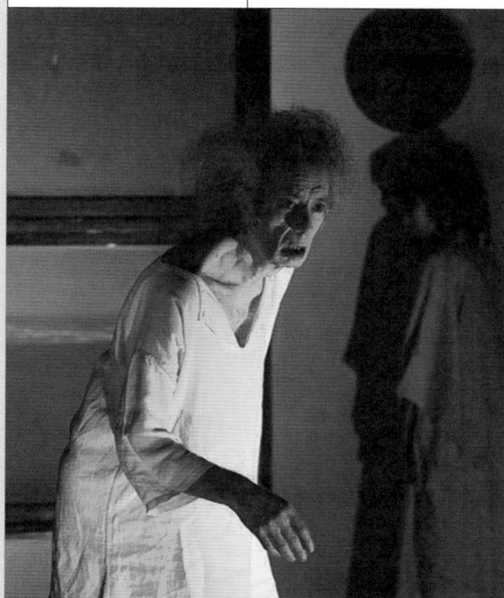

The woman in his dream, duo with Yuri Nagaoka (Tokyo) 2019
Photo: Krzysztof Sienkiewicz

www.bioflexlab.fr
http://www.facebook.com/Bioflexlab

Q1 Reason for Starting Butoh
I started doing Gaga, the body language created by Ohad Naharin and trying to understand the kind of exercises he proposed, I got to butoh. It all started with an article comparing the two practices and I was intrigued by the non-intentionality of Butoh-specific movements. My first experience was with Yumiko Yoshioka.

Q2 Attraction to Butoh
The difference between modern dance and Butoh after Akira Kasai is that the first is interested in movement, while the Butoh is interested in the consciousness who produces the movement. This attract to me because implies questioning the states of consciousness and especially the influence Artaud may have had in Hijikata.

Q3 On Archiving
To preserve the essence of butoh, it is necessary to pursue research on states of consciousness capable of inducing different states of the body. After the language (butoh fu) what role can digital technologies play?

Q1 舞踏をはじめたきっかけ
私はオハッド・ナハリンが生み出した身体メソッド「ガガ」を始め、彼が提案したエクササイズを理解しようとしていた時に、舞踏に辿り着きました。2つの訓練方法を比較する記事を読んだ時、舞踏特有の動きに意図性が無いことに興味をそそられました。私が初めて舞踏を体験したのは吉岡由美子を通じてです。

Q2 舞踏の魅力
モダンダンスと笠井叡以降の舞踏の違いは、前者が動きに関心を置いているのに対して、舞踏は動きを生み出す意識に関心があるということです。私はこのことに興味を持ちました。なぜならそれは意識の状態を疑うこと、そして特にアルトーが土方に与えたかもしれない影響を示唆していると思うからです。

Q3 アーカイヴについて
舞踏の本質を後世に残すためには、異なる身体の状態を生み出す複数の意識の状態について研究を進めることが必要です。言語での保存（舞踏譜）の次は、デジタルテクノロジーがどのような役割を担うことができるでしょうか？

紙田 昇 | KAMITA NOBORU

振付家・舞踏手・ダンサー | 東京（日本） | 27年

Choreographer, Butoh Dancer, Dancer | Tokyo (Japan) | 27 years

http://kamita.net/kdance/

Q1 舞踏をはじめたきっかけ
兄の勧めで銀座で舞踏家の芦川羊子さんの踊りを見てインパクトを受けた。その後、演劇の知人に誘われ、古川杏さんのレッスンに通うようになりました。

Q2 舞踏の魅力
踊りとして表現方法の自由度が非常に高いこと。肉体の形だけでなく内面と外界への意識が必要とされること。美と醜悪が入れ替わること。

Q3 アーカイヴについて
映像、写真、音声、テキストなどあらゆる方法で残すしかないかと。また様々な方のワークショップの映像記録は重要かと思います。踊っている人がどういう仕組みと状態で踊っているかに触れることができます。

Q1 Reason for Starting Butoh
A performance by Yoko Ashikawa that I saw in Ginza on my brother's recommendation had a strong impact on me. After that, I was invited by a theatre acquaintance to attend Anzu Furukawa's lessons.

Q2 Attraction to Butoh
There is a vast freedom of expression in its movement. The importance not only of the shape of the body but of what is inside, and an awareness of what is outside. That the beautiful and ugly are inverted.

Q3 On Archiving
I don't think there's a way to document it other than through video, photography, audio and text, etc. I also think it could be important to film the workshops of various people. This way we can see the structure and conditions people create for their dance.

カナキティ | Kana Kitty

舞踏家・女優 | 東京（日本）・ヨーロッパ | 10年

Butoh Dancer, Actress | Tokyo (Japan), Europe | 10 years

舞踏ペインティング
©bozzo

https://www.kanakitty.com/

Q1 舞踏をはじめたきっかけ
短大在学中、裸婦デッサンの授業でモデルをされていた方が舞踏家でした。彼女が動くとただの教室で森が見え、描く手を止めて見入りました。衝撃を受け、舞踏家を志しました。

Q2 舞踏の魅力
宇宙にアクセスできること、日本で生まれたものであること、哲学を孕んでいること。

Q3 アーカイヴについて
演劇も他のダンスもパフォーマンスアートも、生のものは本当の意味では残すことができませんが、それでも写真や映像や言葉でアーカイヴしようと足掻くことは、冒涜ではなく愛だと信じていたいです。

Q1 Reason for Starting Butoh
While in junior college, there was a life drawing model who was a Butoh dancer. When she moved I saw a forest in the classroom, and had to stop drawing and watch. Awed, I was inspired to become a Butoh dancer.

Q2 Attraction to Butoh
Its ability to access the universe, that it was born in Japan, that it is philosophical.

Q3 On Archiving
No performing art be it theatre, dance style or performance art can be really be preserved, but I believe that to try and archive them in the form of photography, film and text is not blasphemous but comes from a place of love.

Q1 Please tell us how you became involved with Butoh?
Q2 What attracted you to Butoh?
Q3 As a performative art inherently involving the physical body, how can Butoh be preserved? Or, is this even possible?

Q1 あなたが舞踏をはじめたきっかけを教えて下さい。
Q2 あなたにとって舞踏の魅力は何ですか？
Q3 身体芸術である舞踏は、どのようにしたら残すことができるでしょうか？

カセキユウコ | Yuko Kaseki

演出家・振付家・ダンサー・パフォーマー・教師 | ベルリン（ドイツ） | company cokaseki | 28年

Director, Choreographer, Dancer, Performer, Teacher | Berlin (Germany) | company cokaseki | 28 years

Q1 舞踏をはじめたきっかけ
踊る術を持たなかった時、故古川あんず氏のワークショップに行き衝撃を受ける。埋もれていた記憶や感情が体に湧き出る経験をし、その不思議を追求したいと思った。そのままドイツに移住し、踊り続けている。

Q2 舞踏の魅力
舞踏で開かれた身体表現の可能性は限りないと思う。舞踏が蒔いた種から個々の表現という木々が 根を張り、枝分かれして行く。未開発の自分の踊りを刻々と変わる時代と世界と共に生き、変化し、探し続けたい。

Q3 アーカイヴについて
過去を保存し、崇めるだけではなく現在、未来に向けて開かれたアーカイブというものはあるのだろうか？ 学問の見地から生きた進行形の現在形への舞踏とは何なのか。日本に、世界における、舞踏の現時点の立ち位置とは、社会との関係性はなんなのか。

Q1 Reason for Starting Butoh
When I was looking for the way of dance, I went to the workshop of Anzu Furukawa and I got great impact. I experienced the hidden memories and emotions that had flowed into my body. I wanted to pursue mysteries. Since then I continue to dance.

Q2 Attraction to Butoh
I think there is no limit to the possibility of physical expression opened in the butoh. Trees of individual expressions are growing branches and roots from the seeds of Butoh.I want to continue to be and look for transforming my undeveloped dances with the changing time and the world.

Q3 On Archiving
Is there an archive that not only preserves and worships the past but is open to the present and future? What is the Butoh from the academic point of view to the progressive form in present? What is the current position of Butoh as (living) art in Japan and foreign countries? And its relationship with society?

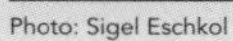

Photo: Sigel Eschkol

www.cokaseki.com

川本裕子 | Yuko Kawamoto

舞踏家 | 東京（日本） | 東雲舞踏 | 28年

Butoh Dancer | Tokyo (Japan) | Shinonome Butoh | 28 years

『豚＝0』
Photo: Hiroyasu Daido

https://shinonomebutoh.jp/

Q1 舞踏をはじめたきっかけ
17歳の時、深夜テレビで舞踏の特集を見て。舞踏家に憧れ高校生活を送った後、大学進学を機に上京。アスベスト館の門を叩く。最初に和栗由紀夫のWSを受けそのまま好善社のメンバーとして活動。

Q2 舞踏の魅力
それぞれの個性が違うことが魅力であるといえる多様性と、自分の中や、人と係る中から何かを見出すことができる可能性を秘めているところ。変でいいんだと胸を張って生きていけるところ。

Q3 アーカイヴについて
例えば、土方巽の映像は何度見ても鳥肌が立ちます。しかし大抵の場合、映像資料では難しいと考えます。身体表現ならではの空気感を残すことは難しいのかもしれません。ただ今後アーカイブの可能性が広がることはあるのではと楽しみにしています。

Q1 Reason for Starting Butoh
When I was 17, I saw a special feature on Butoh on late night TV. Enamored, after high school I moved to Tokyo for university, and beat on the doors of Asbestos-kan. I first took workshops with Yukio Waguri before going on to become a member of the company.

Q2 Attraction to Butoh
The diversity that comes from each individual being different, and the potential to discover something inside yourself, or in interactions with others. That I can be proud to live strangely.

Q3 On Archiving
I get goosebumps no matter how many times I see Tatsumi Hijikata's films. But in most cases I think it is difficult to preserve dance on film. It may be difficult to preserve the atmosphere of any performing art. That said, I look forward to the possibilities of archives being expanded in the future.

Sinéad Keogh

Performance Installation Artist | Dublin (Ireland) | 7 years

パフォーマンスインスタレーションアーティスト | ダブリン（アイルランド） | 7年

Q1 Reason for Starting Butoh
I was researching Butoh in art college, writing and reading about it. I wanted my own practice to be influenced by this form of art which I admired so greatly. I designed a Butoh inspired installation called *The Black Sea* to try bring my practice together with this research.

Q2 Attraction to Butoh
The brutal honesty of raw humanity is expressed more clearly in Butoh then in any form of live art. It is the ultimate representation of the pit of the soul. Darkness, lightness and revelation all at once. Kazuo Ohno was a primary source of inspiration for me.

Q3 On Archiving
In Ireland Ambra Gatto Bergamasco held Moving Bodies, a festival to celebrate Butoh, enlisting artists such as Minako Seki and Master Masaki Iwana. Nothing compares to live experiences which are not supported internationally like they should be. That being said I learned about Butoh from books and written sources and written archives are of a crucial importance for preservation.

Performance shot from *The Black Sea*, 2017.

www.sineadkeogh.net

Q1 舞踏をはじめたきっかけ
アートカレッジで舞踏を研究している頃に、舞踏について書いたり、本を読んだりしていました。自分のやっていることが、敬愛するこの芸術形式に影響を受けたいと思っていました。私自身の実践とこのリサーチとを結びつけるために、舞踏にインスパイアされたインスタレーション「The Black Sea」をデザインしました。

Q2 舞踏の魅力
生々しい人間性の残酷なまでの正直さが、舞踏では、他のあらゆるライブで表現される芸術形式よりも明確に表現されていると思います。舞踏は魂の底深さを表す、究極の表現です。暗闇と光、そして啓示が全て同時にあります。大野一雄は、私にとって第一のインスピレーションの源でした。

Q3 アーカイヴについて
アイルランドでは、Ambra Gatto Bergamascoが舞踏を称えるフェスティバル「Moving Bodies」を開催しており、関 美奈子や岩名雅記といった舞踏家を招いています。ライブ体験に勝るものはありませんが、思うような国際的な支持を得ていません。とは言うものの、私も書物や文字資料から舞踏を学んだので、テキストのアーカイヴは舞踏を残すためには決定的に重要だと思います。

K-K

木野彩子 Saiko KINO

踊子 | 鳥取・神奈川（日本） | 40年

Dancer | Tottori, Kanagawa (Japan) | 40 years

「死者の書　再読」(2018)
Photo: igaki photo studio

https://saikokino.jimdo.com

Q1 舞踏をはじめたきっかけ
私は自分が踊子で、舞踏家としては捉えていませんが、ピンクレディに憧れて一生懸命踊っていたそうです。言葉が出なくて、心配した両親が近くのモダンダンスのお稽古場に通わせ始めました。当時の記憶はありません。

Q2 舞踏の魅力
舞踏に限らず身体には言葉を超えて伝わっていく力があると思っています。また、いろんな人の想いを預かって私もまた踊り続けています。

Q3 アーカイヴについて
残りません。消えるからこそ美しく、その場に立ち会わねば見ることができません。しかしその残像は写真、映像、文字など伝説となりのこる。そこから私たちは想像し、新しい舞踏なりダンスを創造し続けるのだと思います。

Q1 Reason for Starting Butoh
I see myself as a dancer rather than Butoh dancer, I admired Pink Lady and apparently danced with great focus. I couldn't speak as a child, and my concerned parents started taking me to a modern dance class. I have no recollection of this time.

Q2 Attraction to Butoh
I believe the body has the power to express what words cannot, not only in Butoh. I continue to dance with the creative thoughts of all kinds of people.

Q3 On Archiving
It cannot be documented. It is beautiful precisely because it disappears, and you have to have been there to see it. However in the aftermath the photographs, videos and text become legends, and from these we can use our imagination to create new Butoh and dances.

Q1　Please tell us how you became involved with Butoh?
Q2　What attracted you to Butoh?
Q3　As a performative art inherently involving the physical body, how can Butoh be preserved? Or, is this even possible?

BUTOHBUTOHBUTOHBUTOHBUTO

精神のリレー 2019

A Spiritual Relay 2019

鈴木ユキオ
Yukio Suzuki

Photo: bozzo

私は、舞踏に出会えたことで、何も知らない自分の身体でも踊って良いのだと感じさせてもらえました。別の言い方をすると、ダンスしても良い。パフォーマンスしても良い。と思わせてくれたのです。
大人になって舞踏を始めた自分にとって、当初は、舞踏がダンスだという認識はありませんでした。芝居がありダンスがあり、舞踏があるというように分けて考えていたのです。続けていくうちにダンスの歴史を理解し、また自分自身も海外に行くとButoh dancerとして紹介されることで、これもダンスだと理解するようになりました。
アスベスト館に通い色々な講師の方に教わり、大駱駝艦出身の振付家のグループに参加する時期などを経た後、室伏鴻さんと出会い、10年彼の作品に関わることになりました。
ソリストである室伏鴻さんに師事できたことは、私にとってその後の作品作りに大きな影響を与えています。
ソリストであるということは、彼にしかできない、強固な身体から生み出されるものに価値があるわけで、もちろんそこに影響を受け、自分自身も身体を投げ出すような、いわゆるダンスの世界ではみられないような、強度のある身体の提示を試み、トヨタコレオグラフィーアワード2008では『沈黙とはかりあえるほどに』という作品でグランプリをいただきました。
彼の背中を見て、彼とともに過ごし、様々な話をしてきたことが今の自分の根底にあります。
室伏さんが常に言っていたことは、ダンスを疑え、ダンスがあると思うなよ、ということでした。ダンスが1から習うものだとするならば、舞踏は胎児から、歩行から捉え直し、ゼロからダンスを考えるもの。ダンスでないものをどうダンスにするか、ダンスをどう発見するか、ということを常に考えていた人だと思います。

My encounter with Butoh made me feel as though my body could dance, even though I knew nothing about it. In other words, it made me think that it was alright to dance, and that it was alright to perform in public.
As someone who started performing Butoh as an adult, I initially didn't consider Butoh as a dance form. Just as with theatrical pieces and dance works, I felt that Butoh was something apart. As my career progressed, however, I came to better understand how dance had evolved over time. Moreover, while performing overseas, I was introduced as a "Butoh dancer," leading me to realize that Butoh, too, was a dance form.
After having attended Asbestos-kan to receive instruction from various teachers and participating in a piece by a group of choreographers from Dairakudakan, I met Ko Murobushi. I ended up being involved with him on a creative level for ten years.
The fact I was able to study under a soloist such as Ko Murobushi had a huge impact on my subsequent career. There were things that he alone could achieve as a soloist. A powerful physique such as his could generate something truly effective. He naturally exerted a great influence on me, and for my part I strove to present a strong physique that was not to be seen in the so-called dance world, a body in which one utterly sacrifices everything. Ultimately, I was awarded the Grand Prix award at the 2008 Toyota Choreography Awards 2008, for a work called *Confronting Silence*. What now underpins my dance can be boiled down to having observed Muroboshi's back, and spending time together with him to discuss various things. He would constantly remark that when it came to dance he was skeptical and he would question its true nature. If dance had to be learnt from the first basic steps, the Butoh should seek its roots in the fetus, from the act of walking, and in taking a fresh look at dance. He was constantly thinking about how to turn things unrelated to dance into dance and how to explore dance.
I myself am constantly aware of this approach and still use

BUTOHBUTOHBUTOHBUTOHBUTO

鈴木ユキオ

振付家・ダンサー。世界40都市を超える地域で活動を展開し、しなやかで繊細に、空間からはみだすような強靭な身体・ダンスは、多くの観客を魅了している。モデル、音楽家との共同制作、子供や障害のある方へのワークショップなど、活動は多岐に渡る。2008年トヨタコレオグラフィーアワード「次代を担う振付家賞」等受賞多数。

Yukio Suzuki

Choreographer and dancer. He has performed in more than forty cities around the globe. At once flexible and delicate, his dance and powerful physique that seem to transcend space has charmed many audiences. His activities range from modeling, collaborations with musicians, and conducting workshops for children and people with disabilities. He has received many awards, notably the 2008 Next Generation Choreography Award.

自分自身もそこを常に意識しており、今も大事にしています。しかし同時に、動けなくなるまでダンスを疑った上で、そこからダンスしにいくというのも面白いのではないかと、ある時期から考えるようになりました。そこから始まるダンスは、1から習ういわゆるダンスとは絶対に違うところの「ダンス」だと確信しており、そんな思考するカラダが生み出すダンスを追求しています。表面的には舞踏では全くない、しかしいわゆるダンスでもない場所を自分の居場所として、創作活動をしていると感じています。

舞踏譜で理解できる範囲の群舞ではなく、舞踏譜を超えたところにあるソリストの舞踏に自分が惹かれてきたように、また、土方巽が唯一無二のダンサーであり、ダンスの方法論を考えたように、自分自身も唯一無二のダンサーであり、方法論を身につけていくことが重要なのではないかと考えています。結果として舞踏から離れていくようにも感じますが、本質を突き詰めていく限り、芯の部分では舞踏という精神を引きずっている—。それが自分自身の根底であり、舞踏を常に意識し、引き継いでいる部分でもあると自覚しています。同時にそこから離れ、「自分自身」がジャンルであり、探求の過程を見せ続けるという姿勢、生きていく様を晒していけたらと考えています。

it as a reference point. And yet, I started thinking from a certain stage that it would be interesting to question dance until one can no longer move, and to then take the dance from there. I'm convinced that such a dance would utterly differ from the so-called dance one learns from scratch. What I'm seeking is a dance created by such thinking bodies. In terms of expression, it's not in any way connected to Butoh, yet I still feel as though I'm creatively active somewhere that's not directly related to so-called dance.

I was attracted to a soloist's Butoh that had gone beyond notational Butoh-fu and not group dances that could be understood in terms of Butoh-fu. And just as Hijikata was a unique dancer and developed a methodology for his performances, I, too, am a one-of-a-kind dancer and I think it essential to equip myself with my own methodology. Consequently, it feels as though I'm moving away from Butoh, but as far as its essence is concerned, my dance's core elements are still imbued with the spirit of Butoh. These are my roots and I'm constantly conscious of Butoh and of the elements in my work that I've acquired from my encounter with it. And yet, I'm parting ways with Butoh and developing my own genre. I would like to continue pursuing an explorative process and approach to living.

室伏鴻 | Ko Murobushi (1947-2015)

1969年、土方巽に師事。72年、大駱駝艦の旗揚げに参画。78年、自らが主宰するアリアドーネの會と舞踏派背火を率いてパリ公演を実施。80年代からは主な拠点を欧州に移す。2000年より日本での活動を再開し、若手ダンサーによるユニット「Ko&Edge Co」を結成。公演活動と並行して世界各地でワークショップを行い、指導者としても高い評価を得た。

Studied with Tatsumi Hijikata in 1969. Formed part of Dairakudakan in 1972. Led his company Ariadone and Butoh-Ha SEBI in performances in Paris in 1978. Moved his base to Europe in the 80s. Returned in Japan in 2000 and formed the group "Ko & Edge Co." with junior dancers. Held workshops alongwith performances all over the world, and was highly regarded as a leader.

Q1 あなたが舞踏をはじめたきっかけを教えて下さい。
Q2 あなたにとって舞踏の魅力は何ですか?
Q3 身体芸術である舞踏は、どのようにしたら残すことができるでしょうか?

Adam Koan

Butoh Dance Instructor, Performer, X-ray/Cat Scan Technologist | International | Serbia Butoh Retreat | 6 years

舞踏インストラクター・パフォーマー・X線/CATスキャン技師 | 世界各地 | Serbia Butoh Retreat | 6年

Domesticated Hoopee 2.0 (Moving Bodies Festival, Torino, Italy) 2019.
Photo: Emanuele Pensavalle

http://www.shadowbody.com

Q1 Reason for Starting Butoh
I became involved with Butoh at Himalaya Subbody Butoh in Dharamsala, India in fall of 2013. It was a retreat-like space that made us hone into our studies fully. After this, I studied under several Butoh teachers, and also toured 4 times for performance and giving workshops.

Q2 Attraction to Butoh
The first thing that attracted me to Butoh was its uncanny aesthetic. When I discovered it, I was in modern dance school, and I felt that Butoh would widen the creativity factor and engage different fields (such as ritual, performance art, and even serve as a performative vanitas).

Q3 On Archiving
Outside of photography and video, academic articles and books can be archived at a Butoh library where all Butoh media can live. Japanese writings on Butoh can be translated to English and other languages. We can also encourage people like Jordan Rosin. He is putting together a worldwide database of Butoh artists. Creative Commons license makes archiving and accessibility easier.

Q1 舞踏をはじめたきっかけ
2013年の秋に、インドはダラムサラのサブボディ共振塾ヒマラヤで舞踏に関わり始めました。そこはまるで隠れ家のような場所で、集中して舞踏に打ち込むことができました。その後、数名の舞踏の師の下で学び、公演とワークショップ指導の為に4回ほどツアーに回りました。

Q2 舞踏の魅力
私が舞踏の最大の魅力だと思うのは、その神秘的な美学です。私がモダンダンスの学校に在籍していた時に、そのことを発見しました。舞踏は創造的な面を拡張しつつ、儀式やパフォーマンスアート等の異なる領域とも関わることができるので、ヴァニタスのような静物画的パフォーマンスとしても捉えることができると感じました。

Q3 アーカイヴについて
写真と映像に加えて、学術的な記事や書籍が、全ての舞踏のメディアが保存される舞踏ライブラリーにアーカイヴされるべきだと思います。舞踏に関する日本語の書物は、英語や他言語に翻訳されることが可能だと思います。また、Jordan Rosinのような人を促すのも良いと思います。彼は、全世界の舞踏家のデータベースをまとめています。クリエイティブ・コモンズライセンスの仕組みは、舞踏のアーカイヴィングと、アーカイヴに対するアクセスを容易にすることでしょう。

小林嵯峨 Kobayashi Saga

舞踏家 | 東京(日本) | 小林嵯峨+NOSURI | 50年

Butoh Dancer | Tokyo (Japan) | Kobayashi Saga + NOSURI | 50 years

2018年小林嵯峨+NOSURI舞踏公演『にわとり』
Photo: Foumio Takashima

mijikayo-fox@ae.auone-net.jp

Q1 舞踏をはじめたきっかけ
1968年高井富子舞踏公演『まんだら屋敷』を見て。翌年1969年土方巽アスベスト館に入門。

Q2 舞踏の魅力
常に無意識のうちに探し求めているものに出会わせてくれる。それは闇でもあり光でもある。

Q3 アーカイヴについて
基本的に不可能と思います、舞踏は生きているものであり、常に革新的であらねばならない。記述したり再生したりした途端に死ぬものと私は思っています。便利な世の中はそれなりに有効なものを人々に与えてくれますが、また、一方ではまたそれなりの弊害も生まれるのではないでしょうか。しかし、大切な仕事でもあるとは思っています。

Q1 Reason for Starting Butoh
Saw Tomiko Takai's performance *Mandala Yashiki* in 1968. Began attending Tatsumi Hijikata's Asbesto-kan in 1969.

Q2 Attraction to Butoh
It lets us meet that which we aim to find in our unconscious. This is both our darkness and light.

Q3 On Archiving
I think it is fundamentally impossible. Butoh is a living thing, and must always be innovative. I think it dies as soon as one tries to define it or redo it. Although in this convenient world we are given access to many useful things, it can also cultivate some harmful consequences. Nonetheless, I think it is important work.

鼓代弥生 | Yayoi Kodai

美術家・音楽家｜札幌（日本）｜8年

Artist, Musician | Sapporo (Japan) | 8 years

木彫平面作品「月の満ち欠け」（2018年 木製パネル、アクリルガッシュ 728×1030）
舞踏家・紅月鴉海さんを描いた作品です

https://yayoi-kodai.themedia.jp
Twitter: @YayoiKodai

Q1 舞踏をはじめたきっかけ
舞踏家が持つ、空間へ働きかける力にとても興味を持ちました。
空間に届ける力の秘密を少しでも知りたくて、ワークショップに参加しました。

Q2 舞踏の魅力
日常と非日常の境目が鮮やかになりながら溶け合って行って、心や魂の在り処を暴かれていくところです。表現の根元と符合する割合に非常に高いジャンルだと思います。

Q3 アーカイヴについて
写真・映像、受け手の感想、内側に持っているものをメディアにしていくこと。舞踏の持つ働きかける力の強さと人は人を超えるという神秘性が伝わっていくといいなと思います。

Q1 Reason for Starting Butoh
I became interested in Butoh artists' power to move the space.
I wanted to learn even just a little of this secret, and so participated in a workshop.

Q2 Attraction to Butoh
The border between the ordinary and extraordinary is melted even while being made vividly clear, and the heart and soul are revealed. It's a genre that closely matches the root of its expression.

Q3 On Archiving
Photos, film, people's impressions and their inner experiences should be well communicated. It would be nice if it could convey the strength Butoh has to move, and the mysteries of how humans transcend.

Sara Koller

Performance Artist | International | 6 years

パフォーマンスアーティスト｜世界各地｜6年

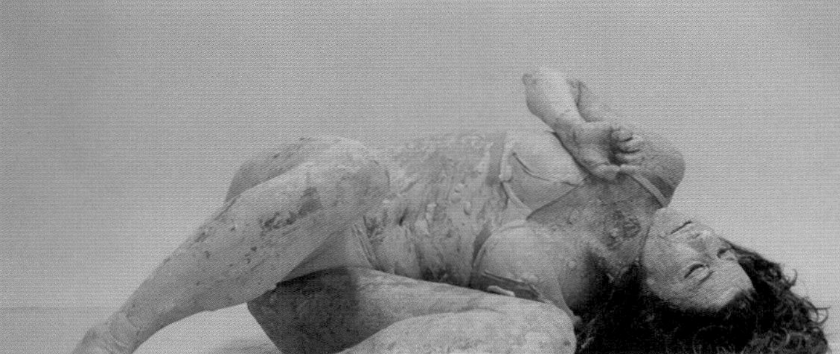

Disambiguation

www.sarakoller.ch

Q1 Reason for Starting Butoh
I am a very moody person and with it also my body. For me, content is more important than aesthetics and truth is the greatest beauty. The workshop with Tamar Borer in Tel Aviv in summer 2014 opened my eyes to the dance of the unconscious.

Q2 Attraction to Butoh
I couldn't dance anymore the same every day because my body has a life of its own. It didn't feel right to force it to obey a choreography, it wanted to talk differently from day to day. In Butoh I found a way to express the authentic movement.

Q3 On Archiving
Butoh has a very strong visual component. Video is therefore suitable for documenting the performance. However, video alone would not be able to capture the entire depth of the work. So in my opinion it is very important to include experience texts of both the audience and the performer in the documentation as well.

Q1 舞踏をはじめたきっかけ
私はすごく気分屋で、それは自分の身体に対しても同じくそうです。私にとって、内容は美学よりも大切で、真実が最も偉大な美だと思っています。2014年の夏に、テルアビブでTamar Borerのワークショップを受けてから、無意識のダンスに開眼しました。

Q2 舞踏の魅力
私の身体はそれ自体が生命を持っているので、毎日同じダンスを踊ることができなくなってしまいました。振付に屈することを身体に強要することが、正しいとは思えなくなってしまい、身体が日々違うように話をしたがっていると感じました。舞踏では、本物の動きを表現することができると感じました。

Q3 アーカイヴについて
舞踏はとても強い視覚的要素を持っています。従って、映像はパフォーマンスの記録に適しています。しかし、映像だけでは、作品全体の深度を捉えることはできないでしょう。観客とパフォーマー両方の体験を記したテキストを記録に含めることが、非常に大切だと思います。

Q1 Please tell us how you became involved with Butoh?
Q2 What attracted you to Butoh?
Q3 As a performative art inherently involving the physical body, how can Butoh be preserved? Or, is this even possible?

Q1 あなたが舞踏をはじめたきっかけを教えて下さい。
Q2 あなたにとって舞踏の魅力は何ですか？
Q3 身体芸術である舞踏は、どのようにしたら残すことができるでしょうか？

近藤基弥 | Motoya Kondo

ベルリン（ドイツ）| Motimaru Dance Company | 10年

Berlin (Germany) | Motimaru Dance Company | 10 years

舞台作品 "Human Installation B.O.D.Y." より。
Photo: Yozy Zhang Garvey

www.motimaru.net

Q1 舞踏をはじめたきっかけ
ふと大野一雄舞踏研究所を訪れ大野慶人先生の稽古を受け、天と地の間に立つ、極小の蝶が巨大な海を渡る等の稽古で二元的な言葉の世界を超えた空間に心身が開いて感動した事。

Q2 舞踏の魅力
日本や東洋、欧米、世界中の芸術や思想の歴史が古今東西、縦横無尽に交差し、さらにより根源的な存在の探求に知的のみならず体験的に向かっている事。

Q3 アーカイヴについて
写真やビデオを残す事も重要であると同時に、稽古や舞台創造の具体的な方法論を探求研磨し、過去に向かうのみならず現在に新たな舞台を生み出す力を舞踏から学び、それを人から人へ伝えて行く事が重要だと思います。

Q1 Reason for Starting Butoh
I took a class with Yoshito Ohno at the Kazuo Ohno Dance Studio, and through exercises of standing between heaven and earth, becoming a butterfly crossing a huge ocean etc, my mind was opened and I was impressed by the atmosphere created beyond the world of words.

Q2 Attraction to Butoh
The philosophies and histories of Japan, the East, the West and all the world endlessly intersecting, not only intellectually, but experimentally in pursuit of a fundamental existence.

Q3 On Archiving
As well as archiving photographs and videos, I think it is important to find and share a concrete methodology for classes and performance creation, and learn to create new performances from Butoh without holding on to the past.

今野眞弓 | Konno Mayumi

介護職 | 東京（日本）| 38年

Care Worker | Tokyo (Japan) | 38 years

彼女たちの理由#02「ゆらりゆられて」2011年5月7日　pit北/区域

Facebook: 今野眞弓

Q1 舞踏をはじめたきっかけ
演劇学校 に通っていたころ、たまたま舞踏という分野の踊りがあることを知り、自分の気持ち、今思っていることを素直に表現できることに強く心が惹かれたこと。

Q2 舞踏の魅力
舞踏の精神があらゆるものを救うこと。表現として、技術だけでなく精神的なものによってその人の負であるものがひっくり返され、人を感動させることができること。

Q3 アーカイヴについて
踊った時代背景もあるし、技術はその人だけのものなので 正確に残すことはできないと思う。しかし、どうしても残すならば、それを見た人がどうして感動したかを言葉（文章）で伝えることが必要。

Q1 Reason for Starting Butoh
I happened to learn about the genre of Butoh while at theatre school, and my heart was strongly drawn to its capacity to express thoughts and feelings in an amenable manner.

Q2 Attraction to Butoh
That the Butoh spirit can rescue anything. As a form of expression, it is not only an art but a spiritual phenomenon that can overturn a person's weaknesses, and make them impressive.

Q3 On Archiving
I don't think it's possible to preserve it authentically, considering the era of the dance, and that techniques are uniquely personal. However if it must be preserved, I think it's important for people who have seen it to share why it was impressive using words (in essays).

工藤丈輝 | Taketeru Kudo

舞踏家｜東京（日本）｜29年

Butoh Dancer | Tokyo (Japan) | 29 years

ソロ公演『業曝（ごうざらし）』テルアビブ公演より（2008年）

http://www.kudo-taketeru.com/

Q1 舞踏をはじめたきっかけ

二十の頃、言葉への絶望感に駆られ、文学の導きで舞踏を知りました。渡仏中、山海塾など知りますが、のちの師となる玉野黄市との出遇いが針路を決定づけます。その後はあれよあれよと舞踏の側に拉致されていく肉体を見まもり、さまざまな影響のもとに成った自らの方法論で現在もつづけています。

Q2 舞踏の魅力

何ものにもなりかわれること。身体を空っぽにする術さえ獲得すれば、水にも植物にも、ケモノにも妖怪にも、鉱物にも火にも気体にも、風にも、光にだってなれるかもしれません……。（こんな仕事がどうして辞められるでしょう。）

Q3 アーカイヴについて

そもそも残すという発想が老婆心なのであり、これまで一体、滅ばなかったものなどあるでしょうか?アカデミーがなまの生活、芸術を制御できるはずはなく、個人でさえどうしたって時代の子どもです。伝統芸能でなく現在時のものであるべき舞踏は、どう生まれ変わっていくかを見とどけるべきでしょう。私見では次代の舞踏家はいわゆる舞踏の世界ではなく、どこから生まれるか分かったものではありません。

Q1 Reason for Starting Butoh

At around 20, totally disillusioned with language, I came to know of Butoh through literature. I heard of Sankai Juku etc while in France, but it was my experience with Koichi Tamano that determined my path. Since then, I have been watching over the changes in Butoh, and drawn from many different influences to create my own methodology which I continue to this day.

Q2 Attraction to Butoh

The potential to change into anything. As long as one has a technique to clear the body and mind, it may be possible to become water or plant, beast or ghost, an element, fire or gas, wind, light... (is it possible to ever stop this kind of work?)

Q3 On Archiving

The very idea of preservation is old fashioned, is there anything until now that hasn't perished? Academies cannot control real life or art, and individuals are but the children of their era. Butoh cannot be seen as a traditional art, it is by definition current, and we should be watching how it changes in the present. In my opinion, the next generation of Butoh artists will not come from the Butoh world, but from somewhere we cannot know.

久世亜紀 | Aki Kuze

書道家・舞踏家｜横浜（日本）｜10年

Calligrapher, Butoh Dancer | Yokohama (Japan) | 10 years

AsiaTry参加作品より（2018.9 秋田千秋公園）

Q1 舞踏をはじめたきっかけ

BankARTにて大野慶人舞踏講座を2ヶ月間受講し、今までに体験したことのない身体と空間の関わりに深い感動と数々の稽古の言葉から大きな衝撃を受けたこと。

Q2 舞踏の魅力

肉体があらゆる空間を自在に創り出し、時空を超えて存在していると感じること。肉体から宇宙へ放たれる存在の粒子。

Q3 アーカイヴについて

舞踏から得る感動の根源を研究して行くこと。逆に全てのものが消えても、最後まで消えないもののひとつが舞踏と思います。

Q1 Reason for Starting Butoh

I took a course with Yoshito Ohno for 2 months at BankART, where I experienced the body and space in a way I had never done before. The words from these classes had a big impact on me.

Q2 Attraction to Butoh

Any scene can be created freely with the body, as though it exists beyond space or time. Particles of existence are released from the body into space.

Q3 On Archiving

Study the cause of feelings that arise from Butoh. On the other hand I think that if everything were to disappear, the last thing left would be Butoh.

Q1 あなたが舞踏をはじめたきっかけを教えて下さい。
Q2 あなたにとって舞踏の魅力は何ですか？
Q3 身体芸術である舞踏は、どのようにしたら残すことができるでしょうか？

久世龍五郎 | Ryugoro Kuze

舞踏家｜東京・横浜（日本）｜久世 龍五郎 and circustik orchestra｜12年

Butoh Dancer | Tokyo, Yokohama (Japan) | Ryugoro Kuze and circustik orchestra | 12 years

ソロ作品「蝉の脇腹(2017.12 中野テルプシコール)」より
Photo: bozzo

Q1 舞踏をはじめたきっかけ

大学の吹奏楽部で指揮者に関心を持った際、たまたま観た映像の大野一雄の踊りに、まさに「空間を指揮している」と感じたため

Q2 舞踏の魅力

繊細さ・ダイナミックさなど、心身や空間に対するアプローチが非常に革新的かつ日本的で、自身の世界観に大きな刺激を与えてくれるところ

Q3 アーカイヴについて

作品の映像記録を残すことも重要ですが、作品そのものではなく「その舞踏家が求めたところが何なのか」「それをどう後世者がキャッチアップしていくのか」を言語化することが重要と考えます。

Q1 Reason for Starting Butoh

I was interested in conducting at university, and around the same time happened to see a film featuring Kazuo Ohno; I felt his dance was really ‘conducting space’.

Q2 Attraction to Butoh

The delicacy and timing of the body and space is incredibly innovative and Japanese in a way that gives great stimulation to one’s worldview.

Q3 On Archiving

Although it is important to film performances, I think it is important to verbalise questions such as “what was this Butoh artist trying to do?”, “how will future generations interpret it?” rather than just see the work as it is.

http://circustik.web.fc2.com/
https://www.facebook.com/ryugoro.kuze

Lorna Lawrie

Dancer, Choreographer, Teacher | France | 20 years

ダンサー・振付家・教師｜フランス｜20年

Q1 Reason for Starting Butoh

I studied classical dance first, then contemporary, but dance was empty for me until I knew butoh in 1996 in Argentine with Rhea Volij. She transmitted butoh to a first generation in Argentine. I made part of “La Brizna” Company, directed by R. Volij in Buenos Aires during 5 years.

Q2 Attraction to Butoh

The “philosophical” aspect. Butoh goes further than other dances, further than the individual, something so necessary nowadays... I didn’t find this in other dances. I was attracted because it’s not just moving. In a deep way butoh opens questions. And it goes to the body for answers; to find maybe not only one answer...

Q3 On Archiving

It would be paradox to fix butoh expression in a closed concept. Diversifying data sources, and renewing them periodically is necessary.
Maybe butoh archives should be a place that welcome dancers to dance, share, leave real traces of new butoh understanding and development. As it is about body construction, destruction, transformation... body should be its main place to continue alive.

Festival “En chair et en son” 2016 Issy les Moulinex, Grand Paris
©Fabrice Pairault

https://www.facebook.com/Danse-Butoh-LORNA-Lawrie-284382618389126/

Q1 舞踏をはじめたきっかけ

私はまずクラシックダンスを、それからコンテンポラリーを学びました。1996年にアルゼンチンでRhea Volijの下で舞踏を知るまで、ダンスは私にとってからっぽなものでした。彼女はアルゼンチンにおける舞踏の最初の世代を創った人です。私はブエノスアイレスで彼女が演出する「La Brizna」カンパニーのメンバーとなり、5年間在籍しました。

Q2 舞踏の魅力

舞踏の「哲学的」な側面です。舞踏は他のダンスを凌駕しており、個人を超越しています。今日の世界にとても必要なものです。他のダンスの中に、私はこのようなことを見出すことがありませんでした。私が惹かれたのは、ただ単に舞踏が感動的だからではありません。深いレベルで、舞踏は問いを投げかけてくれます。そしてその答えを求めるために身体に向かうのです。おそらく見つかる答えは、一つだけでは無いでしょう..

Q3 アーカイヴについて

舞踏の表現を閉じられた概念の中で固定化しようとするのは矛盾していると思います。データソースを多様化し、それらを定期的に更新していくことが必要です。おそらく、舞踏のアーカイヴはダンサーが踊ること、ダンサーがそれぞれの課題を共有すること、ダンサーが新しい舞踏についての理解と発展についての形跡を現実に残すこと、それら全てを歓迎する場として機能するべきだと思います。舞踏は身体の構築、脱構築、変化を扱っているので、舞踏が生き続ける場所は身体の内にあるべきです。

Tiziana Longo

Choreographer, Butoh Dancer, Yoga and Dance Teacher | Berlin (Germany) | 15 years

振付家・舞踏家・ヨガとダンスの教師 | ベルリン（ドイツ） | 15年

"The rose" from latest butoh performance *Spaghetti*
Photo: Yozy Zhang Garvey

www.motimaru.net

Q1 Reason for Starting Butoh
The first encounter was at the Bologna University's Kazuo Ohno's archive. When I saw the video *The written face* there was nothing that stopped me to go to Japan to meet Kazuo Ohno. Then I learnt, studied and worked with my teacher Yoshito Ohno at the K. Ohno Dance Institute.

Q2 Attraction to Butoh
The spirit of butoh in its essence and its embodiment of peculiarity

Q3 On Archiving
Enrolling more direct disciples into re-make of old pieces; constitution of new archives; implementing video material and documentation; creating a butoh course at the University.

Q1 舞踏をはじめたきっかけ
ボローニャ大学での大野一雄アーカイヴが、舞踏との初めての出会いです。映画『書かれた顔』を観た時に、私が大野一雄に会うために、日本に行くことを止めるものは何もありませんでした。それから大野一雄舞踏研究所で、私の師である大野慶人の下で学び、彼と共に作品を創りました。

Q2 舞踏の魅力
舞踏の精神の本質的部分と、その特異性が具現化されたもの。

Q3 アーカイヴについて
旧作品の作り直しには、直弟子をもっと絡ませること。新しいアーカイヴの構築。映像の資料化と記録。大学で舞踏の講義を設けること。

松村智恵子 Chieko Matsumura

渡る風舞踊舎 | 30年以上

Wataru Kaze | over 30 years

Q1 舞踏をはじめたきっかけ
高校時代のダンス部。感じ合いや即興で踊ることを教えて下さった恩師（山口直永氏）が大野一雄氏と親交があり、何度か私達の公演会で踊られた。無意識の涙、感動した。

Q2 舞踏の魅力
目に見えない静けさ、深さ。陰と陽ならば「陰」（無意識の世界）にある根源的なものに触れられる感じがする。こころの奥底にあるいのちの叫びが立ち上がる。

Q3 アーカイヴについて
大野一雄らの映像を大画面で体感できる空間、資料も閲覧、購入できる場所を造る。形を真似ようとすると陳腐になる、と大野氏も語っていた。型にはめようとすれば不自由になるだけ。精神性、心身のありようの伝達を。

前橋の店「kigi」の作品を纏って店前で踊る。2015.9月

https://www.odoruhitono1.com/

Q1 Reason for Starting Butoh
High school dance club. My instructor Naoe Yamaguchi taught me how to dance with feeling and without sound, and was friends with Kazuo Ohno who danced many times at our performances. I was moved to tears.

Q2 Attraction to Butoh
The invisible silence and depth. It seems touched by the fundamentals of 'yin' (the unconscious world) of yin and yang. It's the scream of life from the depths of the soul.

Q3 On Archiving
Create a space where Kazuo Ohno's films etc. can be experienced on a big screen, and one can browse and buy documents. Ohno spoke of copied forms becoming stale. Try to fit a stereotype and become less free. We need a way to communicate this spirituality and mentality.

Q1 Please tell us how you became involved with Butoh?
Q2 What attracted you to Butoh?
Q3 As a performative art inherently involving the physical body, how can Butoh be preserved? Or, is this even possible?

Q1 あなたが舞踏をはじめたきっかけを教えて下さい。
Q2 あなたにとって舞踏の魅力は何ですか？
Q3 身体芸術である舞踏は、どのようにしたら残すことができるでしょうか？

松岡 大 | Dai Matsuoka

舞踏家｜東京（日本）｜山海塾、LAND FES、ダンスアーカイヴ構想｜14年

Butoh Dancer | Tokyo (Japan) | Sankai Juku, LAND FES, Dance Archive Network | 14 years

YOUTUBE「ODORE」チャンネル「土方三章」より

http://daimatsuoka.com

Q1 舞踏をはじめたきっかけ
大学在学時に、山海塾「金柑少年」のVHSを授業で見たのがきっかけ。その直後、土方巽の写真集にも釘付けとなる。

Q2 舞踏の魅力
身体と結びつき、身体経験を変容し得る豊富なイメージと語彙。

Q3 アーカイヴについて
トレーニング方法の共有を進める。アーカイヴを活用して、舞踏の名作のレパートリー化を試みる。

Q1 Reason for Starting Butoh
While at university, I saw Sankai Juku's *Kinkan Shonen* on VHS in class. Immediately after, I found and was hooked on Tatsumi Hijikata's photo books.

Q2 Attraction to Butoh
Connecting with the body, changing the body's experience with rich images and language.

Q3 On Archiving
It's a way to share training methods. By utilising the archives, we can create a repertoire of Butoh masterpieces.

Ana Medeiros

Dancer, Teacher | Porto Alegre (Brazil) | Kazuo Ohno Dance Studio | 5 years

ダンサー・教師｜ポルトアレグレ（ブラジル）｜大野一雄舞踏研究所｜5年

Q1 Reason for Starting Butoh
After seeing Kazuo Ohno's performance I decided to go to Japan, and since 2015 I have gone every year to immerse myself in Yoshito Ohno's universe and teachings. So far I have brought sensei's teachings to where I live in Brazil, and continue to follow his philosophy of life and Butoh.

Q2 Attraction to Butoh
I saw Kazuo Ohno dance in New York in 1996 at the Japan Society. I can truly say that experiencing Kazuo Ohnos's dance changed my life. It was the transformation element in his dance as well as the unveiling of himself so profoundly and tenderly, which took me by the heart.

Q3 On Archiving
I believe Butoh can be preserved byoral transmission from the first generation of Butoh dancers to their students and from their students to others. Such is the legacy of dance which spreads itself around the world from one generation to the next. Books and videos are another very necessary tool to connect the roots of Butoh to new generations.

Photo: Ryo Ichii and David Ceccon

anamedeiroscoreografia.blogspot.com.br

Q1 舞踏をはじめたきっかけ
大野一雄の公演を観た後に、日本に行こうと決めました。そして2015年以降は毎年日本を訪れて、大野慶人の世界観と教えに没頭しています。今は慶人先生の教えをブラジルの私が住んでいるところに持ち帰り、彼の人生と舞踏に対する哲学を追い続けています。

Q2 舞踏の魅力
1996年にニューヨークのジャパン・ソサエティーで大野一雄の踊りを観ました。大野一雄の踊りを観たことで私の人生は変わったと本当に言えます。踊りの中で変化していく姿だけでなく、とても深く、そして優しく、彼自身が露わになっていく様子に心を打たれました。

Q3 アーカイヴについて
第一世代の舞踏家からの口承によって、その生徒たちに伝わり、そして生徒たちからまた他の人々へと伝わることで、舞踏は残されていくと信じています。これこそが、一つの世代からまた次の世代へと、そして世界に広がっていく踊りの遺産だと思います。それとは別に、書籍や映像もまた、舞踏のルーツを新たな世代へと繋げる為に必要なツールだと思います。

南 阿豆 | Azu Minami

舞踏家・グラフィックデザイナー｜東京（日本）｜15年

Butoh Dancer, Graphic Designer | Tokyo (Japan) | 15 years

2019年solo作品「Any Day Now」より
Photo: Bozzo

Q1 舞踏をはじめたきっかけ
徹夜や終電続きの仕事で過労、虚弱体、病気になり、健康のためにできる体操を求めて、たまたま行ってみたのが、舞踏経験のある方のWSでした。

Q2 舞踏の魅力
踊ること、観ること両方で生命の体験。ダンスの振付やカウントなしで、イメージや感覚、自然、体、内面の存在など様々なことを踊りにできる。芸術の遊びがある。

Q3 アーカイヴについて
私の立場からお伝えします。表現を止めない、し続けること。舞踏としてではなく、表現、個として作品を作ること。作品が様々な人に触れられることへ向き合うこと。それらをサポートしてくれる存在への交流と感謝。

Q1 Reason for Starting Butoh
I became ill and frail after working overnight or until the last train, and while searching for an exercise for my health, happened to go to a workshop with a person with Butoh experience.

Q2 Attraction to Butoh
Experiencing life either by dancing or watching. All kinds of things can become dance without choreography or counting such as images, senses, nature, the body, or exposing the inner self. It is an artistic play.

Q3 On Archiving
I'll say this from my point of view. Don't stop expressing, keep doing it. Not as Butoh, but as personal expression. Work on creating pieces that touch all kinds of people. Associate with and appreciate the people who support it.

https://minamiazu-dance.jimdo.com/

M–M

三好由貴 | Yuki Miyoshi

コンテンポラリーダンサー｜関東地区（日本）｜6年

Contemporary Dancer | Kanto (Japan) | 6 years

Q1 舞踏をはじめたきっかけ
コンテンポラリーダンスの創作活動をして行く中で、山海塾の舞台を観た時、私が観たいもの、表現したいもの全てをやっていると思った。私が最も探していたものだと感じた。

Q2 舞踏の魅力
自分の身体の中側と身体の外側の空間や時間を魅せる。卓越してる方は、例え音がなくても、美術がなくても、身体一つで情景が見えてくる。

Q3 アーカイヴについて
どの伝統のある芸術も、色々資料を残しても、やはり直接伝えていくことが最も大事だと思います。これからの世代も入りやすい様な受け皿をもっと広めて行く必要があると思います。欧米を例に挙げると、普通のダンススタジオでもどんどん舞踏のワークショップがあると良いと思います。もちろん、確立された舞踏の訓練をされた方が講師で。

Q1 Reason for Starting Butoh
I saw Sankai Juku perform whilst working on a contemporary dance piece and found it was everything I wanted to see, wanted to perform. I felt it was exactly what I had been searching for.

Q2 Attraction to Butoh
The way it performs space and time inside and outside the body. With the best you can see the whole spectacle with just one body, without even music or scenography.

Q3 On Archiving
Regardless of how traditional an art form is, or how much documentation is left, I think the most important thing is to convey it directly. I think it is necessary to share in a way that is easy for future generations to understand. If I take the West as an example, I think it would be good to have more dance workshops in just regular dance studios. Of course, with properly trained Butoh instructors.

http://yukimiyoshi.com

Q1 Please tell us how you became involved with Butoh?
Q2 What attracted you to Butoh?
Q3 As a performative art inherently involving the physical body, how can Butoh be preserved? Or, is this even possible?

BUTOHBUTOHBUTOHBUTOHBUTOH

精神のリレー 2019

A Spiritual Relay 2019

笠井瑞丈
Mitsutake Kasai

Photo: Keiko Onoda

「四人の師」
私は踊りを通して沢山の人と出会いました。その中で私の踊りに大きな影響を与えてくれた舞踊家が四人います。

元藤燁子さん
初めて舞踏に触れたのが、私が19歳の時に、今は無き「アスベスト館」で行われた短期ワークショップ「アイコンとしての身体」に参加した時です。そのワークショップで中心的に教えてくださったのが、土方巽さんの奥様でもあり舞踏家の故・元藤燁子さんでした。彼女の最初のワークショップは、寝たところから立つという事から始まりました。それを何度も何度も繰り返しました。身体の中の時間を探り、植物的な時間を探り、闇の中を歩く。いろいろなテーマで「立つ」という事だけを掘り下げて行いました。その時の元藤さんの言葉は「踊るという事はまず立つ事から始まる」。当時の私は「踊る」という事は飛び跳ねたり走ったり回ったりする事であり、どうして立つという行為にそんなに時間をかけてカラダを探らなければいけないのか、よく分からずにいました。あれから時間が経ち、いろいろな事を経験しました。今では自分でワークショップを行うこともありますが、あの時の体験をよく話します。元藤さんから受け取った言葉は、私の舞踊 — ダンスそして舞踏 — の扉を開いた。時間が経ち、そんな大切な事に気づきました。あの言葉は、今では私のダンスの原点になっています。

山崎広太さん
1997年、山崎広太さんの作品『ピクニック』を青山スパイラル劇場で観ました。チラシを私の兄・笠井爾示が撮影していたということもあり、観に行こうと楽しみにしていた公演です。初めて観るダンス公演。幕が開き、私

Four Mentors
I've encountered many different people through dance. Among them are four dancers who have greatly influenced my dance.

Akiko Motofuji
The first time I came in contact with Butoh was at nineteen, when I participated in a short workshop, *Body as an Icon* that was held at Asbestos-kan (Tatsumi Hijikata's rehearsal studio). I was taught at that workshop by the late Hijikata's wife and dancer, Akiko Motofuji. At the first workshop, we had to practice how to wake from sleep.
I repeated this action over and again. Exploring time in the body, exploring botanical time, walking in the dark. We delved deeply into how to "stand," availing of various themes. At that time, Motofuji said, "Dancing starts with standing." For me, however, I thought at that point that "dancing" entailed jumping, running around, and pirouetting, and I had a hard time understanding why we had to spend so much time exploring the body in order to stand. In the meantime, however, I've accumulated many experiences. Now that I myself sometimes conduct workshops, I often talk about my experiences at that time. Motofuji's words opened the door to my dance and to Butoh. With the passing of time, I realized just how important that was. Her words have now become the starting point for my dance.

Kota Yamazaki
In 1997, I saw Kota Yamazaki's *Picnic* at the Aoyama Spiral Theater. I had been looking forward to seeing the performance, more so because my brother, Chikashi Kasai, had shot the flyer. This was to be the first dance performance I attended. As soon as the curtain lifted I was completely drawn into his world. I can still recall returning home, excitedly, knowing that there was such a world. The performance flyer included a notice for a workshop to be given by Yamazaki, so I applied immediately. That was my

笠井瑞丈

笠井叡に舞踏を、山崎広太にダンスを師事。1998年より自作のソロダンスを開始。様々なスタイルのダンスのエッセンスを取り入れながら独自の世界観を持つ作品を発表している。近年はソロだけでなく作品振付や客演でも注目を集めている。2009年、平成20年度文化庁新進芸術家海外留学研修員としてニューヨークで1年間研修。10年、横浜ソロ×デュオ・コンペティション・プラス審査員特別賞受賞。16年、テロ・サーリネンカンパニーの作品にゲスト出演。2017年5月、笠井叡振付『花粉革命』を踊る。第12回日本ダンスフォーラム賞受賞。

Mitsutake Kasai

Mitsutake Kasai studied Butoh under his father Akira Kasai and dance with Kota Yamazaki. He embarked on a solo dance career in 1998. Incorporating the essence of various styles of dance, he has created works with a unique perspective on the world. In recent years, he has garnered attention not only for his solo creations but also for his choreographic output and guest appearances. In 2008, he trained in New York for one year as part of the Program of Overseas Study for Upcoming Artists. In 2010, he won the Yokohama Solo x Duo Competition Plus Special Jury Prize. In 2016, he made a guest appearance with the Tero Saarinen Company. In May 2017, he performed *Pollen Revolution* a piece choreographed by Akira Kasai. He was awarded the 12th JaDaFo Award.

はその中の世界に完全に引き込まれました。こんな世界もあるんだと興奮して帰ったことを今でも思い出します。その公演のチラシの中に山崎さんのワークショップのお知らせが入っていました。私はすぐに申し込みをしました。それが初めてのダンス経験です。舞踏の時とは全く違う経験でした。そこからオープンクラスも受けるようになりました。当時山崎さんが立ち上げたグループ『ゴールデンヘアーズ』にも全く踊れないのに声をかけて頂き参加させてもらいました。そこで私は初めてグループワークというのを学びました。どのように人を配置し、どのように群舞を作っていくのかを学びました。ワークショップ後やリハーサル後には山崎さんと飲みに行く事がよくありました。帰れなくなり、泊めてもらったりする事もよくありました。そのような付き合いの中でまた多くの事を学びました。私にとってはダンスを教えてくれた師であり、大きな影響を受けた存在です。

テロ・サーリネンさん

テロ・サーリネンさんはフィンランドを代表するダンサーであり振付家です。自身でテロ・サーリネン・カンパニーというカンパニーを持ち、世界各国でツアーを行なって活動をしています。私が初めてテロさんと会ったのは2014年、埼玉舞踊協会がテロさんに委託をし、日本で作品を作る事になった時です。私はこの時の作品『MESH』に参加する事になりました。30人くらいダンサーが参加している大きな作品でした。こんな大人数で、そして海外の振付家の作品に参加するというのは初めての経験でした。私はその作品の中でソロパートを任されました。テロさんはいつも踊り終わると「気のチカラ」「火のチカラ」「水のチカラ」「地のチカラ」について色々なアドバイスをしてくれました。そして否定的な事は一切言

first experience with dance. It differed completely from my experience with Butoh. From that point on, I started to take open classes. Even though I could hardly dance at that stage, I was still asked to participate in the dance troupe Golden Hairs that Yamazaki had founded, and eventually ended up performing with them. This was my first introduction to group work. I learned how to position dancers on stage and how to create a group dance. After workshops and rehearsals, I would often go for a drink with Yamazaki. At times I wouldn't be able to make it back home and I would stay at his place. I learned a lot from that kind of relationship. For me, he was both a teacher who taught dance and an enormous influence on me.

Tero Saarinen

Tero Saarinen is one of Finland's prominent dance-artists and choreographers. He is the artistic director of Tero Saarinen Company, with which he performs around the globe. I first met Tero in 2014 when the Saitama Dance Association commissioned him to create a work in-situ in Japan. It was on this occasion that it was decided that I participate in his work *MESH*. It was a large-scale piece involving about thirty dancers. As well as being my first experience with such a large cast, it was also the first time I worked with an overseas choreographer. I was assigned a solo part in the work. After we would finish performing, Tero would constantly advise us about the force inherent in the natural elements, the power of *ki*, of water, of fire, of the earth. He would never speak in negative terms. I was able to experience being wrapped in Taro's work of such a vast imaginative force. For me, this was a key experience. The process involved linking with nature's four energies — *Tenkamizuchi* (heaven-fire-water-earth) — within our bodies and to create a dance. This remains the source of my dance to this day. And in 2016, I was able to participate in a performance by the Tero Saarinen Company in Finland.

う事がありませんでした。そんなテロさんの大きなイマジネーションのチカラに包まれ作品が作られていくのを体験する事ができました。私にとってこの時の体験はとても大切な体験でした。「天火水地」の四つのチカラを身体から産み出し踊りを作っていく。これは今の私の踊りを作る源流みたいなものになっています。そして2016年、私はフィンランドでテロ・サーリネン・カンパニーの公演に参加することができました。

笠井叡さん
人は生まれる場所を選べない。そう考えると、私が踊りを踊る事になったのも、偶然であり必然でもあったのかもしれません。私が初めて舞台の立ったのが父・笠井叡の作品「人は肉体をたずさえて死者の世界へおもむくか」(サンフランシスコ)、私が22歳の時でした。それまであまり踊る事に真剣になれなかったのですが、これを機にちゃんと踊りを学ぼうと決意しました。その道を作ってくれた公演でした。踊りの道を歩み始めた事で私はたくさんの事を学び、たくさんの人に出会えました。父から教わったことは、自分のダンスは自分で切り拓いていくしかないということです。ダンスを学ぶ事も大切ですが、思考することがカラダを作り踊りを作るということを学びました。父と息子という関係の中、そして家族という関係の中で、踊りを通して繋がっていくことは、時と場合によっては難しい時もあります。それは最高の苦しみでもあり最高の喜びでもあります。人は生まれる場所を選べないのだから。

ダンスは人と出会うことでまだ知らない自分と出会うこと。
その中で偶然に出会える『師』はとても大切な存在です。
私はこの四人の『師』から多くの事を学びました。

Akira Kasai
We can't choose where we are born. Bearing that in mind, it may have either been a coincidence or an inevitability that has made me dance. The first time I set foot on stage was at the age of twenty-two together with my father, Akira Kasai, in San Francisco in his piece, *Are We Carrying Our Bodies into the World of the Dead?* Until that point, I hadn't taken dance that seriously, but I then decided to learn it properly. That performance was the turning point. As I started to dance, I learned a lot and was to encounter many people. What I've learnt from my father is that I have to develop my own dance. While learning to dance is essential, I learned that reflection also plays a role in creating a physical presence and in making dance. In a father-son relationship, as in all familial relationships, connecting through dance can be challenging at times. It at once involves the greatest suffering and the greatest joy. That comes down to the fact that we can't choose where we are born.

Dancing is about encountering new people and coming to know yourself.
The "mentors" we can encounter by chance play a vital role in our evolution.
I've learnt most of what I know from these four "mentors."

元藤燁子 | Akiko Motofuji (1928-2003)

1952年、のちのアスベスト館を東京・目黒に設立。59年に土方巽と出会い、以来活動をともにする。稽古場兼劇場であった同館には先鋭的な芸術家や文化人が数多く集まり、舞踏創造の場となった。87年土方巽記念資料館を設立、98年に慶應義塾大学アート・センターに資料を寄託する。代表作に、土方演出による「EMILYの薔薇」、アスベスト館改築記念イベント「アイコンとしての身体」等。

Established what later became Asbestos-kan in Meguro, Tokyo in 1952. Worked with Tatsumi Hijikata after meeting him in 1959. Her rehearsal studio and theatre attracted a lot of cutting edge artists and cultural figures, and became a space for Butoh creation. Established the Tatsumi Hijikata Memorial Archive in 1987, and donated materials to the Keio University Art Center in 1998. Key works include *Emily's Rose* directed by Hijikata, and *Body as an Icon*, which commemorated the renovation of Asbestos-kan.

山崎広太 | Kota Yamazaki (1959-)

舞踏を笠井叡に、クラシックバレエを井上博文に師事。1998年、ダニエル・ラリューに招かれ、フランス国立現代ダンスセンターでの作品制作に参加したことをきっかけに、振付家として活動を開始。96-01年、カンパニー rosy Co.を主宰。2002年、アメリカを拠点に、Kota Yamazaki/Fluid hug-hugを新たに立ち上げ。セネガルで1年間滞在制作するなど、アフリカとの関わりも深い。ボディ・アーツ・ラボラトリー代表。

Studied Butoh with Akira Kasai, and classical ballet with Hirofumi Inoue. Began working as a choreographer after being invited by Daniel Larrieu in 1998 to participate in a production at the French National Center for Contemporary Dance (CNDC). Established rosy Co. 1996-2001. Founded Kota Yamazakui/Fluid hug-hug based in America in 2002. Also has a deep connection with Africa after residing in Senegal for one year. Body Arts Laboratory representative.

テロ・サーリネン | Tero Saarinen (1964-)

1985-92年、フィンランド国立バレエ団でダンサーとして活躍。アジアの舞踊を学ぶたびを経て、92年来日し、大野一雄のもとで1年間舞踏を学ぶ。帰国後、本格的に振付家としての活動を開始。96年、テロ・サーリネン・カンパニー立ち上げ。2014年、埼玉県舞踊協会の委嘱を受け、日本人ダンサーに振り付けた『MESH』発表。これまでに40カ国以上でツアーを行い、世界の著名なカンパニーからも作品を委嘱されている。

Danced with the Finnish National Ballet 1985-92. In the hopes of studying Asian dance, travels to study with Kazuo Ohno for one year in 1992. Began working as a choreographer on his return. Founded the Tero Saarinen Company in 1996. Presented *MESH*, commissioned by the Saitama Dance Association and choreographed for Japanese dancers in 2014. Has so far toured in over 40 countries and had works commissioned by internationally renowned companies.

笠井叡 | Akira Kasai (1941-)

モダンダンス、パントマイム、バレエ等を学んだのち、63年に大野一雄、64年に土方巽と出会い、舞踏草創期の活動を支える。71年、天使館を創設。79-85年、ドイツにてルドルフ・シュタイナーの人智学とオイリュトミーを研究。94年、14年ぶりの舞踏公演『セラフィータ』を行い、以後精力的に活動を展開。東京・国分寺の同館では、オイリュトミスト養成講座を開講する。

After studying modern dance, pantomime and ballet, he met Kazuo Ohno in 1963, and Tatsumi Hijikata in 1964. Established Tenshikan in 1971 in support of early Butoh works. Studied Rudolf Steiner's anthropology and eurythmy in Germany 1979-85. Came back to Butoh after 14 years with his piece *Saraphita* in 1994, and has been active ever since. Runs a eurythmy school in Kokubunji, Tokyo.

Q1 あなたが舞踏をはじめたきっかけを教えて下さい。
Q2 あなたにとって舞踏の魅力は何ですか？
Q3 身体芸術である舞踏は、どのようにしたら残すことができるでしょうか？

Jocelyne Montpetit

Dancer, Choreographer, Teacher | National Theater School of Canada | 22 years

ダンサー・振付家・教師 | National Theater School of Canada | 22年

Foreign female dancer festival, Tatsumi Hijikata's Keio university archives (Isamu Noguchi space, Tokyo)
Photo: Makoto Onozuka

https://www.facebook.com/jocelynemontpetitdanse

Q1 Reason for Starting Butoh
In the 80's I saw Buto at Avignon festival. That year I did workshops with Min Tanaka, who later invited me to join Maĭjuku. In 1985 I joined Tatsumi Hijikata at l'Asbestokan studio. After Hijikata died, I joined Kazuo Ohno studio. I came to the hearth of Buto. I continued there until he retired.

Q2 Attraction to Butoh
What attracted me to Buto was the interiority, a way to make an encounter with your deep self and others. It was a very deep road not in surface. Emptiness/ To be in the moment/to not express yourself but your soul/To understand who you are/to meet the space/to meet others.

Q3 On Archiving
I think archives are a fantastic way to communicate Buto, but not enough. There must be international meetings, festivals, film presentations, videos, conferences. Workshops are also very important. We should teach also actors, performers. As Kazuo Ohno told me: “Buto will survive if dancers don't stay in imitation of Buto forms but start their dance from their own souls”.

Q1 舞踏をはじめたきっかけ
1980年代に、アヴィニョン演劇祭で舞踏を観ました。その年に、田中泯のワークショップを受けて、その後彼は私を舞塾に誘ってくれました。1985年に、アスベスト館で土方巽の教えを受けました。土方の死後は、大野一雄舞踏研究所に入り、舞踏という火のある場所に辿り着きました。大野一雄が引退するまで、私はそこで踊りを続けていました。

Q2 舞踏の魅力
私が舞踏に惹かれたのはその内面性、自己の深部が他者と出会うための方法でした。表層にはない、とても深い道のりでした。空になること、瞬間を生きること、自分自身ではなく魂を表現すること、本当の自分が何者かを理解すること、空間と出会うこと、他者と出会うこと。

Q3 アーカイヴについて
アーカイヴは舞踏を伝える上で、素晴らしい方法だと思いますが、それだけでは十分ではありません。国際的な会合、フェスティバル、映画でのプレゼンテーション、映像、会議などが必要です。ワークショップもまた、とても重要です。俳優やパフォーマーにも、教えるべきでしょう。大野一雄は以前私にこう言いました。「ダンサーが舞踏の形を真似るのではなく、彼ら自身の魂から踊り始めれば、舞踏は残り続けるでしょう」。

向 雲太郎 Kumotaro Mukai

舞踏家 | 洲本（日本）| 舞踏家集団デュ社 | 25年

Butoh Dancer | Sumoto (Japan) | The Butoh Tribe Duex Shrine | 25 years

「舞踏?プレゼンテーション・ショウ」
Photo: bozzo

duexshrine.com

Q1 舞踏をはじめたきっかけ
大駱駝艦からの勧誘。

Q2 舞踏の魅力
魅力は計り知れないが、一つ挙げるとすれば“常識を疑う”ということ。自分のそして社会の常識を疑って既成概念をぶち壊すのです。

Q3 アーカイヴについて
映像に本質は映らないのだとしたら、身体芸術を残すことは難しく観た人の記憶の中に残っていけばそれで良いのかもしれない。記録ということだけでいえば、映像や写真を残して共有するのは可能だし必要であると思う。

Q1 Reason for Starting Butoh
By invitation from Dairakudakan.

Q2 Attraction to Butoh
It's impossible to measure my impression, but if I were to give one it would be that it “betrays common sense”. It betrays both personal and society's common sense, and breaks preconceptions.

Q3 On Archiving
In terms of capturing truth on camera, I think it's difficult to preserve performing arts and it's probably fine for it to be left in the memories of those who saw it. In terms of simply keeping a record, I think it's both possible and necessary to take photos and films and share these.

長岡ゆり Yuri Nagaoka

舞踏家・振付家 | 東京（日本） | Dance Medium（主宰） | 30年

Butoh Dancer, Choreographer | Tokyo (Japan) | Dance Medium (Artistic Director) | 30 years

Dance Medium舞踏公演「見えない森2019」より

https://www.dancemedium.net/

Q1 舞踏をはじめたきっかけ
バレエをやっていた中学生の時に母から見せられた土方巽の写真に興味を持ち、高校生から舞踏公演を見に行っていた。その後20代で一人で独自に始めた。

Q2 舞踏の魅力
どんなに緻密な訓練を積み重ねても新たな課題が生まれてくることで、飽きない。また、自分の身体や魂、知性のレベルの変化によっても　踊る中で日々発見があること。

Q3 アーカイヴについて
優れた作品を世界中で公演できるようなサポート作りと、ワークショップを広く行うことによって人々の理解を深めること。ビデオ、文章などの記録保存。などの情報発信により、後進を育てること。

Q1 Reason for Starting Butoh
I became interested in a photo of Tatsumi Hijikata my mother showed me while doing ballet as a junior high school student, and saw Butoh performances from when I was in high school. I started my own solo work in my 20s.

Q2 Attraction to Butoh
I never get bored, because no matter how much precise training is accumulated, there will always be new challenges. Also there are discoveries made every day through dancing that depend on the shifting levels of the body, soul and intelligence.

Q3 On Archiving
Create support to put on excellent performances all over the world, and deepen peoples' understanding by doing workshops in many places. Keep record with videos and essays etc. Foster renewal through such sharing of information.

中西晶大 Masahiro Nakanishi

劇作家・演出家・ディレクター・ダンサー | 東京（日本） | Tokyo Diamond | 12年

Playwright, Director, Dancer | Tokyo (Japan) | Tokyo Diamond | 12 years

Q1 舞踏をはじめたきっかけ
言葉の行き詰まり。体の不自由さ。心のゆきばの無さ。石井満隆の言葉と佇まい。

Q2 舞踏の魅力
そのひと、それぞれの姿が眺められるところ。また、現世にないものを経験できる可能性。

Q3 アーカイヴについて
表面的な記録は写真や映像に任せ、内面的な記録は語りつぐしかないと思う。生の記憶が残っているうちに音声データをどんどん残すのが良いかと。

Q1 Reason for Starting Butoh
Speechlessness. Immobility. Nowhere else for the heart to go. Mitsutaka Ishii's words and presence.

Q2 Attraction to Butoh
That the presence of each individual can be seen. Also, the potential to experience something not of this world.

Q3 On Archiving
For recording the external, take photos and films; for the internal, I think all that can be done is to teach. It would be good to collect more audio data while people are alive.

写真日和 × Tokyo Diamond 作品

https://masahirock.wixsite.com/tokyodiamonddance

Q1　Please tell us how you became involved with Butoh?
Q2　What attracted you to Butoh?
Q3　As a performative art inherently involving the physical body, how can Butoh be preserved? Or, is this even possible?

Q1 あなたが舞踏をはじめたきっかけを教えて下さい。
Q2 あなたにとって舞踏の魅力は何ですか？
Q3 身体芸術である舞踏は、どのようにしたら残すことができるでしょうか？

Anna Ventura Natsuki

Choreographer, Director | Paris (France), La Bisbal (Spain) | L'Universelle Ilustre Dance Company, FPOCI (Fund for the Preservation of the Work of Carlotta Ikeda) | 29 years

振付家・演出家 | パリ（フランス）・ラビスバル（スペイン） | L'Universelle Ilustre Dance Company・FPOCI（カルロッタ池田の作品を保存する財団） | 29年

Genius Loci show, tribute to Carlotta Ikeda.
Photo: Jacques Crenn

http://universelleillustree.free.fr

Q1 Reason for Starting Butoh
As a student of dance in 1986 I attended a performance of Carlotta Ikeda's *UTT* show in Barcelona, Spain, and I identify it as a form of dance that inspires my future journey. Collaborates with the company Ariadone of C Ikeda 1998 - 2014. Founder of the FPOCI in 2016.

Q2 Attraction to Butoh
Artistic curiosity. Connivence and community of ideas with a woman dance artist. The buto of Carlotta Ikeda.

Q3 On Archiving
The immaterial arts are transmitted by contamination, from generation to generation, of the different artists who represent it. The body, the flesh, are the incarnation of thought. Theorization, the archives give words to the flesh and make it possible to disseminate this information to those who do not practice this language. technology and means of communication facilitate the movement of ideas. Here lies the interest of archives and its disclosure.

Q1 舞踏をはじめたきっかけ
1986年にダンスの学生だった時に、スペインのバルセロナで行われたカルロッタ池田の公演『UTT』を観て、私の将来に影響を与えるダンスだと確信しました。1998年～2014年に、カルロッタ池田率いるアリアドーネの會とコラボレーションを行い、2016年にFPOCIを創立しました。

Q2 舞踏の魅力
芸術的な好奇心。女性のダンスアーティストと共謀し、共同体を作ること。カルロッタ池田の舞踏。

Q3 アーカイヴについて
無形の文化は一つの世代から次の世代へと、それを表現するアーティストが接触し合うことで、伝えられます。身体、あるいは生身の肉体は、思想が具現化されたものです。理論化とアーカイヴは、肉体に言葉を与え、舞踏を実践しない人々にも情報を広めることを可能にします。テクノロジーとコミュニケーションの手段は、思想のムーヴメントを容易にします。この点において、アーカイヴの存在と、アーカイヴを公開することのメリットがあると思います。

Marco Nektan

Performance Artist | Belgrade (Serbia) | Jugoslovenska Kinoteka | 12 years

パフォーマンスアーティスト | ベオグラード（セルビア） | ユーゴスラビア・フィルムアーカイヴ | 12年

Q1 Reason for Starting Butoh
In the beginning of 2000s I saw some performances and I was so impressed, so I take workshops and start researching. Since 2012, I dropped all other art form, and I am full dedicated to Butoh practice.

Q2 Attraction to Butoh
Engagement of full body, soul and universe in creation. No limitations, true freedom, and possibilities of endless source of inspiration and tools. Idea that all things in universe is beautiful and no judgement in it.

Q3 On Archiving
If we use principle of Performance art, we can preserve with documentation – catalogues, posters from events, photo and video documentation, artist notations (libretto for performances), critics, written impressions by audience, artifacts (props, costumes...), artist statement and oral stories.

Q1 舞踏をはじめたきっかけ
2000年代の初頭に、私は幾つかの公演を観て感銘を受けたので、ワークショップを受けてリサーチを開始しました。2012年より、他の全てのアート活動を止めて、舞踏の稽古だけに専念することにしました。

Q2 舞踏の魅力
身体と魂、宇宙の全てを創作に結びつけられること。限界が無いこと。真の自由。そして限りないインスピレーションの源泉とツールの数々。宇宙の全ての事象は美しく、その中に批判するものは無いという考え方です。

Q3 アーカイヴについて
もし私たちがパフォーマンスアートの原則に従うならば、イベントのカタログやポスター、写真や映像、アーティストによる譜面（パフォーマンスの台本）、批評、観客からの反応、舞台に使用する物（小道具や衣装など）、アーティスト・ステイトメントや口承などの記録物によって舞踏を残すことができると思います。

Patient 418 (Japanese Serbian Film Festival) 2019.
Photo: Igor Madjinca

http://nektanart.com/

大橋可也 | Kakuya Ohashi

舞踏家｜東京（日本）｜一般社団法人大橋可也&ダンサーズ（代表理事・芸術監督）｜25年

Butoh Dancer | Tokyo (Japan) | Kakuya Ohashi and Dancers (Representative, Artistic Director) | 25 years

「The Lustrous」ショーイングより
Photo: Kiyoharu Mochizuki

http://dancehardcore.com

Q1 舞踏をはじめたきっかけ
自分自身のパフォーマンス作品をつくるために舞踏を学ぼうと思ったため。

Q2 舞踏の魅力
舞踏の創作過程には人間を捉えなおし再定義することができる可能性があると思います。

Q3 アーカイヴについて
舞踏の創作過程に影響を受けたアーティストが活動を続けることだと思います。

Q1 Reason for Starting Butoh
I thought studying Butoh would help create my own performances.

Q2 Attraction to Butoh
I think the creative process of Butoh provides the opportunity to reclaim and redefine human beings.

Q3 On Archiving
I think this is the continuing work of artists who have been influenced by the creative process of Butoh.

Lori Ohtani

Dance Teacher, Butoh Artist | Honolulu (USA) | Tangentz Performance Group | 31 years

ダンス教師・舞踏家｜ホノルル（アメリカ合衆国）｜Tangentz Performance Group｜31年

dancing in concrete forest….
Photo: Franco Salmoiraghi

www.butoh.net

Q1 Reason for Starting Butoh
Butoh began with Cheryl Flaharty's company Iona Pear from 1989-1994. I left in 1994 to form Tangentz (Performance Group) with my husband. I concentrated on learning the roots of where the Butoh form originated and to learn from Butoh Masters that were closely affiliated with the art form.

Q2 Attraction to Butoh
An initial connection to the visual images that butoh created. There is a wonderful layering of meaning. Very deep and abstract. A similar essence that my visual arts background also contained, however, Butoh also crossed over to all other forms of art as it was all encompassing.

Q3 On Archiving
Ongoing digital archiving, oral history, writings and research. However, to really preserve an actual documentation of a Butoh performance it does become static and ceases to lose the "aliveness" of the form. I don't think it is possible to acquire the total experience if one were not present on that day, date, time, etc…

Q1 舞踏をはじめたきっかけ
1989年から1994年の間、Cheryl Flahartyのカンパニー Inona Pear に在籍していた時に舞踏を始めました。1994年にカンパニーを去り、パフォーマンスグループTangentzを夫とともに立ち上げました。舞踏の型がどこから生まれたのか、その起源を、舞踏の技術にとても精通した師から学ぶことに集中しました。

Q2 舞踏の魅力
舞踏が生み出した視覚イメージに最初に惹かれました。素晴らしい意味の層が作られています。とても深く、抽象的です。もともと私がやっていた視覚芸術にも似たような要素が含まれていたのですが、舞踏は他の全ての芸術様式を越境し、包含します。

Q3 アーカイヴについて
現在進められているデジタルアーカイヴ、オーラルヒストリー、文字による記録やリサーチは必要です。しかし、舞踏の公演の記録を実際に残すと、それは静的なものになり、舞踏の「生き生きとした」要素が失われてしまいます。その日、その時間に立ち会っていなければ、総合的な経験を得ることは不可能だと思います。

Q1 Please tell us how you became involved with Butoh?
Q2 What attracted you to Butoh?
Q3 As a performative art inherently involving the physical body, how can Butoh be preserved? Or, is this even possible?

精神のリレー 2019

A Spiritual Relay 2019

大橋可也
Kakuya Ohashi

Photo: GO

僕は舞踏を和栗由紀夫さんから学びました。和栗さんに出会う前にも舞踏のワークショップに参加したこともありますし、他の舞踏家の作品に出演したこともありますが、「学んだ」といえるのは和栗さんからだけです。
現在、僕は大橋可也&ダンサーズとして振付作品の制作を中心とした活動をおこなっていますが、その活動は「舞踏」であるという認識はありません。
しかしながら、僕たちが用いている振付の方法は和栗さんから受け継いだ「舞踏譜の舞踏」の方法から受け継いだものだと考えています。「土方巽の舞踏譜」と呼ばれることが多い舞踏譜ですが、実際に舞踏譜を書いたのは土方に振り付けられたダンサー（弟子たち）であり、書き記した本人の解釈をもってはじめて振付の記録として成立するものです。僕が学んだ舞踏譜も和栗由紀夫の解釈にもとづくものであり、僕は「和栗由紀夫の舞踏譜」として受け止めています。
では、僕たちは「舞踏譜の舞踏」から何を受け継いでいるのか。
それは、テキストを介して世界を身体に取り入れ、自分自身をつくり変えること（を目指すこと）です。
僕たちは日常生活を過ごすなかで、社会から定められた「私」としての役割をこなし、その役割に沿った振る舞いをおこなっています。日常から自由であるはずの舞台空間においても、「私」から自由ではないと感じます。どんなに技巧を凝らしたダンスであれ、どんなに趣向を凝らした演出の作品であれ、そこに登場する人間はその人自身あるいは外部によって決められた人格（キャラクターという「私」）から離れられてはいない、そのように感じるのです。
「私」から逸脱しようという試みは、ポストモダンダンスなど多くの現代芸術でおこなわれてきました。しかしながら、

I studied Butoh under Yukio Waguri. Before I encountered Waguri, I had been participating in dance workshops and also appeared in works by other dancers, but in terms of actually learning something, Yukio Waguri was my only teacher.
I'm currently active with Kakuya Ohashi & Dancers, primarily focusing on producing my own choreographic works, though what we're doing could not be considered as "Butoh."
That said, however, I do consider that the choreographic methods we use derive from the *Butoh-fu no Butoh* (Notational Butoh) method, which we picked up from Waguri. This particular method is often referred to as "Hijikata Tatsumi's Butoh-fu", but the dancers who notated this method were actually dancers or disciples for whom Hijikata choreographed, and upon whose interpretation the first documented annotation for this choreographic method was based. The Butoh-fu I studied is also based on Yukio Waguri's interpretation, and I personally regard it as "Yukio Waguri's Butoh-fu."
So, in answer to the question of what we've learnt from Butoh-fu, I would say that it involves absorbing the world into the body by means of texts and with the intention of transforming oneself.
In our day-to-day lives, each and every one of us plays the role of "I" as determined by society and we behave in accordance with that role. Even on stage, a space that should be free from the constraints of everyday life, it doesn't feel as though one is liberated from this imposed role of "I." It as though irrespective of how skillful the dance is or how elaborate the direction is, the person we behold appearing in front of us on stage is not uncoupled from that imposed person or personality, in other words the "character" called "I."
In modern art, numerous attempts have been made to deviate from the "I," as can be seen in postmodern dance. Many of those attempts, however, seem to start by modifying the framework. I have come to understand the

大橋可也

振付家。一般社団法人大橋可也&ダンサーズ代表理事。1967年生れ。1993-1997年、和栗由紀夫に舞踏を師事。1999年、大橋可也&ダンサーズを結成、振付作品の発表を開始する。主な作品に秋葉原連続殺傷事件に想を得た『帝国、エアリアル』(2008年)、飛浩隆の長編SF小説を題材にした『グラン・ヴァカンス』、リサーチから振付を制作するプロジェクト「ザ・ワールド」(2014-2019年)がある。

Kakuya Ohashi

Choreographer. Director of Kakuya Ohashi & Dancers. Born in 1967, from 1993 to 1997, Ohashi studied Butoh under Yukio Waguri. In 1999, he founded Kakuya Ohashi & Dancers and started presenting his choreographic works, notably *Empire; Aerial*(2008), inspired by Hirataka Tobi's feature-length SF novel *Les Grandes Vacances*, and *The World*, a choreographic project that was the cumulative result of research. (2014-2019).

その多くの試みは枠組みを変えることから始まっているように思います。

「舞踏譜の舞踏」のアプローチは内側から自分自身をつくり変えようというものだと理解しています。そのためのツールがテキストなのです。ある世界の事象に対してテキストを与える(土方巽は絵画などを参照することも多かったですが)ことによって、その事象の再解釈、再定義をおこなうことができるようになる。再解釈する方法には文脈からの逸脱や意図的な誤読もあります。再解釈し再定義した事象を身体に取り入れることで、世界と「私」との関係は書き換えられ、「私」から逸脱した身体が出現する。

このとき、「私」は「私自身」から自由になるといえるのではないでしょうか。もちろん、それは一時的なものであり、舞台が終われば過ぎ去っていくものかもしれません。しかし、この「舞踏譜の舞踏」の振付から得られる体験は、今の社会に生きづらさを感じる僕たちが生きていくうえで必要なものだと思うのです。そして、その体験が僕たちだけのものでなく、「舞踏譜の舞踏」を受け継いだこれからの作品から生まれることを願っています。

Butoh-fu approach as a means to transform oneself from the inside out. The tool to achieve such a transformation is the written word. Applying the written word or texts to phenomena in our surroundings—Tatsumi Hijikata, for example, would often refer to paintings and so forth—enables us to reinterpret and redefine those phenomena. Reinterpretative methods can also deviate from a given context and be misread intentionally. By incorporating the reinterpreted and redefined phenomena into the body, the relationship between the outer world and "I" is rewritten, and a physical presence that deviates from "I" emerges. When this happens, one could say that the "I" has been uncoupled from "oneself." Naturally, it's a transitory phase; it may well dissipate after the performer has exited the stage. Yet, I feel that the experience acquired from availing of Butoh-fu's choreographic methods is indispensable to overcome the challenges we face to live in contemporary society. I hope that this experience will not only benefit us, but that the *Butoh-fu no Butoh* we have inherited will also emerge in future works.

和栗由紀夫|Yukio Waguri (1952-2017)

1972年より土方巽に師事し、数多くの作品に参加。90年から和栗由紀夫+好善社を主宰し、群舞やソロを発表する。98年、CD-ROM『舞踏花伝』を出版、舞踏譜を用いた土方巽独自の作舞法に焦点をあて、舞踏再評価の契機を作った。早稲田大学や慶応義塾大学で教鞭を執るほか、海外での舞踏の指導にも力を入れていた。

Studied with Tatsumi Hijikata from 1972 and appeared in a number of his works. Founded Yukio Waguri + Kozensha in 1990 and made solo and group performances. Released a CD, "Butoh Kaden" in 1998 using Butoh-fu (notations) focussing on Tatsumi Hijikata's unique dance, and created an opportunity to re-evaluate Butoh. Taught at Waseda and Keio Universities as well as teaching Butoh abroad.

Q1 あなたが舞踏をはじめたきっかけを教えて下さい。
Q2 あなたにとって舞踏の魅力は何ですか?
Q3 身体芸術である舞踏は、どのようにしたら残すことができるでしょうか?

岡 登志子 | Oka Toshiko

振付家・ダンサー | 兵庫(日本) | アンサンブル・ゾネ | 26年

Choreographer, Dancer | Hyogo (Japan) | Ensemble Sonne | 26 years

「緑のテーブル2017」2017年3月初演/神戸アートビレッジセンター於

http://ensemblesonne.com/index.html

Q1 舞踏をはじめたきっかけ
大野一雄さん、慶人さんの舞台を見て感動し、興味を持ったこと。

Q2 舞踏の魅力
身体そのものが作品となって生きていることを直接的に表現できること。

Q3 アーカイヴについて
踊りそのものを残すには限界があると思うが、映像や資料で舞踏の本質を探求しその精神を受け継ぎ、今の価値観によって作品を創り出すことで、残すことができないかと思っている。

Q1 Reason for Starting Butoh
I was impressed by Kazuo and Yoshito Ohno's performance, and took an interest.

Q2 Attraction to Butoh
The body itself becomes an artwork, and its aliveness is expressed directly.

Q3 On Archiving
There is a limit to how much of a dance can be preserved, but I think the essence of Butoh can be explored and its spirit inherited through film and documentation, and so it can continue through the creation of current works.

奥村万琵 | Okumura Bambi

舞踏家 | 東京(日本) | 7年

Butoh Dancer | Tokyo (Japan) | 7 years

Q1 舞踏をはじめたきっかけ
役者として活動していた時に舞踏をしている方と知り合い、稽古に参加したこと。

Q2 舞踏の魅力
人間の体から醸し出されるエネルギーや、体を越えて漂ってくる香りや景色が広がったりするなどの無限の空間を感じられるところ。また、良い踊りは人を癒せると思う。

Q3 アーカイヴについて
現実的にどうしたらいいか分からないが、踊り手は昔の身体技術や精神を学び尊重しつつ、かつ自分がパイオニアであること。また、その時その場で踊ることに感謝し責任を持つこと。

Q1 Reason for Starting Butoh
While working as an actor I became acquainted with someone doing Butoh, and participated in a class.

Q2 Attraction to Butoh
That infinite space that can be felt, the exuding energy coming off the human body, the transcending scents, and the way it expands one's perspective. I also think that good dances can heal.

ウユニ塩湖にて

http://zekkeibutoh.mods.jp/

Q3 On Archiving
I'm not sure how to manifest this into reality, but dancers should respect and study old physical skills and philosophy while being pioneers. We should also be thankful and responsible for the time and place in which we dance.

凡例 肩書き | 活動拠点 | 所属団体 | 活動年数

Reference Occupation | Base | Affiliation | Years of Activity

奥村 薫 | Kaoru Okumura

シアトル（アメリカ合衆国）| DAIPANbutoh Collective | 11年

Seattle (USA) | DAIPAN butoh Collective | 11 years

Q1 舞踏をはじめたきっかけ
1993年、アスベスト館のワークショップ「アイコンとしての身体」（未経験者可）に参加して。

Q2 舞踏の魅力
非日常の世界を現出させる力と、理由や意味づけを超えたところにある感動を持ち来る可能性。It's a mystery.

Q3 アーカイヴについて
舞踏の写真や映像は、それ自体で強いインパクトを与える。だが、場を共にした際の、異界を垣間見させる力は格別である。残された作品は既に独自のものであり、導入編、あるいは過ぎ去った時へのオマージュであろう。

Q1 Reason for Starting Butoh
I participated in the *Body as an Icon* (beginners) workshop at Asbestos-kan in 1993.

Q2 Attraction to Butoh
Its power to present the world's extraordinariness, and impress beyond reason or meaning. It's a mystery.

Q3 On Archiving
Butoh photographs and films have a strong impact. But its power to give a glimpse into a different world when experienced in person is exceptional. The preserved materials are originals in themselves, as introductions, or an homage to the past.

「太古の夢」
Photo: David Joshua Jennings @roaddiaries

http://kaoruokumura.com/
https://www.facebook.com/kaoru.okumura

大村憲子 | Noriko Omura

フリーランスダンス講師 | 高知（日本）| 舞踏土佐派 | 6年

Freelance Dance Instructor | Kochi (Japan) | Butoh Tosaha | 6 years

Q1 舞踏をはじめたきっかけ
ダンス歴50年を経て、桂勘らと出会い 舞踏土佐派設立。1971年「天象儀館」荒戸源次郎主宰に入団、田村一平、中島夏らの振付で踊り、麿赤兒らとの交流もベースにあると思う。

Q2 舞踏の魅力
私含め土佐派メンバーが本来の自分を発見し、自他の特異性を認め、解されていくのが分かる。

Q3 アーカイヴについて
土方巽、大野一雄に始まる舞踏だが、日本各地で様々な取組がなされており、その多様性は目を見張る。京都、福岡、岩手他の多様な舞踏家達。隈なく種を蒔き続けた方々により日本以上に海外の舞踏人口は多い。それらを残す今回の書籍の意義は大きい。

Q1 Reason for Starting Butoh
After dancing for 50 years, I met Katsura Kan and established Butoh Tosaha. In 1971 I joined Genjiro Arato's Tenshogikan and danced in works choreographed by Ippei Tamura and Natsu Nakajima etc, and also had exchanges with Akaji Maro.

Q2 Attraction to Butoh
Seeing the Tosaha members, including myself, discover their true selves, and recognise and understand each person's uniqueness.

Q3 On Archiving
Although it was Tatsumi Hijikata and Kazuo Ohno who started Butoh, there are many continued efforts all over Japan. There are Butoh dancers in Kyoto, Fukuoka and Iwate among others. And thanks to those who planted the seeds of Butoh overseas, there are now more who practice it abroad than in Japan. I think the collection in this book is hugely significant.

公演「月と山と精霊と」2017

omura.koha@gmail.com

Q1 Please tell us how you became involved with Butoh?
Q2 What attracted you to Butoh?
Q3 As a performative art inherently involving the physical body, how can Butoh be preserved? Or, is this even possible?

Q1 あなたが舞踏をはじめたきっかけを教えて下さい。
Q2 あなたにとって舞踏の魅力は何ですか？
Q3 身体芸術である舞踏は、どのようにしたら残すことができるでしょうか？

Cécile Raymond

Dancer, Choreographer, Dance Teacher | France | 19 years

ダンサー・振付家・ダンス教師 | フランス | 19年

Q1 Reason for Starting Butoh
I was a contemporary dance student and was interested in Japanese language. I discovered Japanese culture and was then curious to see what the Japanese contemporary dance area looked like. That's how I came to discover butoh. I read a lot about butoh before doing my first workshop.

Q2 Attraction to Butoh
To abandon intentional, conventional, codified movements and go back deep inside your body and let it resonate outside. To find authentic and singular movements in response to our surroundings. Human and not societal movements.

Q3 On Archiving
By transmission (workshops), video captation, texts and notes relating butoh research (teaching, creation, audience feelings...).

Q1 舞踏をはじめたきっかけ
私はコンテンポラリーダンスを学ぶ学生で、日本語にも興味を持っていました。日本文化を発見してから、日本のコンテンポラリーダンスがどのようなものか、非常に興味を持ちました。そのような経緯で、舞踏を見つけました。最初のワークショップを受ける前に、舞踏について沢山の資料を読みました。

Q2 舞踏の魅力
意図的で、型にはまった、コード化された動きを捨て、自分の身体の深く内側に戻り、それをまた身体の外側に共鳴させること。本物の、この世に一つしかない動きを環境に対する反応の中で見つけ出すこと。人間的であり、社会的ではないムーヴメント。

Q3 アーカイヴについて
（ワークショップのような）伝承、映像記録、（教え、創作、観客の反応などの）舞踏のリサーチに関するテキストとノート。

Body in turmoil.
Photo: Cécile Dégremont

http://cietransit.weebly.com

Katharina Roll

Dance, Mime and Performance Artist | Germany | 15 years

ダンス・マイム・パフォーマンスアーティスト | ドイツ | 15年

don't come on!, solo performance

https://www.facebook.com/katharina.roll.1069

Q1 Reason for Starting Butoh
After a classical dance education I decided to search for skills that allowed me to go inside, to follow the body's inherent feelings and emotions. A TV report about Butoh caught my attention in 2004. The images moved me unexpectedly and since then I have been trying to discover the methodology of Butoh.

Q2 Attraction to Butoh
Butoh is not afraid to include the full range of aliveness. Regardless of "ability and knowledge" the focus is more of "sensibility", "truths". The idea of being "real", "authentic", creates a specific body. It's a body that easily takes other bodies with them by not being judged by conventional standards.

Q3 On Archiving
To preserve the origins of Butoh, it is important to archive existing film and texts and make it accessible to the public. Passing on the original methodology of Butoh from one generation to the next. Although Butoh is more about an individual journey, documenting rehearsals, improvisations, performances can be a way of preservation.

Q1 舞踏をはじめたきっかけ
クラシックダンスの教育を受けた後に、身体の内側に向かい、その欲求に従いながら、身体固有の感覚や感情に向き合うことのできる技術を探し求めようと心に決めました。パントマイムから始めた私は、2004年に舞踏を紹介する短いテレビ放送に釘付けになりました。その映像は予想外に私の心を強く動かし、それからは舞踏の方法論を、実践のなかで継続して探求し続けています。

Q2 舞踏の魅力
舞踏は生き生きとした感性を全て包み込むことを恐れていません。「能力や知識」や高度な技術にとらわれずに、舞踏は「感覚」や「真実」に対し、他のダンスパフォーマンスよりも重点を置いています。「本物」である、または「正真正銘」といった概念は、一つの身体性を形成します。それは因習的な基準によって判断されることなく、容易に他の身体を巻き込むことのできる身体です。

Q3 アーカイヴについて
舞踏の起源を残すためには、現存する映像やテキストをアーカイヴし、一般公開することが重要だと思います。舞踏の方法論を一つの世代から次へと受け渡すことも大切です。舞踏は個人的な旅のようなものですが、稽古や即興、公演を記録することは、後世に残すための一つの方法となり得るでしょう。

Jordan Rosin

Director, Choreographer, Researcher, Teacher | USA | The Ume Group (Artistic Director) | 10 years

演出家・振付家・研究者・教師 | アメリカ合衆国 | The Ume Group（主宰） | 10年

The Ume Group's *Facet* with Yoshiko "Yokko" Usami, 2013.
Photo: Anton Martynov

www.jordanrosin.com

Q1 Reason for Starting Butoh
I started studying Butoh in 2010 with Joan Laage in Seattle. I became interested in Butoh as a style of physical theatre, which I incorporated into my work as a director/choreographer. *Butoh Electra* was my undergraduate thesis which launched my company, The Ume Group in New York City.

Q2 Attraction to Butoh
Originally, it was the grotesque and alien qualities of Sankai Juku & Dairakudakan which attracted me to Butoh. As I began to study the form myself, I started to value its poetry, expressiveness, and emphasis on the uniqueness and beauty of each individual practitioner.

Q3 On Archiving
Dance Archive Network and Hijikata Tatsumi Archive are doing great work to organize and increase access to original photographs, videos, and writings pertaining to the origin of Butoh. However, another important way that the Butoh must be preserved is through direct transmission of lineage teachings from experienced practitioners who acknowledge the inherent paradox that such a personal dance cannot be taught.

Q1 舞踏をはじめたきっかけ
2010年にシアトルで、ジョン・ラーグの下で舞踏を学び始めました。フィジカルシアターの一種として舞踏に興味を持ち始め、演出家／振付家としての私の作品に取り入れるようになりました。大学で学部論文「Butoh Electra」を書いたことをきっかけに、自分のカンパニーThe Ume Groupをニューヨークで立ちげました。

Q2 舞踏の魅力
元々は、山海塾や大駱駝艦のグロテスクでエイリアン的な質に舞踏の魅力を感じていました。自分で舞踏の型を学び始めると、その詩的要素や表現力、それぞれの表現者の個性や美しさを重要視することなどに、共感を持ち始めました。

Q3 アーカイヴについて
ダンスアーカイヴ構想と土方巽アーカイヴは、舞踏の起源に関わるオリジナルの写真や映像、書物をまとめ、アクセスを増やしている点で、優れた事業を行なっていると思います。しかし、舞踏が残されるためにもう一つ重要な方法は、舞踏のようなパーソナルなダンスは人から人に教えることができない、という矛盾を認識している経験豊かな実践者が、技術体系の継承を直々に行うということです。

Marie-Gabrielle Rotie

University Lecturer, Choreographer, Performer, Artist, Producer | Cambridge, London, Wales (UK) | Goldsmiths, University of London | 28 years

大学講師・振付家・パフォーマー・アーティスト・プロデューサー | ケンブリッジ・ロンドン・ウェールズ（イギリス） | Goldsmiths, University of London | 28年

Q1 Reason for Starting Butoh
I was searching for a dance that was rigorous but also creative, and accidentally discovered Butoh. I established Butoh UK in 1997 and have been very active organising over 70 workshops in London and Wales with many teachers and several Butoh Festivals.

Q2 Attraction to Butoh
I originally trained as a painter, and am attracted to the embodiment of visual images, and the emphasis on the imagination, but also material body of the dancer. Butoh offers dancers a holistic, metaphysical and phenomenological approach to thinking through the body and also how dance connects to daily life.

Q3 On Archiving
Butoh strictly exists beyond any material archive, and is transmitted through the bodies of those who have studied. Butoh exists as an idea, as a transmission of possibility. The archive is always a ghost of itself, an impossibility. However, the attempts to preserve videos and writings of historic practitioners is important, to give context.

www.embodiedimages.space
www.butohuk.com

Black Mirror, solo.
Photo: Rachael Cherry

Q1 舞踏をはじめたきっかけ
苛烈でありながら創造的なダンスを探し求めている時に、偶然に舞踏を見つけました。1997年にButoh UKを創立し、多くの舞踏家と共に、70回以上のワークショップと幾つかの舞踏フェスティバルを、ロンドンとウェールズで積極的に開催してきました。

Q2 舞踏の魅力
元々は画家としての訓練を受けていました。舞踏の視覚イメージを具現化するところと、想像力に重点を置くところと、そしてダンサーの身体を物質的に捉えるところに魅了されています。舞踏は身体を通じて思考するための全体論的、形而上学的、現象学的なアプローチをダンサーに提案します。そしてダンスがどのように日常生活と繋がっているかということ。

Q3 アーカイヴについて
舞踏はあらゆる物質的アーカイヴを超えて存在し、舞踏を吸収した身体を通して伝承されるものです。舞踏は概念として、そして可能性の伝達として存在します。アーカイヴは常に、それ自体の幽霊、つまり不可能性のようなものです。しかし、歴史に残すべき舞踏家の映像や文章は、舞踏に文脈を付与するために重要です。

Q1 あなたが舞踏をはじめたきっかけを教えて下さい。
Q2 あなたにとって舞踏の魅力は何ですか？
Q3 身体芸術である舞踏は、どのようにしたら残すことができるでしょうか？

酒井直之 | Naoyuki Sakai

ダンサー・振付家 | 東京（日本） | Co. 山田うん | 8年

Dancer, Choreographer | Tokyo (Japan) | Co.YAMADAUN | 8 years

酒井直之「stand」2019 画像提供：スパイラル

https://naoyukis330.wixsite.com/naoyukisakai330

Q1 舞踏をはじめたきっかけ
細江英公の『鎌鼬』や森下隆『土方巽：肉体の舞踏誌：写真集』などを始めとする写真群とその歴史を知ったことがきっかけです。

Q2 舞踏の魅力
汚いもの、醜いものこそ美しいと言える思想だと思います。そこには、広く人類を包み込む懐を感じます。

Q3 アーカイヴについて
残せる部分と残せない部分があると思います。しかし、残せる部分から私が舞踏に興味を持ち、新たな表現に向かえたように、アーカイヴとその時代の表現が重なることで、真の意味での「舞踏」が生きると信じています。

Q1 Reason for Starting Butoh
Photo books such as Eikoh Hosoe's *Kamaitachi* and Takashi Morishita's *Tatsumi Hijikata: Rebellion of the Body: Photography*, and the history I learnt from them.

Q2 Attraction to Butoh
I think it is to do with the idea of being able to call dirty, ugly things beautiful. There is a nostalgia there that speaks to many.

Q3 On Archiving
I think there are parts that can be preserved and parts that can't. However, in the same way that I came to find a new form of expression having developed an interest in Butoh from those parts that can, I believe "Butoh" lives on in a true form through the overlapping of archives and the expressions of those times.

坂本博美 | Hiromi Sakamoto

パーソナルトレーナー・舞踏家 | 東京（日本） | 22年

Personal Trainer, Butoh Dancer | Tokyo (Japan) | 22 years

Q1 舞踏をはじめたきっかけ
過去様々なダンスをしている中で大駱駝艦の方々との共演がきっかけ。

Q2 舞踏の魅力
日本の身体の極みだと思っています。舞踏表現に於いての表現の奥行きは底知れぬ深さをかんじています。地球から宇宙までを内包していると感じます。

Q3 アーカイヴについて
私個人、舞踏を学びたいと思った時に、なかなか情報にありつけずもどかしい思いをしたため日本で稽古場を提供くださっている舞踏家の方々を見られる一覧があり世界中からアクセスできるようになったらもっと開かれた門になるのではないかと思います。残らない可能性としては、今活躍なさっている方々の生の舞踏作品に出会うことのないまま時が経過してしまうことの怖さ、であるような気がしています。

Q1 Reason for Starting Butoh
Performing with people from Dairakudakan while doing other forms of dance.

Q2 Attraction to Butoh
I believe it's the extremity of the Japanese body. The intensity of Butoh expression has an incomprehensible depth. I feel it includes everything from Earth to Space.

Q3 On Archiving
When I started studying Butoh, what I personally found frustrating was a lack of information. I think it would be more accessible if there was a list of all Butoh dancers in Japan that offered classes, which could be accessed from anywhere in the world. As for the possibility of it not being preserved, I think there is a fear of not being able to see a live Butoh performance by successful performers before their time passes.

いけ花と舞踏2019

Instagram: hiromi.sakamoto
Facebook: 坂本博美

凡例 肩書き | 活動拠点 | 所属団体 | 活動年数
Reference Occupation | Base | Affiliation | Years of Activity

櫻井郁也	Sakurai Ikuya

Dancer | Tokyo (Japan) | Sakurai Ikuya / Cross Section | 26 years

舞踊家 | 東京(日本) | 櫻井郁也/十字舎房 | 26年

櫻井郁也 ルクセンブルク公演『Hakobune (2012)』より

Q1 舞踏をはじめたきっかけ
85年の舞踏懺悔録集成や土方巽さんの東北歌舞伎計画を観た。師事していた笠井叡が吉岡実さん逝去直後に舞踏活動を再開する現場を手伝うなか、深く共感し影響を受けた。

Q2 舞踏の魅力
未完の思考であること。常に新しくあること。個体を重視すること。多様さが前提にあること。規定できないこと。歴史や地域性や既成文化や思想に依存しないこと。

Q3 アーカイヴについて
記録や資料保存を願う反面、「残す」という意思に付随して「舞踏」の概念規定やジャンル化や方法化への方向も出てくる可能性を危惧します。多様さ多義性をいかに反映して保存してゆくかが論点と思います。

Q1 Reason for Starting Butoh
I went to Butoh Festival '85 and Tatsumi Hijikata's *Tohoku Kabuki Plan*. I felt deeply empathetic and influenced in Kasai Akira's efforts to set up a place for Butoh to continue after the passing of Minoru Yoshioka.

Q2 Attraction to Butoh
It's an incomplete thought. It's always new. It emphasises individuality. Its prerequisite is diversity. It cannot be defined. It doesn't depend on history, place, established culture or thought.

Q3 On Archiving
By recording or saving documentation with the intention to "preserve", I fear that there is an incidental possibility of creating conceptual rules, genre and method of "Butoh". I think the more pressing issue is how to save its diversity and ambiguity.

http://www.cross-section.x0.com/

関 典子	Noriko Seki

ダンサー | 兵庫(日本) | 神戸大学(准教授)・薄井憲二バレエ・コレクション(キュレーター) | 20年

Dancer | Hyogo (Japan) | Kobe University (Professor), Kenji Usui Ballet Collection (Curator) | 20 years

Q1 舞踏をはじめたきっかけ
故・和栗由紀夫氏に、「舞踏とコンテンポラリーダンスの融合を!」と、誘われて。『Labyrinth』『肉体の迷宮』の共同振付、ブラジル・東京公演を行いました。

Q2 舞踏の魅力
想像力を総動員して「動かざるを得ない」状況に身を置くこと。舞踏譜(数多の図版や言葉)を徹底的に想像し体現し尽くすことで、超現実(強度の現実)に至ること。

Q3 アーカイヴについて
ダンサーの存在や動きそのものを残すことはできません。しかし、キュレーター業務で資料を手にする時には、当時の息吹や経てきた時間をまざまざと感じます。この体感と想像力こそ、アーカイヴの鍵だと考えます。

Q1 Reason for Starting Butoh
I was invited by the late Yukio Waguri to "fuse Butoh and contemporary dance!". Co-choreographed *Labyrinth* and *Nikutai no Meikyu*, which were performed in Brazil and Tokyo.

Q2 Attraction to Butoh
Total mobilisation of the imagination to state in which you "can but move". Achieving surreality (stronger reality), through picturing and embodying Butoh-fu (many images and words) thoroughly.

Q3 On Archiving
It is not possible to preserve dancers' existence or movement itself. However as a curator, when I hold archived materials I can feel the breath of the past and passing of time. I think this experience and imagination is the key to archiving.

Photo: Naoya Ikegami

http://www2.kobe-u.ac.jp/~sekinori/

Q1 Please tell us how you became involved with Butoh?
Q2 What attracted you to Butoh?
Q3 As a performative art inherently involving the physical body, how can Butoh be preserved? Or, is this even possible?

Q1 あなたが舞踏をはじめたきっかけを教えて下さい。
Q2 あなたにとって舞踏の魅力は何ですか？
Q3 身体芸術である舞踏は、どのようにしたら残すことができるでしょうか？

Katia Shklyar

Actor, Dancer | Helsinki (Finland) | 5 years

俳優・ダンサー | ヘルシンキ（フィンランド） | 5年

Evol Ralullec (Helsinki Butoh Festival) 2019

www.utouto.fi/

Q1 Reason for Starting Butoh
I found butoh through a workshop held by a butoh artist and teacher Ken Mai, who lives in Helsinki. After that, I took part in longer courses and shorter workshops to learn more. Since then almost every my performance has been strongly inspired by butoh.

Q2 Attraction to Butoh
I experience butoh as a very sincere and raw artistic language, it often goes beyond the performance itself. When I dance butoh I can establish a connection with the audience on the level much deeper than visual or performative, it goes from heart to heart, it involves the whole universe.

Q3 On Archiving
Good quality photographs and video can transmit technical value through visual and auditoryal channels. But it is very hard to transmit the energy, the feeling of the performance, the invisible waves moving between audience and dancer. Perhaps, a combination of video, photo and narration (written or audio recorded) could be the closest way to preserve Butoh dance.

Q1 舞踏をはじめたきっかけ
ヘルシンキに住む舞踏家のケン五月のワークショップを通じて、舞踏に出会いました。それからもっと学びたいと思い、より長いコースや、より短いワークショップなどを受講しました。以降、私の全ての公演は舞踏に強く影響を受けています。

Q2 舞踏の魅力
私は舞踏を、とても誠実で、生々しい芸術言語と感じています。しばしば、舞踏は公演そのものを超える力を持っています。舞踏を踊るときには、視覚的・パフォーマンス的なものよりも深いレベルで観客との繋がりを築くことができます。心から心へと伝わり、宇宙全体を巻き込むことができるのです。

Q3 アーカイヴについて
質の高い写真や映像は、視覚そして聴覚の経路を通じて、技術的な価値を伝えることができます。しかし、公演のエネルギーやフィーリング、ダンサーと観客との間に動く、目に見えない波動を伝えることはとても難しいです。おそらく、映像、写真そしてナレーション（文字あるいは記録された音声）の組み合わせが、舞踏を保存するのに一番近い方法ではないでしょうか。

祖父江洋子 Yoko SOBUE

ダンサー・振付師・ベネッシュノーテーター | パリ（フランス） | Après le silence & Cie | 20年

Dancer, Choreographer, Benesh Notator | Paris (France) | Après le silence & Cie | 20 years

Q1 舞踏をはじめたきっかけ
私は舞踏の実践者ではありません。フランスでは舞踏の影響を受ける人たちに遭遇することが多く、舞踏はコンテンポラリーダンスの一種と考えられている節もあり、舞踏について考えざるを得なかった。

Q2 舞踏の魅力
三途の川、お彼岸、四十九日とか、生と死の間の様な存在。お地蔵さんを見たら手を合わすとか、仏壇に手を合わせる、神社で自然と神様にお祈りをするとか、アニミズム的感覚。

Q3 アーカイヴについて
土方巽や大野一雄が実在しない現在、戦後から時代も変わって、同じ形で継承することは難しい。舞踏はどんどん国際化しているが、舞踏のエッセンスの様なものは残すことができるのでは。

Q1 Reason for Starting Butoh
I am not a Butoh practitioner. In France I encounter many people who are influenced by Butoh, or factions that consider Butoh to be a type of contemporary dance, so I had no choice but to think about Butoh.

Q2 Attraction to Butoh
It exists between life and death, like the Sanzu river, Higan shores, or 49 days after death. Like a form of animism, similar in feeling to praying to *jizo* [Buddhist figurines], family altars, or to the gods and nature at a Shinto shrine.

Q3 On Archiving
In a world without Tatsumi Hijikata and Kazuo Ohno, that has changed a lot since the post-war era, it is difficult to inherit the same form. Butoh continues to grow internationally, but could something of its essence be preserved?

Dans l'ombre du tissu (2017)

http://apreslesilenceetcie.free.fr/

凡例 肩書き | 活動拠点 | 所属団体 | 活動年数
Reference Occupation | Base | Affiliation | Years of Activity

鈴木 仁 | Jin Suzuki

サーカスパフォーマー | 東京・群馬（日本）| 5年

Circus Performer | Tokyo, Gunma (Japan) | 5 years

ジャグリングオムニバス公演「秘密基地vol.10」より
©Tatsuru Someya

jinjinjinsei.com

Q1 舞踏をはじめたきっかけ
最初はただ趣味でジャグリングをしていました。興味が舞台全般に広がっていくうちに、いつしか舞踏に魅せられ、自分の演技も舞踏に近づいていきました。

Q2 舞踏の魅力
飾らないところです。私は私ではない何かになりたい訳でも、より良い自分になりたい訳でもないので。

Q3 アーカイヴについて
影響を受け、また人に影響を与える。そうして繋いで行けば、作品が忘れ去られても、残っていくことになるでしょう。影響を受ける機会が増えるなら、なんでもする価値があると思います。

Q1 Reason for Starting Butoh
At first I was just juggling as a hobby. When my interests in performance in general broadened, I became fascinated by Butoh, and my performances became closer to Butoh.

Q2 Attraction to Butoh
It's not decorative. Even if I want to be something that isn't me, it doesn't mean I want to be a better version of myself.

Q3 On Archiving
Be inspired, and inspire others. If we do so, these connections will remain, even if the works are forgotten. I think it's worth doing anything in order to increase opportunities to be inspired.

髙橋瑞乃 | Mitsuno Takahashi

6児の母・舞踏家 | 福岡（日本）| 舞踏青龍會 | 21年

Mother of 6, Butoh Dancer | Fukuoka (Japan) | Butoh Seiryu-kai | 21 years

Q1 舞踏をはじめたきっかけ
美術の高校を中退後、創作の場を求めて彷徨っていた時期、友人に誘われてパフォーマンスをしたところ、舞踏青龍會のダンサー（山口千春）にスカウトされたことがきっかけ。

Q2 舞踏の魅力
奥深い精神性の探求の記録と、相対を越える秘密の鍵と、冷や汗と滂沱の涙と暴風雨と響き渡る沈黙が魅力です。

Q3 アーカイヴについて
残すことはできます。書籍でも、音映でも、写真でも、あるいは美術作品でも、オリジナルであればそこに意識はしっかり残ります。

Q1 Reason for Starting Butoh
After dropping out of art school I was looking for a creative space when a friend invited me to do a performance, where I was recruited by a Butoh Seiryu-kai dancer (Chiharu Yamaguchi).

Q2 Attraction to Butoh
The profound quest for spirituality, the key to transcending the self, the cold, sweat, tears, storms and resonating silence.

Q3 On Archiving
It is possible to preserve. Whether as documentation, sound, photographs, or even an artwork, if it is an original then the sense of it is well preserved.

第2回京都国際舞踏祭（2019年5月1〜4日）において、作品提出時の画像です。
Photo: Kazuo Yamashita

Facebook：髙橋瑞乃

Q1 Please tell us how you became involved with Butoh?
Q2 What attracted you to Butoh?
Q3 As a performative art inherently involving the physical body, how can Butoh be preserved? Or, is this even possible?

精神のリレー 2019

A Spiritual Relay 2019

高松真樹子
Makiko Takamatsu

Photo: Kohichi Tamauchi

黒いドレスを着た女性が会場の階段奥から降りて来ました。美しく退廃的な空気を身に纏っており、しかし容姿の印象は無くただ影だけ（に見えた）がズルズルっと闇を引きずって、永遠のような目眩む深い闇が降りてきました。
それが師・上杉満代氏をはじめて目にした瞬間の感動でした。

私はそれまでモノクロ16mmフィルムを扱う映像作家でしたが、現実でモノクロームを体感した初めての一瞬でした。こんな事が表現しうるのかと。
それが私の舞踏のはじまりです。
目の前にいるのは一人のダンサーではなく一つの世界。彼女の背後にはまるでスクリーンで映画を観ているかのように風景が拡がり、その世界の質感、触感が明確に伝わってきました。現実の身体から離れた影が、生き生きと別次元に解き放たれたようで、私の身体のなかは喜びに震えました。
舞踏とは何か？— 舞踏する者にとっては自分に一生かける問いであると思いますが、私は「存在が空間を変容させる事」が大前提にあると思っています。
優れた先達の舞踏に共通するのは、流派を問わず、そこに身体が存在するだけで、空間を自在に操り、振動を起こす事。重要なのは、身体と空間が同様にメタモルフォーゼするという部分です。ここが舞踏とダンスの違いなのではないか、と私は思っています。
空間が変容するとは、不可視な現象です。しかし、不可視なものを可視化する事こそが舞踏なのではないでしょうか？それはスピリチュアルな現象ではなく、身体技術を伴うものであると思います。様々な方法で師から伝えられた舞踏の身体技術である、と。
上杉満代氏の師である大野一雄氏は、ミクロとマクロ、

From the back of the venue a woman in a black dress descends the stairwell.
Shadow-like, barely perceptible, imbued with a beautifully decadent air but without the semblance of a shape, she continues coming down and in her wake she trails darkness, a pitch darkness that dazzles like eternity.
That was my first encounter with my mentor Mitsuyo Uesugi.

Until that point, I had been working as a video-artist using monochrome 16mm film, but this was the first time I experienced monochrome in reality. I had to ask myself how was it possible to express oneself in such a way?
And thus began my involvement with Butoh.
What I was beholding in front of me was not a dancer, but rather an entire universe. Behind her, the landscape was expanding as though one was watching a film projected on screen, the universe's texture and tactile sensations clearly conveyed. My body trembled with joy as that shadow slipped away from her "real" body, as though assuming a life of its own, and released into a vibrant dimension.
What is Butoh?—Any Butoh practitioner will wrestle with this question their entire lives, but I think it is based upon the notion that "existence transforms space."
A common feature in all outstanding Butoh performances, irrespective of the performer's affiliations, is how the performer's sheer physical presence freely manipulates space and generates vibrations. What is paramount is that the body as well as space undergo a metamorphosis. Herein lies what I believe to be the critical difference between Butoh and dance.
The transformation of space is an invisible phenomenon. Yet, isn't Butoh the key to rendering invisible things visible? Here, I'm not referring to a spiritual phenomenon, but rather to physical techniques, which Mitsuyo Uesugi transmitted to me in various forms.
Kazuo Ohno, Mitsuyo Uesugi's teacher, was thoroughly convinced that dance comes into being at that intersection

高松真樹子
多摩美大映像学科在学中1998年より土方巽創業のショークラブ「将軍」にてショーダンサーとして働く。2002年より舞踏家・上杉満代氏に師事。現在までソロ公演を中心に活動。2016年よりダンサー名をラヴィから本名の高松真樹子に改名。メタモルフォーゼする身体空間、舞踏における影像身体を追究している。

Makiko Takamatsu
As of 1998, while a student at Tama Art University's Department of Art and Media, I worked as a show dancer at the show club *Shogun* founded by Tatsumi Hijikata. As of 2002 I studied under the Butoh dancer Mitsuyo Uesugi. To date, I have focused on solo performances. In 2016, I changed my assumed stage name "Ravi" to my real name, Makiko Takamatsu. Currently I am pursuing my research on metamorphosing body-space and the image-body as created through Butoh.

個と宇宙の交わる一点に踊りは存在すること、に徹底されていたように思います。その過剰なスケールの振り子。身体が空間に溶けだし、輪郭とともに消失してしまうような踊りは、継承し得ない個的秘儀です。しかし、その極微細な空間把握、即興性において上杉氏は大野氏の完全に継承者であり、かつ全く違う一世一代の舞踏者です。師から影響を受けた思想や技術、それらを世代の違う私が享受し、生み出されたものが第三者としての私という「存在」です。身体のありようは常に現在であり、師から全てを継承するのは不可能ですが、肉体から精神を引き上げる垂直の糸が、師から受け継いできた他者の力であると思います。操り人形の糸のように。
今の時代に幻想という言葉は死んでしまったのかもしれませんが、私にとって幻想こそが真の現実です。幻想のなかを肉体を持って生きられるということが舞踏の喜びです。常識や人間であることに支配された身体の中に、宇宙があり、生き物の歴史があり、闇があり、光があり、私が所有できない「存在」があります。
生き物の普遍的な欲求が舞踏にはあり、時代が変化してもその欲求は「存在」し続けるのだと思います。

where the micro and macro converge, where the individual and the universe intersect, at an excessive level on the pendulum. A dance through which the body melts into the ether and whose contours vanish is a unique secret that cannot be transmitted. While Mitsuyo Uesugi is true descendent of Kazuo Ohno on account of her ultra-fine understanding of space and her improvisational skills, she utterly differs as a Butoh performer.
As somebody from a later generation, I have thoroughly benefited from Mitsuyo Uesugi's ideas and techniques. They impacted me in such a way that my "existence" now manifests itself as that of "an other." While my physical presence constantly manifests itself, some things are absolutely impossible to access, even with my mentor's assistance. The vertical thread that lifts the spirit from my physical body, as though I were a puppet on a string, is none other, however, than that "other's" power I acquired from my mentor.
While nowadays the word "fantasy" might no longer mean anything, fantasy is reality as far as I am concerned. The joy of Butoh consists in being able to inhabit one's body within a fantasy. Within my body, a body steered by common sense and the fact of being human, lives the universe, the history of mankind, darkness and light, even those "existences" I cannot possess.
Butoh encapsulates all living creatures' universal desires, and these desires persist even as the generations change.

上杉満代 | Mitsuyo Uesugi (1950-)

幼少よりクラシック・バレエを学び、谷桃子バレエ団に入団。70年に退団し、大野一雄氏に師事。75年よりソロ活動を開始する。80年、大野一雄のヨーロッパツアーに参加。87-90年、渡仏。舞踏家として上杉貢代を名乗るが、2006年に上杉満代に改名。太田省吾や岡本章等の演劇作品にも出演している。

Studied ballet from a young age and joined the Tani Momoko Ballet company. Resigned in 1970 and went to study with Kazuo Ohno. Began creating solo performances in 1975. Participated in Kazuo Ohno's 1980 Europe tour. Stayed in France 1987-90. Also appeared in works by Shōgo Ōta and Akira Okamoto.

Q1 あなたが舞踏をはじめたきっかけを教えて下さい。
Q2 あなたにとって舞踏の魅力は何ですか？
Q3 身体芸術である舞踏は、どのようにしたら残すことができるでしょうか？

高松真樹子 | Makiko Takamatsu

舞踏家 | 東京（日本） | 18年

Butoh Dancer | Tokyo (Japan) | 18 years

Q1 舞踏をはじめたきっかけ
美大、映像学科卒業後に舞踏家・上杉満代氏の出演していた舞踏公演を観て、まさしく女性が女性であることの踊りだった事と背景に明確な風景が見えた事に感銘を受けた。

Q2 舞踏の魅力
体という最も普遍的な媒体のまま誰しもが可能でそして不可能であるということ。この世に生きながらにして別次元の幻影の世界に息づけること。

Q3 アーカイヴについて
舞踏をアーカイブする事自体が逆説的であるように思えるのですが、舞踏が生まれた時代それが革命の時代だとすれば、それに感銘を受けた個々人がその源泉を探りながら社会と共有できない個の最小単位の革命を起こし続けること。

Q1 Reason for Starting Butoh
After graduating in Art and Media, I saw a Butoh performance by Mitsuyo Uesugi and was impressed by a woman dancing what it is to be a woman, and the clarity with which her surroundings were revealed.

Q2 Attraction to Butoh
That even though the body is the most universal medium, it is possible and impossible for everyone. Breathing in the illusory world of another dimension even while living in this one.

Q3 On Archiving
Although archiving Butoh at all seems somewhat paradoxical, if we see the age in which Butoh was born as an era of revolution, those who are impressed by it may continue the revolution of socially unshareable individualities on the smallest scale by exploring these sources.

Photo: Koichi Tamauchi

Facebook: 高松真樹子
Twitter: 高松真樹子 @laviemonde

田辺知美 | Tomomi Tanabe

助産師 | 東京（日本） | 35年

Midwife | Tokyo (Japan) | 35 years

田辺知美「カリントン」ーアンフォルムからフォルムへ時間と身体を紡ぐ踊りー
2015年スタジオサイプレスにて Photo: Koichi Tamauchi

Q1 舞踏をはじめたきっかけ
20歳頃、生きるのがやや大変な時に土方巽に出合い、「不安や恐怖は自分の内の鳥かごに入れて、大切に飼いなさい」という言葉を頂き、それを支えに身体で自身や世界を確認、探求することから。

Q2 舞踏の魅力
思いがけない領域を体験、汚いものや役に立たないものや病が美しいことになる、価値の逆転。踊ることで自分の中の他者に触れる瞬間。

Q3 アーカイヴについて
先人の残した舞踏という身体芸術を大切にしつつ、新たな領域を模索探求する経過が大事。その在り方を提供（未完成、現在進行形でも）することから、身体に向き合うことの面白さや大切さが伝わると良いと思う。

Q1 Reason for Starting Butoh
When I was 20, going through a difficult time, I met Hijikata Tatsumi who told me to “put your anxieties and fears in a bird cage and keep them precious”, and with this began establishing and exploring myself and the world through my body.

Q2 Attraction to Butoh
Experiencing the unexpected: dirty, useless and weak things become beautiful, a reversal of values. That moment you find something within yourself while dancing.

Q3 On Archiving
While I appreciate that what is left by our Butoh predecessors is precious, the progression of exploring new areas in important. I think it would be good if the fun and value of facing oneself can be passed on by teaching ways to do this (even if it’s incomplete or unfinished).

田仲ハル | Hal Tanaka

舞踏家・振付家・グラフィックデザイナー｜北海道（日本）｜38年

Butoh Dancer, Choreographer, Graphic Designer | Hokkaido (Japan) | 38 years

北海道舞踏フェスティバル2019より
Photo: yixtape

https://www.facebook.com/hal.tanaka.7

Q1 舞踏をはじめたきっかけ
高校時代に舞踏を見て、気がついたらツアーに出ていた。

Q2 舞踏の魅力
不条理。

Q3 アーカイヴについて
人類が存続する限り、舞踏は残ります。

Q1 Reason for Starting Butoh
I first saw Butoh during high school, next thing I know I'm on a tour.

Q2 Attraction to Butoh
Absurdity.

Q3 On Archiving
As long as humans exist, so will Butoh.

田中トシ | Toshi Tanaka

パフォーマンスアーティスト・教師｜サンパウロ（ブラジル）｜40年

Performance Artist, Teacher | São Paulo (Brazil) | 40 years

performance Fugaku, Tabibito 風楽/旅人2019 in São Paulo.
Photo: Fábio Pazzini

www.jardimdosventos.com

Q1 舞踏をはじめたきっかけ
十代後半絵画からロックへ、声から身体へ目覚めた時そこに舞踏があった。そのことは今に繋がる出発だった。

Q2 舞踏の魅力
誰もが自らの体を通じて内的創造力を回復し人生と社会、自然と関わりより良い世界を作り出せると思うから。

Q3 アーカイヴについて
地に触れ、体に触れる、その触れ方を伝え僅かな言葉を口承し、そこから響き伝わる風を謙虚に受け継ぐ他になかろうか。

Q1 Reason for Starting Butoh
In my late teens I moved from painting to Rock, then from singing to the body, where I found Butoh. That was the point that led to the present.

Q2 Attraction to Butoh
Because I think anyone can restore inner creativity with their body, and create a better world by interacting with life, society and nature.

Q3 On Archiving
There is no more to do than to touch the earth and body, convey the ways to touch, and to humbly receive the winds that resonate from there.

Q1 あなたが舞踏をはじめたきっかけを教えて下さい。
Q2 あなたにとって舞踏の魅力は何ですか？
Q3 身体芸術である舞踏は、どのようにしたら残すことができるでしょうか？

点滅 TEMMETSU

舞踏家・演出家｜東京（日本）｜B機関（主宰）｜27年

Butoh Dancer, Director | Tokyo (Japan) | B-kikan (Artistic Director) | 27 years

Q1 舞踏をはじめたきっかけ
1993年、土方巽記念アスベスト館にて舞踏ワークショップ「アイコンとしての身体」（講師：大野一雄・大野慶人・笠井叡・和栗由紀夫・元藤燁子・他）を受講したことから。

Q2 舞踏の魅力
見えないものが見られるところ。自分以外の何ものかの存在を意識させられるところ。自分が自分の体から抜けていく様を体感できるところ。

Q3 アーカイヴについて
世界と日本では状況が違いますが、舞踏がマイナーな分野になっている日本では、他分野の舞踊、演劇などと組み合わせてハイブリッドな舞踏手を育成するというのも一つの手段だと考えます。

Q1 Reason for Starting Butoh
I attended the *Body as an Icon* Butoh workshop (with Kazuo Ohno, Yoshito Ohno, Akira Kasai, Yukio Waguri, Akiko Motofuji, etc.) at the Tatsumi Hijikata Memorial Asbestos-kan in 1993.

Q2 Attraction to Butoh
The way the invisible can be seen. The way it creates an awareness of something beyond yourself. The way you can experience your own body escapism.

Q3 On Archiving
Japan is different from the rest of the world, but in Japan where Butoh is a minor field, I think one method would be to join with other fields such as dance and theatre, and cultivate hybrid dancers.

B機関『青森県のせむし男』より
Photo: Muga Miyahara

http://www.temmetsu.link/

Ana Rita Teodoro

Choreographer, Dancer | Lisbon (Portugal), Paris (France) | 15 years

振付家・ダンサー｜リスボン（ポルトガル）・パリ（フランス）｜15年

Orifice Paradis (Laurent Friquet)

https://parasita.hotglue.me/?Ana%20Rita%20Teodoro/

Q1 Reason for Starting Butoh
When I read the book *House of the Sleeping Beauties* by Yasunari Kawabata, I was profoundly touched by the way Kawabata described the moments just before old Eguchi enters into a dream. I thought that it might exist, a dance in Japan that works between awakening and dreaming. Then I found Butoh.

Q2 Attraction to Butoh
The practice of a dance that is not based in models to copy but based on the exchange of an imaginary background as poetry or paintings. It also attracted me how the butoh practice was connected to a way of living and taking care of the surrounding environment.

Q3 On Archiving
Although butoh is a physical practice, it's more important what's underneath the "dance form". That is, the way butoh thinks choreography and how the dancer creates his motivations, imagination, concentration. Butoh can only be preserved through the accessibility of its archives, where we can have a glimpse of the thoughts of its authors and continue an artistic dialogue with them.

Q1 舞踏をはじめたきっかけ
川端康成の「眠れる美女」を読んだ時に、江口老人が夢の世界に入っていく様子の描画に深く感動しました。日本には、目を醒ましている状態と夢を見ている状態の間に存在する踊りがあるのかもしれないと思いました。そして私は舞踏を発見しました。

Q2 舞踏の魅力
型を真似るのではなく、詩や絵画などの想像上の背景を交換することに基づいた踊りであることに惹かれます。舞踏の稽古が、人としての生き方や、周りの環境を大切にする方法と繋がっていることも、私にとっては魅力です。

Q3 アーカイヴについて
舞踏は身体的な訓練ですが、その「踊りの形式」の下に潜むものの方が、より重要です。それは、舞踏がどのように振付を考えているか、そしてダンサーが踊る動機や創造性、集中力をどのように生み出しているのか、ということです。アーカイヴへのアクセスのしやすさこそが舞踏を残すことにつながります。アーカイヴを通して、私たちは舞踏家の考えを垣間見、彼らとの創造的な対話を行うことができるのです。

凡例 肩書き｜活動拠点｜所属団体｜活動年数
Reference Occupation | Base | Affiliation | Years of Activity

TO-EN Butoh Company

Butoh Dancer, Choreographer | Poland, Europe | 10 years

舞踏家・振付家 | ポーランド・欧州 | 10年

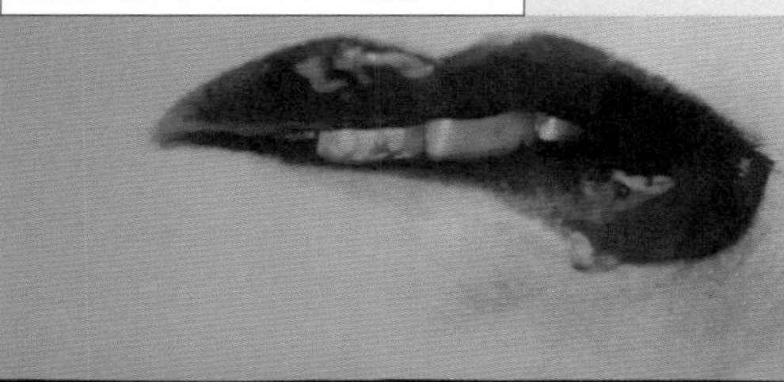

DESERT ROSE by TO-EN Butoh Company
photo: Natalia Osuch

www.toenbutoh.com

Q1 Reason for Starting Butoh
I have participated in Butoh workshops where I have met my master SU-EN (Artistic director of SU-EN Butoh Company based in Sweden). She has invited me to be her apprentice.

Q2 Attraction to Butoh
I was attracted by the means of expression in Butoh dance. What happens to the body, the transformative aspect and the sphere of choreographic matter in the form of body materials.

Q3 On Archiving
In the era of cibernetisation it is important to archive Butoh in print and digital form. I strongly recommend collecting audio-visual documentation, photography, texts, PR materials as an imprint of creation and preservation of heritage. I also believe in meetings with all generations of Butoh dancers, holding conferences, workshops and keeping the stage works alive. This process can also help to clarify our body work in terms of a "method" as to separate from all who give a vague and misleading idea of Butoh dance.

Q1 舞踏をはじめたきっかけ
舞踏のワークショップに参加して、私の師であるSU-EN（スウェーデンを拠点とするSU-EN舞踏カンパニーの主宰者）に出会いました。彼女から、自分の下で学ばないかと誘われました。

Q2 舞踏の魅力
舞踏の表現方法に魅了されました。身体に起きていること、変化を扱う点、そして物質として身体を捉える中での振付作業。

Q3 アーカイヴについて
サイバー空間で情報が行き交うこの時代においては、舞踏を紙資料だけでなく、デジタルでもアーカイヴしていくことが大切です。映像資料、写真、テキスト、PR資料をクリエーションの刻印として、そして文化遺産として収集していくことを強く勧めます。また、全ての世代の舞踏家たちが集まり、会議やワークショップを行い、舞台作品を残していくことが大切だと思います。このプロセスは、「メソッド」としてのボディワークを明らかにすることにも役立つため、舞踏に対する曖昧で、誤った考えを広める人々を遠ざけることができるでしょう。

トマツタカヒロ | Takahiro Tomatsu

肉態表現 | 東京（日本） | 25年

Martial Butoh | Tokyo (Japan) | 25 years

Q1 舞踏をはじめたきっかけ
中学生の頃、図書室で見た土方巽の写真集にショックを受けて以来、そのイメージが脳裏から離れず独自の「肉態」という身体表現を継続中。

Q2 舞踏の魅力
戦後、欧米に抗うように、また日本にさえ牙を剥くような凶暴、狂気、滑稽、卑猥、哀愁、、日本が溢れる身体表現に日本人として惹かれる。

Q3 アーカイヴについて
残す残らないと言うより変容しながら伝播すると思う。私は25年以上精神医療に関わるが、精神疾患は時代を写し変化、今や疾病か人格かさえ曖昧、舞踏も精神疾患に似ていると思う。

Q1 Reason for Starting Butoh
When I was a junior high school student, I was shocked by photographs of Tatsumi Hijikata I found in a library. Those images never left me, and now I continue the search for new forms of presenting the"body".

Q2 Attraction to Butoh
A post-war resisting of the West, or even Japan, baring the teeth of ferocity, craze, humour, obscenity and despair... As a Japanese person, I am drawn to this abundantly Japanese bodily expression.

Q3 On Archiving
Whether it can be preserved or not I think it will change as it proliferates. Having been involved in psychiatry for over 25 years, I find mental illnesses change in the contexts of their times; whether someone is ill or its their personality is ambiguous, and I think Butoh is similar.

2019' 11/15 トマツ肉態 London 公演ポスター(@the horse hospital)

https://www.instagram.com/takahiro.tomatsu/

Q1 Please tell us how you became involved with Butoh?
Q2 What attracted you to Butoh?
Q3 As a performative art inherently involving the physical body, how can Butoh be preserved? Or, is this even possible?

Q1 あなたが舞踏をはじめたきっかけを教えて下さい。
Q2 あなたにとって舞踏の魅力は何ですか？
Q3 身体芸術である舞踏は、どのようにしたら残すことができるでしょうか？

友井亮輔 RYOSUKE TOMOI

「Traffic」Choreography: Kazuhiro Nishijima

https://ryosuke-tomoi-michael-jackson.jimdofree.com/

営業・セールス｜横浜（日本）｜5年

Sales | Yokohama (Japan) | 5 years

Q1 舞踏をはじめたきっかけ
音楽や舞踊における自身の限界を感じたため。

Q2 舞踏の魅力
4次元の美的感覚。

Q3 アーカイヴについて
形あるものはいずれ無くなり、精神は受け継がれてゆくということを舞台表現やそれぞれの稽古の中でアーティストが学んでいくことで、舞踏を含むあらゆる表現の世界の可能性は広がり、多様性を伴いながら更に残される（受け継がれてゆく）と思います。

Q1 Reason for Starting Butoh
I felt my limitations in music and dance.

Q2 Attraction to Butoh
4-dimensional aesthetic sense.

Q3 On Archiving
Anything with a form eventually disappears, but if artists learn what can be inherited from predecessors through stage appearances or practice, the potential for all kinds of expression including Butoh increases, and will be preserved (or inherited) as it diversifies.

Kea Tonetti

Dancer, Teacher | Milan (Italy) | Spazio Continuum, Compagniakha | 40 years

ダンサー・教師｜ミラノ（イタリア）｜Spazio Continuum・Compagniakha｜40年

White-hot (Moscow) 2016.
Photo: Eugene Titov

www.compagniakha.it

Q1 Reason for Starting Butoh
During my journey in the art of dance, from ballet to contemporary and theater dance, I started to research eastern cultures practices and philosophy. Meeting Butoh was overwhelming, a part of me felt like if I knew it already, falling in love with this dance of body and soul.

Q2 Attraction to Butoh
The poetry and the Presence given to every part of the body, the slow and micro movements coming from ground, center and skeleton, generating organic movements. The state of Emptiness embracing every life manifestation and permeating the body transformation in inner landscapes, letting various layers come out from the dance.

Q3 On Archiving
For Butoh the Spirit beyond the forms is more important, but to study the technics, the main principles of the founders are important, to understand and respect the original spirit and forms. The meeting between archaic and contemporary is its beauty, but also its evolution in new researches on movement, through maintaining the main energetic state of Butoh.

Q1 舞踏をはじめたきっかけ
ダンスという旅を続ける中で、バレエからコンテンポラリー、そしてシアターダンスに到り、東洋文化で行われている訓練や哲学の研究を始めました。舞踏に出会い、私は圧倒されました。自分の中の一部が、すでに私はこれを知っている、というような感覚でした。この身体と魂の踊りに恋に落ちてしまいました。

Q2 舞踏の魅力
身体のあらゆる部分に与えられる詩情と存在感。ゆっくりとしたミクロな動きが地面、中心軸、そして骨格から生まれ、有機的な動きを創出する。空の状態が、すべての具現化された生命を包み込み、身体変化を内部の風景へ浸透させることで、複数のレイヤーがダンスの中から生まれ出す。

Q3 アーカイヴについて
舞踏において、より重要なのは、形を超える魂です。しかし、技術を学び、本来の（舞踏の）精神や形を理解し、重んずるためには、創始者たちの重要な原理が大切です。舞踏の過去と現在を結びつけるのはその美しさだけではありません。舞踏の主たるエネルギー状態を維持しながら、新しい研究のなかでムーブメントを進化させることもまた、そうだと言えます。

辻 たくや | Tsuji Takuya

舞踏家｜東京（日本）｜天狼星堂｜9年

Butoh Dancer | Tokyo (Japan) | TENROUSEIDOH | 9 years

Q1 舞踏をはじめたきっかけ
俳優活動をしていたが2011年東北大震災、原発事故以降、身体性を強く意識するようになった時に友人に「舞踏」を紹介されたのがきっかけです。

Q2 舞踏の魅力
舞踏を踊ることによって何度でも生まれなおしができること。そして、そのたびに様々な出来事や存在と出会うことができること

Q3 アーカイヴについて
映像、文書、写真などあらゆる手段を使って記録を残す必要があるが、身体芸術である「舞踏」を記録することは不可能ではないだろか。私が「舞踏」を残すためにできることはを踊り続けることではないか。

Q1 Reason for Starting Butoh
I used to work as an actor, but after the 2011 Fukushima Daiichi nuclear disaster, I began to have a stronger awareness of my own physicality, and I was introduced to "Butoh" by a friend.

Q2 Attraction to Butoh
That by dancing Butoh you can be reborn time and time again. And that you meet all kinds of situations and existences by doing so.

Q3 On Archiving
Although it is important to preserve "Butoh" using various methods such as film, documentation and photography, as an art of the body it is impossible to record. All I can do to preserve "Butoh" is keep dancing.

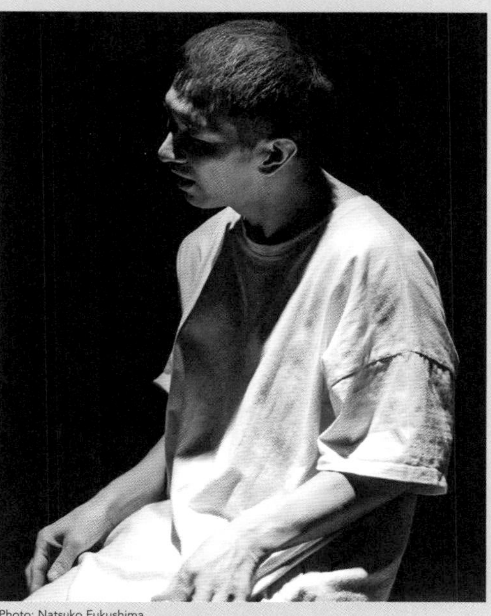

Photo: Natsuko Fukushima

https://odamaki0930.wixsite.com/takuyakikaku

上村なおか | Naoka Uemura

ダンサー・振付家｜東京（日本）｜45年

Dancer, Choreographer | Tokyo (Japan) | 45 years

音楽×ダンス〈ナイトシェード〉「かごの中の鳥」より。　2019年4月　於：世田谷美術館
Photo: Hideto Maezawa

www.naoka.jp
Twitter: naokatombo

Q1 舞踏をはじめたきっかけ
自分のカラダを実感したくて。そしてカラダというものそのものの謎に向かいたくて。

Q2 舞踏の魅力
物質としての肉体のみならず、カラダとは何なのか、果てしなく探求できるところ。

Q3 アーカイヴについて
ナマモノである身体芸術は、その時の空気や匂い、気配、すべての要素を完璧に記録するのは難しいと感じていますが、様々なメディアを通してアーカイヴすることで、その時代に生きられなかった人に対してその存在を想起させることが出来ると考えます。

Q1 Reason for Starting Butoh
I wanted to truly grasp my body.
I wanted to face the mysteries of this thing called a body.

Q2 Attraction to Butoh
That it can endlessly explore not just the material body, but also question what the body is.

Q3 On Archiving
I think it is difficult to record all the elements of live, body-based performing arts in their entirety, such as the air, the smells, and the atmosphere. However by archiving it using various media, I think it can serve to recall its existence for those who were not born in that era.

Q1　Please tell us how you became involved with Butoh?
Q2　What attracted you to Butoh?
Q3　As a performative art inherently involving the physical body, how can Butoh be preserved? Or, is this even possible?

Q1 あなたが舞踏をはじめたきっかけを教えて下さい。
Q2 あなたにとって舞踏の魅力は何ですか？
Q3 身体芸術である舞踏は、どのようにしたら残すことができるでしょうか？

上杉満代

Mitsuyo Uesugi

舞踏家｜東京（日本）｜45年

Butoh Dancer | Tokyo (Japan) | 45 years

『ラブ・レター…貴方へ』より
Photo: Makoto Onozuka

Q1 舞踏をはじめたきっかけ

1972年音楽と演劇とマイムの詩劇「日本武命」に特別出演された大野一雄氏の踊りに感銘を受け上星川の稽古場に通う。古典バレエを学びながら個の身体表現を模索しているなか、土方巽の作品に接しながらも、大野一雄の映画などの孤独な作業に魅せられる。

Q2 舞踏の魅力

一切の観念を捨て体の中に潜む人類の30数億年の記憶。宇宙の生命の誕生。日々の日常にそんな時間軸を体で体感する。それが大変厳しく難しい作業で有るが故に、個の一生の仕事となる肉体表現が舞踏だと思います。

生き方と思想が一致した時、全ての境界が消滅する。大野一雄氏に出逢って魅了された舞踏です。

Q3 アーカイヴについて

舞踏は個の一生に深く関わって産まれる稀有な舞台表現です。それ故に個の舞踏の奥には深い謎と秘密が潜んでいるでしょう。舞踏を学ぶ若い人達は舞踏の創始者である大野一雄氏、土方巽氏の仕事を謙虚に学び、体と社会と格闘し続けて欲しいと思います。舞踏は生き物です。人間が生存する限り舞踏は産まれてこなくてはいけません。

Q1 Reason for Starting Butoh

Kazuo Ohno left a deep impression on me when I saw him in 1972 as part of a music, theatre and mime recital *Yamato Takeru*, and I attended his studio in Kami-hoshikawa. Even as I struggled to find my own form while studying classical ballet and experiencing Tatsumi Hijikata's pieces, I was most fascinated by Kazuo Ohno's solitary work in films etc.

Q2 Attraction to Butoh

Abandoning all ideas to the memory of 3 billion years of humanity lurking in the body. The birth of life in the universe. To experience that timeline every day with your body. While it is a relentless and difficult task, I believe this lifelong work of bodily expression is Butoh. When one's lifestyle matches their ideas, all boundaries disappear. This was the Butoh of Kazuo Ohno that fascinated me.

Q3 On Archiving

Butoh is a rare performative expression heavily connected to one's life. As such, there are deep mysteries and secrets hidden in the depths of Butoh. I would like young people who study Butoh to learn about Kazuo Ohno and Tatsumi Hijikata's work with humility, and continue to contest the body and society. Butoh is a creature. It must continue for as long as human life exists.

Yumi Umiumare

Choreographer, Performer | Melbourne (Australia) | ButohOUT! (Artistic Director) | 29 years

振付家・パフォーマー｜メルボルン（オーストラリア）｜ButohOUT!（主宰）｜29年

TeaBreak (Evocation of Butoh, Asia Topa Festival) 2017.
Photo: Mifumi Obata

www.yumi.com.au

Q1 Reason for Starting Butoh

Classical ballet was the only dance I learnt when I was young so Butoh blew my mind when I saw it. Dancers doing the exact opposite from the discipline of ballet. I was scared initially, but the draw was strong. I participated in various workshops before eventually joining Dairakudakan in 1990.

Q2 Attraction to Butoh

I am attracted to the universality of Butoh, going beyond the confines of individual culture, religion, gender and belief. Butoh touches the soul of humanity, embracing both darkness and light. Butoh inspires me to cross all boundaries, encouraging me to explore the rawness of life and visceral expression.

Q3 On Archiving

Definitely important to preserve archival records of historic works, but to preserve the art form of Butoh itself seems to defeat the inherent anarchic nature. This unique art form must constantly be evolving; challenging and deconstructing ideas of conservatism and social constructs. As performers and creators, our purpose is to keep seeking, yet maintain the deep spirit of Butoh.

Q1 舞踏をはじめたきっかけ

若い時にはクラシックバレエが私にとって唯一のダンスだったので、舞踏を観た時には衝撃を受けました。バレエの基本とは完全に正反対のことを舞踏家たちが行なっていました。最初は怖かったのですが、それでも強く引き込まれました。様々なワークショップを受けた後に、1990年に大駱駝艦に入りました。

Q2 舞踏の魅力

個人の文化、宗教、ジェンダーそして信念に囚われない舞踏の普遍性に魅力を感じています。舞踏は人間性という魂に触れ、闇と光の両方を包み込むものです。舞踏は私に、あらゆる境界を超えることを勧め、人生の生々しさと、本能的な表現の探求を促してくれます。

Q3 アーカイヴについて

歴史的な作品をアーカイヴとして保存することはたしかに大切なことですが、舞踏という芸術形式そのものを残すことは、本来持つアナーキーな性質を覆すことのように思います。このユニークな芸術形式は常に進化し続けるべきです。つまり、保守的な思想や社会構造に挑み、そしてそれらを解体することです。パフォーマーとして、そしてクリエーターとして、私たちの目的は舞踏の深い精神を探し求め続けながら、維持していくことにあると思います。

Annemarijke van Etten (Pacifica)

Artist, Butoh Dancer | Tokyo, Zushi (Japan), Amsterdam (Netherlands), Freiburg (Germany), Neuhaus (Switzerland) | GEDOK | 37 years

アーティスト・舞踏家 | 東京・逗子（日本）・アムステルダム（オランダ）・フライブルク（ドイツ）・ノイハウス（スイス） | GEDOK | 37年

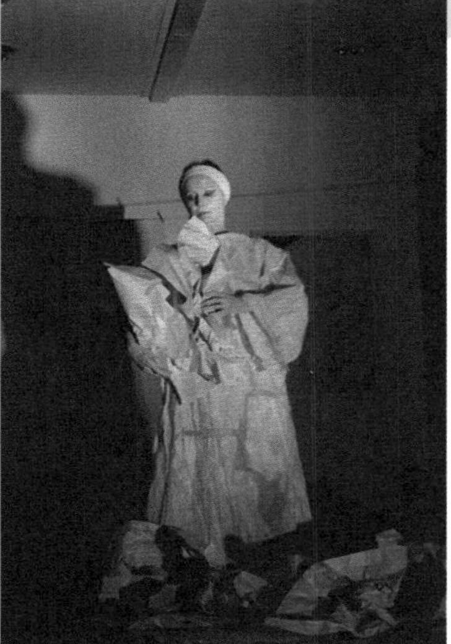

Klangbilder II: Images of Sound II (Schwarzes Kloster, Freiburg, Germany) 1996.

Q1 Reason for Starting Butoh
I first came to Japan in 1972, I saw the film *Himiko*. Only for some minutes Tatsumi Hidjikata was moving. His way of moving and being struck me. In 1982 I came again to Tokyo and lived there for 10 years. I started looking for Butoh-performances, to see their way of moving, started training with some of them.

Q2 Attraction to Butoh
I gradually understood better the inner visualization of their body and face, because of the strong stillness and tension. As a contrast of the classical ballet, the free "letting go" of their being was most interesting for me.

Q3 On Archiving
It is possible! Originally Butoh came from Japanese creative courage to express differently with the body as in the traditional dramatic arts before. It is important to see the films, videos, photos of the past, and of the now-a-days butoh-dancers. Of course it is important to have good examples by teachers who share their experiences with the students.

Q1 舞踏をはじめたきっかけ
1972年に初めて日本を訪れた時に、映画『卑弥呼』を観ました。数分の間でしたが、土方巽が出演していました。彼の動きや立ち振る舞いに、私は衝撃を受けました。1982年に再び東京を訪れ、それから10年間滞在しました。舞踏の公演を探し、舞踏家たちがどのように動いているのかを観るうちに、彼らと共に稽古をするようになりました。

Q2 舞踏の魅力
強固な静止と緊張によって、身体や顔の内側（で起きていること）を（外的に）可視化することについて、徐々によく理解できるようになりました。クラシックバレエとは対照的に、その人の本質を自由に「解放する」感覚が、私にとって一番興味深いです。

Q3 アーカイヴについて
可能だと思います！もともと舞踏は、それまでの伝統芸能にあった身体技法とは異なるものを表現しようとした創造的な試みだと思います。過去の、そして現在も活動する舞踏家の映画、映像、写真を観ることは大切です。もちろん、指導者が生徒たちにその経験を伝え、良い見本に触れさせることも重要です。

Mario Veillette

Dance Teacher | Québec (Canada) | L'École de danse de Québec | 31 years

ダンス教師 | ケベック（カナダ） | L'École de danse de Québec | 31年

Vieille pomme (Old Apple), solo, 2008.

www.culture-quebec.qc.ca/marioveillette

Q1 Reason for Starting Butoh
First classes with Natsu Nakajima (Concordia University, 1987), lots of butoh shows in Festival International de nouvelle Danse (Montreal). Professional workshop with Jocelyne Montpetit (Mtl) and participation in Ex...it 2003 (Schloss Broellin, Germany). Wrote a Master degree thesis on Teaching Butoh and Somatic Practices.

Q2 Attraction to Butoh
The research on humanity through the cultural aspects and the inclusion of the animal, vegetal, mineral and societal sides of the individual.

Q3 On Archiving
Through research and practice of many teachers worldwide who include in their practice their individuality and experiences, the butoh is constantly evolving, taking new flavours and colours. The preservation of the original forms is important but one has to be able to travel beyond images and "clichés" and ask what butoh has to offer now.

Q1 舞踏をはじめたきっかけ
1987年、コンコルディア大学での中嶋夏のクラスで最初に舞踏に出会う。モントリオールのヌーヴェル・ダンス国際フェスティバルで多くの舞踏の公演を観る。Jocelyne Montpetitのプロ対象のワークショップに参加。ドイツのシュロスブロリンにて，Ex...it 2003に参加。舞踏の指導と身体訓練に関する修士論文を執筆。

Q2 舞踏の魅力
（舞踏は）文化的諸側面、そして個人の動物的・植物的・鉱物的・社会的側面の一体性を通じた、人間性の探求。

Q3 アーカイヴについて
それぞれの個性と経験をその訓練内容に含む、世界中の多くの指導者による研究と稽古を通じて、舞踏は新しいテイストを携えながら常に進化を続けています。オリジナルの型を残していくことは重要ですが、舞踏家はイメージやクリシェを超えて旅すること、そして舞踏が今人々に何を届けるべきなのかを問うことができなければいけません。

Q1 あなたが舞踏をはじめたきっかけを教えて下さい。
Q2 あなたにとって舞踏の魅力は何ですか？
Q3 身体芸術である舞踏は、どのようにしたら残すことができるでしょうか？

Orland Verdú

Physical Actor, Butoh Dancer | Barcelona (Spain), International | Oracles Theatre (Director), Grup Cultural EXEO | 9 years

フィジカルアクター・舞踏家｜バルセロナ（スペイン）｜Oracles Theatre（主宰）・Grup Cultural EXEO｜9年

PINOCCHIO / NAGASAKI / MORPHEUS (Onyric Theatre & Butoh Dance) Photo: Justin P Brown

www.orlandverdu.com

Q1 Reason for Starting Butoh
I discovered the butoh dance whilst participating in a workshop led by Atsushi Takenouchi, during my studies of theatre in Barcelona (2011). Atsushi became a reference for my first butoh steps, until I began to expand my knowledge & develop my personal technique, based upon my own artistic background.

Q2 Attraction to Butoh
Butoh revealed to me the mystery of the body & the dance of the soul. It is a profoundly liberating art, where physical activity, creative imagination & magical consciousness coincide. I discovered in butoh the roots of what Nietzsche investigated in *The Birth of Tragedy*. The origin of theatre.

Q3 On Archiving
How to keep an unborn art growing, like a shining tree? How to be a body "sorcerer"? We preserve the code (Apollo - form in Hijikata's way) & the soul (Dyonisus - spirit in Ohno's way) by cultivating both. Butoh is body metamorphosis. The dreamer's dream. Using body & mind, the actor/dancer becomes a puppet of the Mystery.

Q1 舞踏をはじめたきっかけ
2011年にバルセロナで演劇の勉強をしているときに、竹之内淳志のワークショップに参加して舞踏を見出しました。竹之内淳志は私が舞踏を学ぶ最初の段階における参照対象となりました。その後私は自分の知識を広げ、アーティストとして受けてきた教育をベースにした個人的なテクニックを開発し始めました。

Q2 舞踏の魅力
舞踏は私に身体の不可思議さと魂のダンスを開示してくれました。身体運動と創造的想像力、魔法のような意識が同時に起こる、深い自己を解放させてくれる芸術です。私は舞踏に、ニーチェが探し求めていた「悲劇の誕生」のルーツを発見しました。演劇の起源です。

Q3 アーカイヴについて
光り輝く樹木のような、未だ誕生していない芸術を進化させ続けるのは、どのように可能なのでしょうか？身体の魔術師にはどのようにしたらなれるのでしょうか？私たちはコード（土方が志向した型―アポロン的）と魂（大野一雄が志向した精神―ディオニュソス的）を高めることで、その両方を後世に残すことができます。舞踏は身体のメタモルフォーシス（変身）です。夢みるものたちの夢なのです。身体と精神を使い、俳優／ダンサーは神秘という名のパペットになるのです。

Coco Villarreal

Dancer, Theater Director, Opera Singer, Music Composer | International, Spain, Mexico | Teatro Prieto Compañía Internacional | 18 years

ダンサー・舞台演出家・オペラ歌手・作曲家｜世界各地・スペイン・メキシコ｜Teatro Prieto Compañía Internacional｜18年

The expression of Ebro river

https://www.facebook.com/teatroprietomexico/

Q1 Reason for Starting Butoh
I saw a short video on VHS of Kazuo Ohno dancing *Admiring La Argentina*. My acting teacher showed it to us in the university. I felt so impressed and attracted at the same time that I had to try it myself.

Q2 Attraction to Butoh
The search of the purest energy translated in to body movement. The power of the insight and personal research while dancing. The joy of the journey through the mysteries of life and death. The jump in to the abstract world and the alchemy process that is fulfilled with the live performance.

Q3 On Archiving
Butoh will be preserved through the connection between human beings, from one body to the other. Like a DNA molecule that transmits very ancient information to another, affecting, transforming, offering new possibilities. The images which are based on its aesthetic are precious jewels which offer a first approach to the dance itself. The creation of archives is a very important role for its preservation and development.

Q1 舞踏をはじめたきっかけ
『ラ・アルヘンチーナ頌』を踊る大野一雄の短い映像をVHSで観ました。大学で、演技指導の先生が観せてくれました。私はとても感動し、そして惹きつけられ、自分でも舞踏を実践しないといけないと思いました。

Q2 舞踏の魅力
最も純粋なエネルギーを身体の動きへと変換する試み。踊っている間に生じる洞察力と自己の探求。生と死の不可思議さを旅することの喜び。抽象世界へと飛び込むこと。そして、ライブのパフォーマンス中に満ち溢れる錬金術的なプロセス。

Q3 アーカイヴについて
舞踏は一つの身体から別の身体へと、人同士の繋がりの中で、後世へと残されていくでしょう。DNA分子のように、古代から伝わる情報を次の分子へと伝達し、影響や変化を与えながら、新しい可能性をもたらすのです。舞踏の美学の基盤となるイメージは、人々が舞踏にアプローチするきっかけを与える貴重な宝石です。アーカイヴを構築することは、舞踏の存続と今後の舞踏の発展にとって、非常に重要です。

山本 萌 Yamamoto Moe

舞踏家｜金沢・野々市（日本）｜金沢舞踏館（主宰）｜43年

Butoh Dancer | Kanazawa, Nonoichi (Japan) | Kanazawa Butoh Kan (Artistic Director) | 43 years

「ふいご少年と煙玉少女」2016年金沢
Photo: Hajime Hayashi

金沢舞踏館ホームページ/ http://www.spacelan.ne.jp/~butohkan/
Kanazawa Butoh Kan FaceBook/ https://www.facebook.com/KanazawaButohKan

Q1 舞踏をはじめたきっかけ
「静かな家」の舞台を観た事で舞踏を知り、その時の踊り手芦川羊子に感動し、土方巽に興味を持った事が始まりです。その後、舞台のお手伝いから舞台に立つ事になりました。

Q2 舞踏の魅力
日本で生まれたButohがどの様に発展していくのか興味深く、その一端に携わっている事にやりがいを感じ、身体一ツから全ての表現をしている事に魅力を感じています。

Q3 アーカイヴについて
それぞれがはっきりとした技術体系を持つべきと考えます。動きを作り出すことはダンス、踊りの世界でとても重要な課題で技術体系の元が思想につながっていると思います。

Q1 Reason for Starting Butoh
I discovered Butoh when I saw *Quiet House*, and was impressed by Yoko Ashikawa's dance, which led to my interest in Tatsumi Hijikata. Afterwards, I helped out on stage before starting performances myself.

Q2 Attraction to Butoh
I'm interested to see how the Butoh born in Japan develops, and feel rewarded to be a part of it. I'm also fascinated by how so much can be expressed with one body alone.

Q3 On Archiving
I think everyone has to have their own technique clearly defined. How to create movement is an important issue in dance, and I think the origin of our techniques are linked to our ideology.

横滑ナナ

Nana YOKOSUBERRY

舞踏家｜東京（日本）｜大森政秀主宰「天狼星堂」所属（2004〜2015年）｜20年

Butoh Dancer | Tokyo (Japan) | Tenrouseidoh 2004-2015 | 20 years

2019.10.19~20 舞踏ソロ公演「ひやおろし」@テルプシコール
Photo: Koichi Tamauchi

https://nanasuberry.wixsite.com/yuhutsudu-sha
https://www.facebook.com/nana.yokosuberry

Q1 舞踏をはじめたきっかけ
美術家を志していた20代舞踏に出逢う。大野一雄の舞台を観た時、空間に肉体のみで、見えるはずのない軌跡が描かれていく「舞踏体」に感動した。

Q2 舞踏の魅力
舞台芸術のみならず、美術音楽文学全ての芸術、そして全ての人々の生き様に通底する美学として「舞踏性」が絶対的な根底として考察できること。

Q3 アーカイヴについて
土方巽時代から現在に至る、多くの舞踏を志す人々、老若男女問わず経歴問わずその活動をつぶさに観続けていく有識者の平衡感覚が持続できることを願います。それに伴う助成システムの充実が課題です。

Q1 Reason for Starting Butoh
I came across Butoh as an aspiring artist in my 20s. When I saw Kazuo Ohno's performance on stage, I was moved by the "Butoh body", which appeared to make visible an invisible trajectory in the air.

Q2 Attraction to Butoh
That "Butoh" can be considered an absolute foundation not only for the performing arts, but all art, music, literature and aesthetics in everyone's lives.

Q3 On Archiving
I hope that the many people who do Butoh and continue this work, from Hijikata's day to now, regardless of age, gender or career, can continue to keep a sense of equilibrium. The biggest issue is how to fund a system to enable this.

Q1 Please tell us how you became involved with Butoh?
Q2 What attracted you to Butoh?
Q3 As a performative art inherently involving the physical body, how can Butoh be preserved? Or, is this even possible?

Q1 あなたが舞踏をはじめたきっかけを教えて下さい。
Q2 あなたにとって舞踏の魅力は何ですか？
Q3 身体芸術である舞踏は、どのようにしたら残すことができるでしょうか？

芳谷伸二

Shinji Yoshitani

理学療法士｜広島（日本）｜1年

Physical Therapist | Hiroshima (Japan) | 1 year

※自分の中での舞踏をどのように表現しようかと考えていました。いろいろと活動することで，仕事や家庭生活に負担が来るようでは元も子もない，また見る人も「下手な動きを見せられても・・・」ということでも申し訳ないのですが，「自己紹介として」（1分くらいのパフォーマンス）でやってみようと始めました。まだ始めたばかりです。

Q1 舞踏をはじめたきっかけ
友だちが誘ってくれた大野一雄舞踏研究所でのレッスンで，大野先生の「フリースタイルで踊ってください」という誘いかけがきっかけで始めた。

Q2 舞踏の魅力
舞踏は「存在としての自分」をしっかりと感じさせてくれる。また，何でもないような動きに意味や感動が発見でき，日常の生活を豊かにしてくれる。

Q3 アーカイヴについて
舞踏は見る人に感じてもらうことで成立する。写真や映像だけでなく，何かを加え，見る人がより感じられる工夫ができれば良い。パラパラ絵本のような写真集はとてもよい保存法だと思う。

Q1 Reason for Starting Butoh
I started when I went to a lesson at the Kazuo Ohno Dance Studio with a friend, and was invited by Ohno sensei to "dance freestyle".

Q2 Attraction to Butoh
Butoh really makes you sense the "existing self". Meaning and inspiration can be explored in movements that seem like nothing, and it brings richness to everyday life.

Q3 On Archiving
Butoh comes to life by sparking emotions in those that see it. It would be good if there was a way to grasp something that creates this feeling, not just photographs or film. I think something like a photo album made into a flipbook would be a good way to conserve it.

Anita Zdrojewska

Artist | Warsaw (Poland) | Pompka Foundation (President) | 10 years

アーティスト｜ワルシャワ（ポーランド）｜Pompka Foundation（代表）｜10年

Point Zero (Butoh Kai/Butohsfera) 2019

www.fundacjapompka.org.pl

Q1 Reason for Starting Butoh
I was studying Japanology at Warsaw University but mostly in the history and traditional arts' field. Ten years ago, I saw a documentary on New York Butoh Festival and - since then - started researching, participating in workshops and inviting Butoh artists to Poland.

Q2 Attraction to Butoh
Strong, deeply touching and thought provoking visual existence.

Q3 On Archiving
Video is an important documenting tool giving an information and context on who/what/when/where. Still, it's poor: digital material can't share "dancer's existence" / "Butoh spirit" with the audience. Physical body/performer is needed to work not only on the form but also on the essence and to transfer both unique and universal stories to the public.

Q1 舞踏をはじめたきっかけ
ワルシャワ大学で日本学を専攻していた際は、主に歴史と伝統芸能の分野を学んでいました。10年前に、ニューヨーク舞踏フェスティバルのドキュメンタリーを観てから舞踏のリサーチを開始し、ワークショップへの参加や、ポーランドへの舞踏家の招聘を始めました。

Q2 舞踏の魅力
強烈で深い感動を呼び起こし、思想を喚起するビジュアル的存在。

Q3 アーカイヴについて
映像は、「誰が／何を／いつ／どこで」に関する情報や文脈を与える重要な記録ツールではありますが、資料としては不十分です。デジタル資料では、「ダンサーの存在感」や「舞踏の精神」を観客と共有することができません。パフォーマーの身体性は、形だけにとらわれるのでなく、本質と向き合いながら、ユニークであると同時に普遍的なストーリーを伝えるものである必要があります。

凡例　肩書き｜活動拠点｜所属団体｜活動年数
Reference　Occupation | Base | Affiliation | Years of Activity

精神のリレー 2019

A Spiritual Relay 2019

向 雲太郎
Kumotaro Mukai

Photo: bozzo

師から受け継いだ精神ということですが、様々なことを数限りなく受け継いでいると思います。その中で最も大事にしているのは、主宰している『舞踏家集団デュ社』のコンセプトでもある“疑う”ということです。
常識に疑問を持つ、思い込みを疑うというのは、師匠である麿赤兒がそのまた師匠である土方巽から受け継いだ精神でもあります。常識を疑って超えていくのは舞踏にとって、とても大切な魂のようなものだと考えています。

“笑い”というのも師から受け継いで大切にしていることです。「舞踏に笑いは要らない。」と非難されたこともありますが、クソ真面目なんてクソ、真面目は禁物。どこかにユーモアや明るさがないと、暗くて湿った救いようのない、観ていてもつらいだけのものになってしまうのです。舞踏は東北だから暗い方がいいという決めつけがある。では関西の舞踏は違う道を歩きます。麿さんは奈良で自分は兵庫、そんな生い立ちも、師匠のユーモアが好きな理由かもしれません。

“なんでもあり”というのも舞踏のひとつの答えのように思っていますが、師匠から学び受け継いだ精神だと思います。ルールを無視してタブーを破っていく。そのためには不良のこころと豊富な知識と実験精神も必要不可欠だと思います。舞踏家は知的な不良でなくてはならない。そして舞台上でやってはいけないことなどない。それは土方が舞踏の始まり『禁色』でやってみせたことです。

“諦め”のこころも師から受け継いでいます。『天賦典式』と師匠は言いますが、全肯定は全否定の裏返

In terms of the spiritual dimension acquired from my mentor Akaji Maro, I've inherited so much from him. The most important thing was the ability "to question," which also happens to be the underpinning concept for The Butoh Tribe Duex Shrine — the troupe I'm currently leading. This tendency to question conventional beliefs and doubts is also the spiritual approach that my teacher Akaji Maro acquired from his mentor Tatsumi Hijikata. As I see it, going beyond conventional beliefs is a vital spiritual element for any Butoh performer.

The ability to "to make people laugh" is something I acquired from Akaji Maro and something I cherish dearly. Somebody once criticized me, saying that "Butoh shouldn't require laughter." I strongly believe, however, that being ridiculously serious is taboo in Butoh. If there's no humor or merriness, then everything will end up just being grim and heavy, without any redeeming features for those watching. Generally speaking, Butoh originating in Tohoku (the northern region of Japan) is believed to be better on account of its darker hues. Conversely, Butoh from Kansai (the western region of Japan) has taken a different approach. Maro is originally from Nara and I'm from the Kansai region as well— from Hyogo— so perhaps that explains why I like his sense of humor.

While "everything is possible" is one of Butoh's responses, I think this approach is also a spiritual aspect I picked up from Maro. He would break taboos and just ignore any rules. To achieve that one needs a rebellious streak, abundant knowledge, and an experimental spirit. In intellectual terms, Butoh must be outrageous. And there is absolutely nothing that can't be done on stage, as for example when Hijikata performed the opening section of his Butoh performance *Kinjiki*.

I also acquired a sense of "surrendering oneself" from Maro. He would refer to *Temputenshiki* — the fact of being born

向 雲太郎

1994年大駱駝艦に入団、麿赤兒に師事。01年より振付・演出作品の発表を開始。これまでに19作品を発表、国内10ヶ所のほか、海外5カ国11ヶ所で作品を上演。第37回舞踊批評家協会賞・新人賞受賞。12年退団独立。14年舞踏家集団"デュ社"を旗揚げ。13年〜16年、セゾン文化財団 シニアフェローシップ。

Kumotaro Mukai

In 1994, Kumotaro Mukai joined Dairakudakan where he started studying under Akaji Maro. As of 2001, he started choreographing and directing. To date, he has presented nineteen works. In addition to performing at ten locations across in Japan, he has also appeared at eleven locations in five countries overseas. At the 37th Dance Critics Association Award, he won the Newcomers Award. In 2012, he quit Dairakudakan and embarked upon a solo career. In 2014, he founded the Butoh troupe: The Butoh Tribe Duex Shrine. He was a Senior Fellow at the Saison Cultural Foundation between 2013-2016.

しであると考えています。常識を疑うためには一度諦めなくてはならない。「世の中で役に立つ人間でないといけないが…ダメだ、諦めよう…ならばどうすればいいのか…そうだ生まれたというそのことを才能にしてみよう。」そんな諦めの境地から舞踏は生まれてきたのだと思います。

"即興"は、大野一雄さんから学びました。自分のソロで、調子が悪いからとやめてしまう。でもそれでいい。いつやめてもいい。という覚悟は即興の真髄だと思います。いっぽう師匠は、土方さんと同じように即興をあまり信じていないのではないかと思ったりします。
笠井叡さんからは、チャレンジ精神を学びました。いつも「変わったことをしてるなあ。」と感服します。笠井さんからもユーモアと不良の魂を感じます。
不良といえば室伏鴻のハイソサエティーな客の前では踊らなかったという逸話も好きです。嫌いな人が共演者にいると本番中「ずーっ」と寝てたという逸話も「いいなあ。」と、思わずにやり。

こうやって振り返ってみると、大駱駝艦で修業した20年間の日々の中で師・麿赤兒から全身全霊で何もかもを受け継ぎ、師匠のそのまた師匠である土方巽、パイオニアである大野一雄、先駆者・笠井叡、室伏鴻等からも影響を受け精神をしっかりと受け取り「自分のからだの中に血となり肉として受け継いでいるのだ。」と再確認したのでした。

and entering this world—as truly a gift. And yet, all affirmations are just the reverse of all negations. In order to question conventional beliefs, we have to cast ourselves aside. "I've got to be a useful person in this world ... such an approach isn't going to work. If I were to surrender... what should I do ... let's avail of the ability that comes with birth." Butoh emerges from such a situation in which one surrenders.

I learnt how to improvise from Kazuo Ohno. When dancing solo performances, at times I would give up because I felt unwell. But that is OK; one can quit anytime. That is the very essence of improvisation. Conversely, Akaji Maro, just like Hijikata, wasn't such a great believer in improvisation.
I learnt the spirit of challenge from Akira Kasai. I always admired the fact that he was doing something different. Kasai's works are also imbued with humour and a rebellious streak.
Speaking of outrageousness, I liked that anecdote about Ko Murobushi, according to which he would not perform for high-society audiences. I also enjoyed the story about how he would sleep right through a performance if he disliked one of his co-performers.

Looking back over the twenty years of training with Dairakudakan, I am now able to reconfirm that I've inherited absolutely everything from my mentor Akaji Maro, both physically and spiritually; it is now streaming through my blood. I've also been deeply spiritually influenced by his teacher, Tatsumi Hijikata and by the pioneering figure of Kazuo Ohno, as well as those in the vanguard such as Akira Kasai and Ko Murobushi.

麿赤兒 | Akaji Maro (1943-)

1965年、唐十郎率いる状況劇場に参画。66年、役者として活動しながら土方巽に師事。72年、大駱駝艦を旗揚げ。舞踏に大仕掛けを用いたスペクタクル性の強い様式を導入する。82年、フランスとアメリカで初の海外公演。東京・吉祥寺に構えるスタジオ「壺中天」を拠点に、自作の発表だけでなく若手の創作も支援。映画・TV・舞台等でも広く活躍する。

Joined Jōkyō Gekijo with Kara Jūrō in 1965. Began studying under Tatsumi Hijikata while working as an actor in 1966. Founded Dairakudakan in 1972. Introduced a strong "spectacular" style to Butoh using gimmicks. Performed overseas for the first time in France and the United States in 1982. Presents not only his own works but those of younger artists at "Kochuten", a studio in Kichijoji, Tokyo. Also often appears in movies, on TV and stage.

土方巽 | Tatsumi Hijikata (1928-1986)

故郷秋田でモダンダンス（ノイエタンツ）を、上京後は安藤三子のもとでジャズダンス等を学ぶ。1959年、舞踏の最初の作品とされる『禁色』（共演：大野慶人）を発表。文学の影響を受けながら独自のダンスを構想し、三島由紀夫、澁澤龍彦、瀧口修造、中西夏之、細江英公、横尾忠則、寺山修司といった同時代の文化人との交流の中、前衛芸術を先導する。1970年代からは舞踏譜を用いた新たな方法論の開発に打ち込んだ。

Studied modern dance (Neue Tanz) at his hometown in Akita, and jazz with Mitsuko Ando after moving to Tokyo. Presented *Kinjiki* (co-star: Yoshito Ohno), later known as the first Butoh performance in 1959. Conceived his own original dance form inspired by literature, and had exchanges with the cultural elite of his time such as Yukio Mishima, Tatsuhiko Shibusawa, Shūzō Takiguchi, Natsuyuki Nakanishi, Eikoh Hosoe, Tadanori Yokoo and Shūji Terayama, leading the way in avant-garde art. Began using his own form of dance notation, known as *Butoh-fu* from the 1970s.

大野一雄 | Kazuo Ohno (1906-2010)

石井漠、次いで江口隆哉、宮操子にモダンダンスを師事。戦争による長い中断を経て、1949年に最初の自主公演を行う。50年代後半に土方巽と知り合い、59年『禁色（改訂版）』に出演。77年、土方の演出のもとソロ作品『ラ・アルヘンチーナ頌』を発表、代表作となった。73歳で海外デビューし、90歳を超えてなお旺盛な公演活動を継続。横浜・保土ヶ谷の稽古場には世界中から教えを請うものが訪れた。

Studied modern dance with Baku Ishii, followed by Takaya Eguchi and Misako Miya. After a long period interrupted by the war, performed his first solo in 1949. Met Tatsumi Hijikata in 1950, and appeared in the revised *Kinjiki* in 1959. Performed his solo *Admiring La Argentina* directed by Tatsumi Hijikata in 1977, which became a masterpiece. Debuted abroad at age 73, and continued to perform into his nineties. People came from all over the world to be taught by him in Hodogaya, Yokohama.

索引
Index

名前 Name	ページ数 Page

A

Ala-Rashi, Mariam	66
Aldalai, Guyphytsy	66
有科珠々 Alishina, Juju	67
天児牛大 Amagatsu, Ushio	49, 50, 52, 53, 54, 57, 76-77
Ang, Lena	58
アオキ裕キ Aoki, Yuuki	67
Aranaga, Anastazia Louise	57
アリアードネの會 Ariadone Company	→ 池田, カルロッタ Ikeda, Carlotta
浅井信好 Asai, Nobuyoshi	68
芦川羊子 Ashikawa, Yoko	50, 52, 53, 56
azumi O E	57

B

B-Floor Theatre	56
Baron-Bonarjee, Dominique	68
Barth, Anna	69
バウシュ, ピナ Bausch, Pina	53
Bergamasco, Ambra G.	57
Bergeron, Mireille	69
Betz, Lucie	58
Bieszczad-Roley, Karolina	70
Bradley, Lynne	70
Brown, Sheri	58
白虎社 Byakkosha	→ 大須賀勇 Ohsuga, Isamu

C

Caron, Claude-Marie	71
Chernobyl, Holly	57
コーカー, ケイトリン Coker, Caitlin	46-47
Collini, Gustavo	49, 57
Cruz Islas, Carlos Iván	71
Cuéllar, Natalia	50, 57

D

DAIPANbutoh Collective	57
大駱駝艦 Dairakudakan	→ 麿赤兒 Maro, Akaji
雫境 DAKEI	72
ダンス・ラヴ・マシーン Dance-Love-Machine	→ 田村哲郎 Tamura, Tetsuro → 古川あんず Furukawa, Anzu
DEREVO	57
Desierto, Mizu	72
Dunsky, Maya	50, 56, 73

E

Edoheart	73
エイコ&コマ Eiko & Koma	50, 57
遠藤公義 Endo, Tadashi	49, 50, 55, 74
榎木ふく Enoki, Fuku	74
Espinosa, Iván Daniel	75
Eugenia Vargas	49, 50

F

Fina, Damiano	75
Fleming, Maureen	56
Frauke	56
藤條虫丸 Fujieda, Mushimaru	49, 58
藤谷由美 Fujitani Yumi	78
Fujiwara, Denise	57
福原哲郎 Fukuhara, Tetsuro	49, 57
古川あんず Furukawa, Anzu	53, 57, 86-87

G

Gaathon, Yael	78
Gaumé, Adrien (aka SIDELANER)	79
五井輝 Goi, Teru	53, 58
Grégoire, Lucie	79
Gutiérrez, Andrés	80

H

Habillé d' eau	→ 岩名雅記 Iwana, Masaki
白桃房 Hakutobo	→ 土方巽 Hijikata, Tatsumi → 芦川羊子 Ashikawa, Yoko
Hanff, Sylwia	56, 80
原田伸雄 Harada, Nobuo	56, 81
哈爾賓派 Harupin-ha	→ 玉野黄市 Tamano, Koichi
長谷川宝子 Hasegawa, Takako	53
秦かのこ Hata, Kanoko	56
Haydon, Caroline	81
Henry, Paul Michael	56
土方巽 Hijikata, Tatsumi	49, 50, 52, 54, 56, 137, 139
筆宝ふみえ Hippo, Fumie	53
Hofmann, Claudia	82
北方舞踏派 Hoppo Butoh-ha	→ 山田, ビショップ Yamada, Bishop

堀内博子 Horiuchi, Hiroko	53
Horváth, Brigitta	82
保坂一平 Hosaka, Ippei	57
胡高阳 Hu, Gao Yang	57, 83
Hurpeau, Claire	83

I

Ianuck, Tiago	58
Iarisoa, Julie Veronirina	84
Ibey, Paul	84
市原昭仁 Ichihara, Akihito	85
池田, カルロッタ Ikeda, Carlotta	49, 50, 54, 57
Ilicic, Aleksandar	85
今貂子 Ima, Tenko	50, 56, 88
石出卓也 Ishide, Takuya	58
石井満隆 Ishii, Mitsutaka	52
石井則仁 Ishii, Norihito	58, 76-77, 88
石本華江 Ishimoto, Kae	55, 89
伊藤キム Itoh, Kim	55, 86-87
岩名雅記 Iwana, Masaki	49, 50, 56
岩下徹 Iwashita, Toru	49, 58, 89

J

Jasmin, Françoise	90
Joao Butoh	56
Job, Jacki	57
Jöbstl, Marlène	90
josie j (divinebrick)	91
Johnson, Kitt	57

K

鏡ざゆら Kagami, Zayura	91
Kajiwara, Judith	92
Kalho, Josma	92
紙田昇 Kamita, Noboru	93
カナキティ Kana Kitty	93
笠井叡 Kasai, Akira	49, 50, 52, 54, 108, 109, 138
笠井瑞丈 Kasai, Mitsutake	106-107
カセキユウコ Kaseki, Yuko	49, 50, 55, 94
桂勘 Katsura, Kan	49, 50, 55
川口隆夫 Kawaguchi, Takao	50, 53, 55
川本裕子 Kawamoto, Yuko	94
ケン五月 Ken Mai	49, 50, 53, 55
Keogh, Sinéad	95
金満里 Kim, Manri	56
木村由 Kimura, Yu	58
金亀伊織 Kinki, Iori	57
木野彩子 Kino, Saiko	95
Koan, Adam	56, 98
小林嵯峨 Kobayahi, Saga	53, 58, 98
鼓代弥生 Kodai, Yayoi	99
Koller, Sara	99
近藤基弥 Kondo, Motoya	49, 100
今野真弓 Konno, Mayumi	100
古関すまこ Koseki, Sumako	49, 58
首くくり栲象 Kubikukuri-Takuzou	52
工藤丈輝 Kudo, Taketeru	49, 50, 53, 55, 101
黒沢美香 Kurosawa, Mika	53
久世亜紀 Kuze, Aki	101
久世龍五郎 Kuze, Ryugoro	102

L

ラーグ, ジョン Laage, Joan	49, 50, 55
Lanckton, Stephanie	58
Lawrie, Lorna	102
リー, リゾーム Lee, Rhizome	58
LEIMAY	58
Lohman, Melissa	57
ロンゴ, ティツィアナ Longo, Tiziana	49, 53, 58, 103

M

麿赤兒 Maro, Akaji	49, 50, 52, 54, 56, 137-139
Martínez, Esparta	57
松原東洋 Matsubara, Toyo	53
松村智恵子 Matsumura, Chieko	103
松岡大 Matsuoka, Dai	104
Medeiros, Ana	104
三上賀代 Mikami, Kayo	58
南阿豆 Minami, Azu	53, 105
Miranda, Calé	57
宮下省死 Miyashita, Seishi	53
三好由貴 Miyoshi, Yuki	105
Montpetit, Jocelyne	110

Motimaru → 近藤基弥 Kondo, Motoya → ロンゴ, ティツィアナ Longo, Tiziana

元藤燁子 Motofuji, Akiko 49, 53, 57, 106, 109

向雲太郎 Mukai, Kumotaro 49, 50, 56, 110, 137-139

Mulvilai, Kage 57

室伏鴻 Murobushi, Ko 49, 50, 52, 54, 96-97

睦美 Mutsumi 53

N

長岡ゆり Nagaoka, Yuri 49, 111

中嶋夏 Nakajima, Natsu 49, 50, 52, 55

中西晶大 Nakanishi, Masahiro 111

成瀬信彦 Naruse, Nobuhiko 53

Natsuki, Anna Ventura 112

根来裕子 Negoro, Yuko 53

寧呂 Neiro 53

Nektan, Marco 112

西山弘志 Nishiyama, Hiroshi 57

O

OddDance 58

Oguri 18-21, 58

大橋可也 Ohashi, Kakuya 113, 114-115

大野一雄 Ohno, Kazuo 49, 50, 52, 54, 124-125, 138, 139

大野慶人 Ohno, Yoshito 49, 50, 52, 54

Ohtani, Lori 113

大岩英夫 Oiwa, Hideo 53

岡登志子 Oka, Toshiko 116

奥村万琵 Okumura, Bambi 116

奥村薫 Okumura, Kaoru 117

Olliveaux, Margot 60-61

大森政秀 Omori, Masahide 53

大村憲子 Omura, Noriko 117

大西小夜子 Onishi, Sayoko 58

Ortuzar, Macarena 58

長内真理 Osanai, Mari 56

大須賀勇 Ohsuga, Isamu 50, 56

Ota, Yuko 58

P

Palacios, Lobsang 57

Piñon, Diego 49, 50, 57

R

Raymond, Cécile 118

Roll, Katharina 118

Ronchi, Maruska 50, 57

Rosin, Jordan 119

Rotie, Marie-Gabrielle 50, 58, 119

S

サーリネン, テロ Saarinen, Tero 107- 108, 109

相良ゆみ Sagara, Yumi 53

酒井直之 Sakai, Naoyuki 120

境野ひろみ Sakaino, Hiromi 53

坂本博美 Sakamoto, Hiromi 120

Sakamoto, Michael 56

Sakurai, Hiroshi 57

櫻井郁也 Sakurai, Ikuya 57, 121

山海塾 Sankai Juku → 天児牛大 Amagatsu, Ushio

正朔 Seisaku 49, 57

関美奈子 Seki, Minako 49, 50, 55

関典子 Seki, Noriko 121

蟬丸 Semimaru 49

島崎徹 Shimazaki, Toru 53

白井剛 Shirai, Tsuyoshi 56

Shklyar, Katia 122

祖父江洋子 Sobue, Yoko 122

SU-EN 49, 50, 56

サブボディ共振塾ヒマラヤ Subbody Resonance Butoh Himalaya → リー, リゾーム Lee, Rhizome

Sugai, Emilie 56

Sutherland, Alan 57

鈴木仁 Suzuki, Jin 123

鈴木ユキオ Suzuki, Yukio 58, 96-97

T

髙橋瑞乃 Takahashi, Mitsuno 123

高井富子 Takai, Tomiko 53

高松真樹子 Takamatsu, Makiko 124-125, 126

竹之内淳志 Takenouchi, Atsushi 49, 50, 54

滝田高之 Takita, Takayuki	58
玉野弘子 Tamano, Hiroko	55, 57
玉野黄市 Tamano, Koichi	49, 50, 53, 55
田村哲郎 Tamura, Tetsuro	53
田辺知美 Tanabe, Tomomi	126
田仲ハル Tanaka, Hal	53, 127
田中泯 Tanaka, Min	50, 52, 55
田中トシ Tanaka, Toshi	14-17, 50, 127
点滅 TEMMETSU	128
転形劇場 Tenkei Gekijo	56
Teodoro, Ana Rita	128
勅使川原三郎 Teshigawara, Saburo	58
Thormann, Imre	55
Tisato, Margherita	58
TO-EN Butoh Company	129
トマツタカヒロ Tomatsu, Takahiro	129
富永真紀子 Tominaga, Makiko	49, 50, 55
友恵しづねと白桃房 TOMOE SHIZUNE and HAKUTOBO	→友恵しづね Tomoe, Shizune
友恵しづね Tomoe, Shizune	56
友井亮輔 Tomoi, Ryosuke	130
Tonetti, Kea	130
とりふね舞踏舎 Torifune Butoh-Sha	→ 三上賀代 Mikami, Kayo
辻たくや Tsuji, Takuya	131
鶴山欣也 Tsuruyama, Kinya	49

U

上村なおか Uemura, Naoka	131
上杉満代 Uesugi, Mitsuyo	52, 56, 124-125, 132
ゆみうみうまれ Umiumare, Yumi	22-26, 57, 130

V

Valente, Gérard-Charles	69
Valentin Tszin	49, 50
van Etten, Annemarijke (Pacifica)	133
Vangeline	49, 50, 55
Veillette, Mario	133
Verdú, Orland	134
Villarreal, Coco	134
Volij, Rhea	58

W

和栗由紀夫 Waguri, Yukio	49, 50, 52, 55, 114-115
若松萌野 Wakamatsu, Moeno	49, 57
Walter, Roland	58
Wannapa P-Eubanks	58
Wenzlik, Alexander	56
Wolfe, Katrina	58

Y

山田, ビショップ Yamada, Bishop	53, 57
山本萌 Yamamoto, Moe	135
山崎広太 Yamazaki, Kota	50, 106-107, 109
横滑ナナ Yokosuberry, Nana	135
吉田光雄 Yoshida, Mitsuo	56
吉本大輔 Yoshimoto, Daisuke	49, 50, 53, 55
吉岡由美子 Yoshioka, Yumiko	27-32, 49, 50, 54
芳谷伸二 Yoshitani, Shinji	136
雪雄子 Yuki, Yuko	53

Z

財津暁平 Zaitsu, Gyohei	49, 50, 53, 55
Zdrojewska, Anita	136
Zen Zen Zo	→ Bradley, Lynne

カバーには、2017・2018年度に実施のアンケート調査で「あなたは舞踏をどのように説明しますか?」という質問に対して国内外から寄せられた回答、全467件を掲載した(掲載順不同)。

Cover design: All 467 Japanese and international responses to the question "How would you describe Butoh?" from the 2017 and 2018 surveys (randomised order).

舞踏という何か

Something Called Butoh

2020年2月11日初版第1刷発行

First edition: 11 February 2020

発行　NPO法人ダンスアーカイヴ構想
140-0004　東京都品川区南品川5-11-19
TEL・FAX：03-3450-6507
Email：info@dance-archive.net

編集　溝端俊夫、松岡大、呉宮百合香、本田舞、石山星亜良
翻訳　本田舞、松岡大、ジョン・バレット、川口隆夫
デザイン　北風総貴(ヤング荘)、松岡未来(ヤング荘)

協力　大野一雄舞踏研究所、
土方巽アーカイヴ(慶應義塾大学アート・センター)
助成　公益財団法人東京都歴史文化財団 アーツカウンシル東京

販売　有限会社かんた
印刷　株式会社シナノ

Publisher: NPO Dance Archive Network
5-11-19, Minamishinagawa, Shinagawa, Tokyo, 140-0004
Phone: +81 (0)3 3450 6507
Email: info@dance-archive.net

Editors: Toshio Mizohata, Dai Matsuoka, Yurika Kuremiya, Mai Honda, Seara Ishiyama
Translation: Mai Honda, Dai Matsuoka, John Barrett, Takao Kawaguchi
Design: Nobutaka Kitakaze (Young Soul), Miku Matsuoka (Young Soul)

In conjunction with: Kazuo Ohno Dance Studio, Tatsumi Hijikata Archive (Keio University Art Center)
Supported by: Arts Council Tokyo (Tokyo Metropolitan Foundation for History and Culture)

Sales/Distribution: Canta Co. Ltd
Printer: Shinano Co. Ltd

 ISBN 978-4-902098-11-2